BEST BIKE RIDES® SERIES

Best Bike Rides
Seattle

Great Recreational Rides
in the Metro Area

GENE BISBEE

FALCONGUIDES

GUILFORD, CONNECTICUT
HELENA, MONTANA
AN IMPRINT OF GLOBE PEQUOT PRESS

FALCONGUIDES®

Copyright © 2014 Morris Book Publishing, LLC

FalconGuides is an imprint of Globe Pequot Press.
Falcon, FalconGuides, Outfit Your Mind, and Best Bike Rides are registered trademarks of
Morris Book Publishing, LLC.

Maps by Trailhead Graphics, Inc. © Morris Book Publishing, LLC
All photos are by Gene Bisbee.

Text design: Sheryl Kober
Layout artist: Sue Murray
Project editor: Ellen Urban

Library of Congress Cataloging-in-Publication Data
Bisbee, Gene.
 Best bike rides Seattle : great recreational rides in the metro area /
Gene Bisbee.
    pages cm — (Best bike rides series)
 Summary: "Best Bike Rides Seattle describes 40 of the greatest
recreational rides in Seattle. Road rides, rail trails, bike paths, and
single-track mountain bike rides all get included. Most rides are in the
5 to 30 mile range, allowing for great afternoon outings and family
adventures"— Provided by publisher.
 ISBN 978-0-7627-8447-9 (paperback)
1. Bicycle touring—Washington (State)—Seattle—Guidebooks. 2.
Bicycle trails—Washington (State)—Seattle—Guidebooks. 3. Seattle
(Wash.)—Guidebooks. I. Title.
 GV1045.5.W22S433 2014
 796.6'409797772—dc23
                                                    2014014865

Printed in the United States of America

10 9 8 7 6 5 4 3 2 1

Contents

Overview

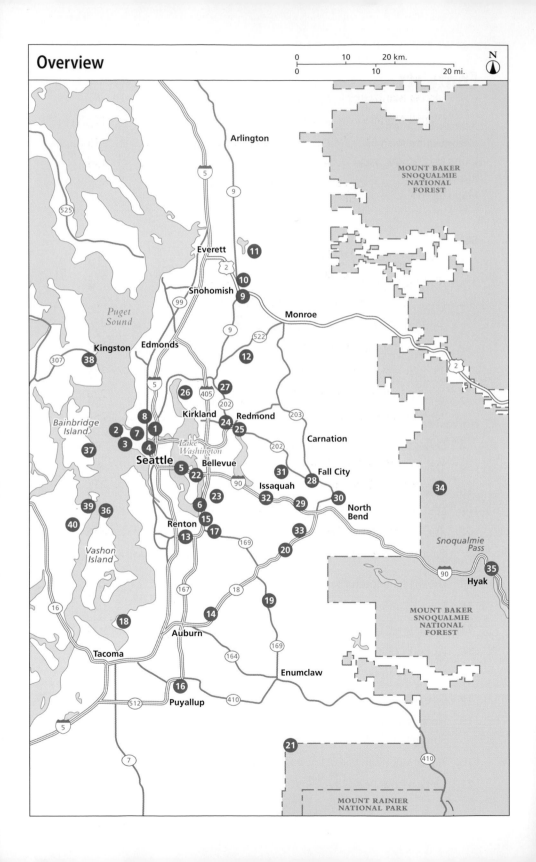

Acknowledgments

First and foremost I'd like to thank my wife, Becky, and children, Emeric and Paige, for helping out on the home front and putting up with my absences and distractions over the months that I worked on this book.

I'd also like to thank all the route-meisters for clubs and charity rides who worked diligently over the years to identify many of the generally accepted best bicycling routes in the Seattle area. This includes, but is not limited to, staff and volunteers for the Cascade Bicycle Club and Washington Bikes (formerly the Bicycle Alliance of Washington). Also, the volunteers for the Evergreen Mountain Bike Alliance and other trail-user groups, who put in countless hours of backbreaking work to build and maintain single track through local forests, deserve recognition.

In particular, I'd like to thank the following for guiding me through some unfamiliar areas: Gordon "Buzz" Grant of the Foothills Rails-to-Trails Coalition, Rick Feeney of West Sound Cycling Club, Glenn Glover of the Evergreen Mountain Bike Alliance, Rick Heinz of the Real Life Church, and Kent Peterson in Issaquah; bike shop owners Brian Backus (Trailside Cyclery in Orting), Mark Everett (Arlington Velo Sport in Arlington), and Martin Mollatt (Snohomish Bicycles in Snohomish); and King County parks and recreation division's David Kimmett, project/program manager for forest stewardship and trails planning; Robert Foxworthy, regional trails coordinator; Duane Evans, King County Parks District maintenance coordinator; and David Vijarro, civil engineering supervisor for Seattle Department of Transportation.

The historical background on the Puget Sound region provided by the writers and editors at Historylink.org was very helpful in explaining the backstories of communities on some bike routes.

I'd also like to thank biking companions Kazuki Sawanoi and Andy Davidson for accompanying me on some rides and for being patient while I took "just one more" picture or stopped to record some notes.

And, finally, thanks to all the friendly bicyclists who I met on the trails and roads and who interrupted their rides to describe some upcoming turns or where to find some tasty food along the route.

Introduction

"Hey, wanna go for a ride?"

That question always quickens my pulse and clicks my mind into gear as it runs through the possibilities of where to go and what to see. If you feel the same way, then this guide is for you.

The greater Seattle area is home to a rich mix of areas for taking your road, mountain, or hybrid bicycle. Bikes lanes and other facilities in urban and suburban areas make riding safer. Even in these days of congested traffic, it's easy enough to find forgotten low-traffic rural roads where you'll encounter a small-town bakery or old-fashioned burger joint.

The rich history of rail transportation here has left behind many rail-to-trail conversions that grace many areas with no-traffic routes that stretch on for miles. Trails accessible to mountain bikers wend deep into many parks and preserves below the towering Douglas fir and western red cedar and over small streams. We can thank the local bicycle clubs, alliances, and those who rode before us for advocating for safer streets and more access to trails. Their work has paid off in creating so many choices when it comes time to go on a bike ride.

It also means recognition. The League of American Bicyclists declared Washington the No. 1 bicycle-friendly state six years in a row—2008 to 2013. Seattle earned a gold-level Bicycle Friendly Community award, the second highest to platinum.

Generally speaking, the topography here is hilly with broad, flat valleys. Glaciers in the last Ice Age carved up the land, leaving behind steep mountainsides and broad floodplains. Streams eroding those mountains and islands chiseled the terrain some more. This creates challenging bike routes with lots of elevation gain. It also creates sensational scenery for cyclists who reach the viewpoints, such as Million Dollar View from Cougar Mountain Loop or the East Tiger Summit trail. All that climbing helps us to appreciate the rides through the rich bottomland along the Snoqualmie, Green, and Carbon Rivers even more. And we can thank the railroad builders for creating the easy grades into the Cascades on the Snoqualmie Valley Regional and John Wayne Pioneer Trails.

A lot has been written about Seattle weather. It is wet. However, we can ride here year-round. We rarely have snow and ice; nor do we get extremely hot and humid weather in the summer. Our annual rainfall of 38 inches actually is comparable to Dallas (37 inches) and Chicago (36 inches). It's just that it comes a little bit at a time; Seattle usually has about 140 days a year with some precipitation.

If rain is in the forecast, it doesn't mean that your planned ride is washed out. It just means that it's a good idea to set out with some rain gear. Often a light, water-repellent jacket that's easily stuffed in a jersey pocket or rack bag will suffice. Even with light rain, however, the roads get wet and your spinning wheels throw lots of sand and grit onto your bike and drivetrain. A good way to reduce the amount of post-ride cleaning is to use fenders and a long mud flap in the front that almost touches the road. A mud flap on the rear fender will help keep your buddy clean, too.

Remember the saying here: "There's no bad weather; just bad gear."

SAFETY

This is a bike-route guide, not a how-to book on bicycling. Even so, there are some topics to touch on that will make your ride safer and more enjoyable.

On the Roads

Local jurisdictions have gone to great lengths to make the streets safer. Bike lanes, sharrow lanes (traffic lanes marked with a bike and an arrow to remind motorists that bicyclists have the right to use the entire lane), greenways, and now cycle tracks are designed to decrease bicyclists' exposure to traffic. There is no defense, however, against a distracted driver or a malicious motorist.

If you're a recreational cyclist who can choose when to ride, it helps to stay off the road during the busiest times of the day—essentially the morning and evening commute hours. Development patterns in the Puget Sound region mean that some two-lane rural roads can get clogged with traffic heading to outlying housing developments. Plan your trips, if possible, to avoid those times. Also, if you think it will become dark before you finish your ride, use a bright headlamp and a red rear flasher or two.

There are some old sayings about safe bicycling that bear repeating: "Know and follow the rules of the road" and "Ride predictably." In other words, ride your bike as if you were driving a car: Stop at stop signs and red lights, signal when you turn, and ride with traffic, instead of the opposite direction. Avoid riding on the sidewalk, if possible, and, if you must, do so in the same direction as traffic on that side of the street.

Also, ride as if you're invisible. Always make eye contact with motorists who are turning left in front of you or coming out of side streets. If they're not looking your way, they may not see you. Stay out of vehicles' blind spots.

When you're riding in the bike lane on the right side of the road, watch for cars making right turns across you path. Make sure they've seen you before entering the intersection.

One of the diciest maneuvers in traffic is making a left turn. Always signal and check behind you before changing lanes to make a left turn; either wait for a break in traffic or make eye contact with a motorist who will allow you to change lanes. Get in line behind other cars in the left turn lane, and then move toward the right after you make the turn. Or you can make a "box left turn," in which you ride across the intersection, stop, turn your bike 90 degrees in your intended direction of travel, and proceed when the light changes on that cross street.

Parked cars can be as dangerous as moving cars. Always give about 4 feet of room for a car door to open, whether you're in a bike lane, traffic lane, or sharrow lane.

On the Rail Trails

Even though there's no traffic on the rail trails, bicyclists need to use caution. These multiuse trails are often busy with people walking their dogs, families with kids, joggers wearing headphones, and bicyclists with varying degrees of expertise. The sections of trail next to parking lots are the busiest.

Always ride to the right and pass on the left. Give a warning to pedestrians you are about to pass. You can usually tell if they've heard you; if not, give them a wide berth. Ride at a reasonable speed and always slow down if you're passing children or if someone looks confused.

Watch for bollards, those posts installed at street crossings to prevent cars from entering the trail. These can create more problems than they fix. If you're in a group, it's a good idea to warn those behind you. Also, watch out for fallen limbs or cracked pavement on the trails.

On Single Track

Trail etiquette applies even to the most remote single track. Essentially, wheels yield to heels. Rules dictate that you move to the side or off the trail for hikers. My experience is that most hikers will move to the side to allow you to pass after you announce yourself from a safe distance.

You'll encounter equestrians on the trails. Horses are skittish creatures; always give a greeting from a distance so they don't spook and stand off the trail on the downhill side. (Horses are a prey animal and can get excited if you stand uphill because carnivores usually attack from above.)

For other mountain bikers, riders heading uphill have the right-of-way. Always announce if you're riding solo or if there are others in your party. Also, take it easy on the trail. Avoid skidding your tires when slowing, as this loosens the dirt. During the rainy months in the Pacific Northwest, you'll face plenty of mud puddles. While it's better to go through a puddle than to widen a trail by going around it, go slowly to avoid creating ruts.

EQUIPMENT

Helmets are required for everyone riding a bicycle in King and Pierce Counties. It's a good idea when riding elsewhere, as well. When buying a helmet, look at the label inside to make sure it meets one of the following standards: CPSC, ASTM F1447, Snell B-90/95, or Snell N-94. More-expensive helmets aren't necessarily better. Cascade Bicycle Club sells perfectly adequate low-cost helmets at Bicycle Sunday on Lake Washington and at other events.

Mirrors allow you to monitor traffic behind you. I use a rectangular one attached to my eyeglasses, but mirrors can attach to your helmet or handlebar. I use my mirror primarily to check for traffic if I have to veer into the lane to avoid some road debris or ride beyond the door zone of parked cars. It also prevents surprises when other cyclists pass without announcing themselves.

A bell is a good idea if you ride trails where there are pedestrians. It's easy to flick a small handlebar bell with your finger and the high-pitched sound carries a good distance.

Lights are a good safety feature, day or night. A small blinking handlebar light in broad daylight catches motorists' attention, as does a red blinker on the back of your bike. State law says that at night, you must have a steady white light on the front and a red reflector on the rear.

Bike locks are a wise item to carry, especially if you're going to leave your bike for a while to go for a hike, go inside to get a bite, or check out a museum. U-locks are heavy, but among the best.

A cyclometer to measure your mileage is necessary for using the Miles & Directions for rides in this book. They come in all styles and prices.

Cyclists pedal past a field of flowers near Carnation.

Using this Guide

The Seattle area offers a wide range of bicycling choices. Urban riding. Hilly terrain. Flat routes. Rail trails. Forest roads. Technical mountain-biking trails. Flowy single track. They're all in this guide.

Most of the rides are in the 5- to 35-mile range and can be finished within 4 hours or less. Don't be fooled by the short mileages; those are mountain-bike rides in which 5 miles over rough terrain can take an hour or more.

The individual ride summaries include the mileage and estimated riding time—that's time in the saddle. If there are going to be climbs, I mention those in the Terrain section.

For many, the excitement of bicycling is not just the fluid motion of propelling yourself across the landscape; it's the sights along the way. I enjoy roadside attractions as well, and mention them under Things to See.

The Getting There section has directions by car and mentions which bus routes serve that location. Transit systems in the Greater Seattle area provide bicycle racks on the fronts of buses. If you're unsure how to operate these, check the instructions and film at metro.kingcounty.gov/tops/bike/bikeride.html.

There are no epic, all-day bike routes in here, although some routes—such as the North and South Lake Washington Loops—can be combined to extend the mileage. You also can consult local county bicycle maps to find adjacent routes to explore.

The rail-trail rides are often the longest. In many cases, I mapped those trails from beginning to end. Studying the map and descriptions, bicyclists can choose whether to ride the entire length or split the ride up into separate rides. Most, such as the Centennial Trail in Snohomish County, the Cedar River Trail in King County, and the Foothills Trail in Pierce County, have multiple midpoint trailheads that can serve as turnarounds. Know your limits. If you know how far you can ride, then simply turn around when you've reached your halfway point. Using the rail trails is a good way to increase your stamina by going a little farther each time.

Where possible, I've offered multiple options for riding the single track in mountain-biking areas. Some routes have their own characteristics; if you're not ready to ride a technical route, then you can choose an easier one.

Ongoing changes to the transportation network here may affect some of these bicycle routes. A new SR 520 Bridge—with its own bike paths—over Lake Washington will change the configuration of bike routes in the Montlake and Medina neighborhoods. The completion of the tunnel-boring project in Seattle will create a bike path along Seattle's waterfront. Mountain-bike trails in parks are being added, moved, or rubbed out all the time.

GPS

The distances for Miles & Directions in this book were calculated with a GPS device I mounted on my handlebars. Your mileages should match if you use your own GPS device. A cyclometer may give a slightly different reading due to its settings or even tire pressure. Also, a short side trip that's not mapped will affect the mileage. Try to take those into account.

Key to icons used in this edition:

 Road Bike   Mountain Bike   Hybrid

A manmade hill dominates Gas Works Park on the Lake Union Loop.

Ride Finder

BEST ROAD RIDES

9. Snohomish–Monroe Loop
11. Snohomish–Granite Falls Loop
14. Black Diamond–Green River Gorge Loop
22. Mercer Island Loop
23. Cougar Mountain–May Valley Loop

28. Fall City–Carnation Loop
36. Vashon–Maury Island Loop
37. Bainbridge Island Loop
38. Port Gamble–Poulsbo Loop
39. The Ride to Port Orchard

BEST RAIL-TRAIL RIDES

10. Centennial Trail
15. Cedar River Trail
16. Foothills Trail Ride

24. Sammamish River Trail
29. Preston–Snoqualmie Trail
35. John Wayne Pioneer Trail

BEST COMBINED ROAD AND TRAIL RIDES

1. Lake Union–Ship Canal Loop
2. Discovery Park Loop
3. Magnolia Loop
4. Space Needle–Fishermen's Wharf Loop
5. North Lake Washington Loop
6. South Lake Washington Loop

7. Seattle Waterfront to Alki Beach Round-Trip
8. Green Lake to Edmonds Loop
25. Lake Sammamish Loop
29. Preston–Snoqualmie Trail
30. Rattlesnake Lake and Snoqualmie Falls Loop

BEST RIDES FOR MOUNTAIN BIKES

12. Paradise Valley Conservation Area
17. Towers of Power
18. Dash Point State Park Trails
19. Henry's Ridge–Black Diamond–Summit Ridge
20. Taylor Mountain Forest Loop
21. Carbon River Road
26. Saint Edward State Park and Big Finn Hill Park

27. Thrilla in Woodinvilla Loop
31. Duthie Hill Mountain Bike Park Loop
32. Grand Ridge Park Trail
33. Tiger Mountain State Forest
34. Middle Fork Snoqualmie Trail
35. John Wayne Pioneer Trail
40. Banner Forest Heritage Park

BEST RIDES FOR SIGHTSEEING

1. Lake Union–Ship Canal Loop
2. Discovery Park Loop
3. Magnolia Loop
4. Space Needle–Fishermen's Wharf Loop
7. Seattle Waterfront to Alki Beach Round-Trip
9. Snohomish–Monroe Loop
10. Centennial Trail
20. Taylor Mountain Forest Loop
21. Carbon River Road
22. Mercer Island Loop
25. Lake Sammamish Loop
28. Fall City–Carnation Loop
29. Preston–Snoqualmie Trail
30. Rattlesnake Lake and Snoqualmie Falls Loop
33. Tiger Mountain State Forest
34. Middle Fork Snoqualmie Trail
35. John Wayne Pioneer Trail
36. Vashon–Maury Island Loop
37. Bainbridge Island Loop
38. Port Gamble–Poulsbo Loop
39. The Ride to Port Orchard

BEST RIDES FOR BEACHCOMBING

2. Discovery Park Loop
3. Magnolia Loop
7. Seattle Waterfront to Alki Beach Round-Trip
8. Green Lake to Edmonds Loop
26. Saint Edward State Park and Big Finn Hill Park
36. Vashon–Maury Island Loop
37. Bainbridge Island Loop
38. Port Gamble–Poulsbo Loop
39. The Ride to Port Orchard

BEST RIDES FOR SEEING MUSEUMS AND HISTORIC LANDMARKS

1. Lake Union–Ship Canal Loop
2. Discovery Park Loop
3. Magnolia Loop
4. Space Needle–Fishermen's Wharf Loop
9. Snohomish–Monroe Loop
10. Centennial Trail
11. Snohomish–Granite Falls Loop
14. Black Diamond–Green River Gorge Loop
23. Cougar Mountain–May Valley Loop
26. Saint Edward State Park and Big Finn Hill Park
30. Rattlesnake Lake and Snoqualmie Falls Loop
38. Port Gamble–Poulsbo Loop
39. The Ride to Port Orchard

BEST RIDES FOR SEEING BIRDS AND WILDLIFE

2. Discovery Park Loop
6. South Lake Washington Loop
9. Snohomish–Monroe Loop
13. Green River–Interurban Trails Loop
14. Black Diamond–Green River Gorge Loop
15. Cedar River Trail
21. Carbon River Road
24. Sammamish River Trail
25. Lake Sammamish Loop
30. Rattlesnake Lake and Snoqualmie Falls Loop
33. Tiger Mountain State Forest
36. Vashon–Maury Island Loop
40. Banner Forest Heritage Park

BEST RIDES FOR FAMILIES

2. Discovery Park Loop
15. Cedar River Trail
16. Foothills Trail Ride
24. Sammamish River Trail
29. Preston–Snoqualmie Trail
35. John Wayne Pioneer Trail

BEST OFF-ROAD RIDES

2. Discovery Park Loop
10. Centennial Trail
12. Paradise Valley Conservation Area
13. Green River–Interurban Trails Loop
15. Cedar River Trail
16. Foothills Trail Ride
17. Towers of Power
18. Dash Point State Park Trails
19. Henry's Ridge–Black Diamond–Summit Ridge
20. Taylor Mountain Forest Loop
24. Sammamish River Trail
29. Preston–Snoqualmie Trail
31. Duthie Hill Mountain Bike Park Loop
32. Grand Ridge Park Trail
33. Tiger Mountain State Forest
34. Middle Fork Snoqualmie Trail
35. John Wayne Pioneer Trail
40. Banner Forest Heritage Park

BEST RIDES FOR CAMPING

13. Green River–Interurban Trails Loop
14. Black Diamond–Green River Gorge Loop
18. Dash Point State Park Trails
21. Carbon River Road
28. Fall City–Carnation Loop
34. Middle Fork Snoqualmie Trail
35. John Wayne Pioneer Trail
37. Bainbridge Island Loop
38. Port Gamble–Poulsbo Loop

Map Legend

Transportation

Interstate/Divided Highway	═══════
Featured US Highway	═════
US Highway	═════
Featured State, County, or Local Road	──────
Primary Highway	───────
County/Local Road	───────
Featured Bike Route	••••••••••••••••
Bike Route	▪▪▪▪▪▪▪▪▪▪▪▪▪▪
Featured Trail	------------------
Trail/Dirt Road	------------------
Railroad	⊢─┼─┼─┼─┤

Hydrology

Reservoir/Lake	⬭
Swamp	
River/Creek	～～
Waterfall	⋰

Land Use

National Forest/ National Park	▭
State/Local Park/ Open Space/ Wildlife Area	▭

Symbols

Interstate	🛡90
US Highway	🛡2
State Highway	(202)
County Road	FR 56
Trailhead (Start)	🔟
Mileage Marker	17.1◆──
Visitor Center	❷
Point of Interest/ Structure	▪
Restroom/Pit Toilet	🚻
Museum	🏛
Parking	🅿
Airport	✈
University/College	🎓
Picnic Table	⨖
Campground	Λ
Viewpoint	◧
Ranger Station	🚹🏠
Mountain/Peak	▲
Bridge	⤳
Gate	⅋
Lighthouse	🗼
Direction Arrow	→

Seattle

Downtown Seattle is visible from the Alki Beach monument that marks the landing spot of the first white settlers.

At first glance, Seattle may not strike visiting flatlanders as a city where bicycling would be a popular pursuit. The land seems to rise right out of Puget Sound. The hilly terrain is a challenge, but bicycle routes avoid the steepest grades.

The bike routes in this section make use of the historic bike thoroughfares and former railroad lines, as well as the newer bike trails and bike lanes. Some of the routes visit tourist attractions such as the Space Needle and the Ballard Locks, while others are scenic workouts that loop around Lake Washington.

Bicycling has been a popular pastime in the Emerald City for a long time. The arrival of the first bicycle in Washington Territory made headlines on November 15, 1879. A *Weekly Intelligencer* reporter predicted, "Another season will find many bicycles here in active use." It did.

Bicycling's early popularity fell off with the advent of the automobile. Since the 1980s, however, a growing contingent of residents has embraced bicycle commuting and recreation for its economic, environmental, and healthful benefits.

Advocates have worked with elected officials and city staff to make Seattle streets as safe as possible for people on bicycles. As of this writing, the city has 78 miles of bike lanes, 47 miles of bike trails, and 92 miles of sharrows (streets marked to remind motorists that bicycles have a right to the road).

An updated Bicycle Master Plan calls for more bicycle facilities with an emphasis on new best practices. Expect more miles of cycle tracks that are separated from traffic and neighborhood greenways where families can feel safe riding in the street.

Lake Union–Ship Canal Loop

You're never far from Seattle's waterfront on this bike ride around Lake Union and the Ship Canal. Starting at a sprawling relic to the industrial age in a city that embraces high tech, the loop passes houseboat communities where Tom Hanks found himself in Sleepless in Seattle *and rolls through a park that's home to nostalgic wooden boats. You can take a boat tour of Lake Union, if you like, or a short side trip to Fremont to visit the troll that lives beneath the Aurora Bridge.*

Start: Gas Works Park

Length: 10.4-mile loop

Approximate riding time: 1 to 1.5 hours

Best bike: Road or hybrid

Terrain: The ride is mostly flat, except for a bridge crossing and a very steep pitch on a side street. Most of the ride is on paved trail.

Traffic and hazards: Expect low traffic on side streets; 2 bridge crossings are on a sidewalk and bike lane. The trail passes through a parking lot, so watch for turning cars. Also, the Burke-Gilman and Ship Canal trails are popular with pedestrians.

Things to see: Gas Works Park; houseboat community; the troll under the Aurora Bridge; and Lake Union Park, home of the Center for Wooden Boats and the Museum of History and Industry (MOHAI)

Maps: Seattle Bicycle Map website, seattle.gov/transportation/ bikemaps.htm; *DeLorme Atlas & Gazetteer—Washington*, page 45, D10

Getting there: By car: From I-5, take exit 169 for Northeast 45th Street. Turn left onto Northeast 45th Street, then left onto Meridian Avenue North. After a little more than a mile, Meridian ends at Gas Works Park. Turn right onto North Northlake Way, then immediately left into the parking lot. **By bus:** Metro Transit Route 26 stops at North 35th Street and Wallingford Avenue North, about 0.3 miles. GPS: N47 38.800' / W122 20.143'

THE RIDE

When the first white settlers arrived in the Seattle area in the mid-1800s, Lake Union sat isolated in the midst of a giant forest. It was called "small lake" by the local Duwamish tribe, but one of Seattle's early mayors renamed it Lake Union with the vision of linking it with the larger Lake Washington to the east and the Puget Sound to the west.

This ride follows the circumference of the lake and crosses the Lake Washington Ship Canal that fulfilled that vision in the 1930s to make the lake a vibrant part of the city's maritime community today. Although the ride starts where the Burke-Gilman Trail passes the Gas Works Park parking lot, the 20-acre park is certainly worth a visit as it boasts sweeping views of the entire lake as well as the Seattle skyline and the city's iconic Space Needle.

It's one of the most bizarre-looking public parks you'll ever see, owing to its former life as a coal gasification facility for the Seattle Gas Light Co. in the first half of the twentieth century. The rusting hulks of gas generator towers, storage tanks, and connecting pipes remain preserved, and a century-old pump house is now a play barn with the pumps, compressors, and a flywheel incorporated into play structures. An earthen mound built on rubble from the facility serves as a platform for kite flying and sightseeing the sailboats, kayaks, large pleasure boats, and seaplanes that ply the lake.

Leaving the parking lot, cross North Northlake Way and turn right onto the Burke-Gilman Trail, a rail trail that rolls for nearly 19 uninterrupted miles. Watch for pedestrians on this busy thoroughfare as you head toward the University of Washington campus.

A sign for the Cheshiahud Loop directs you left from the Burke-Gilman onto Northeast 40th Street, then right onto the University Bridge, which you can cross on a bike lane. The bridge is a draw span that opens occasionally for sailboats or larger pleasure craft passing through Portage Bay along the Lake Washington Ship Canal.

Bike Shops

Cascade Bicycle Studio: 180 N. Canal St.; (206) 547-4900; cascadebicyclestudio.com

Free Range Cycles: 3501 Phinney Ave. North; (206) 547-8407; freerangecycles.com

Herriott Sports Performance: 101 Nickerson St. #105; (206) 816-3436; hspseattle.com

Recycled Cycles: 1007 NE Boat St.; (206) 547-4491; recycledcycles.com

Rosebud Bicycle Builds: 700 NW 42nd St.; (206) 595-287; rosebudbicyclebuilds.com

Speedy Reedy Triathlon: 1300 N. Northlake Way; (206) 632-9879; speedyreedy.com

Wright Brothers Cycle Works: 219 N. 36th St.; (206) 633-5132; wrightbrotherscycleworks.com

A right turn takes you downhill to the waterfront, where you'll find a sprawling community of houseboats and the businesses that serve them. Fairview Avenue is obstructed, so there's a short, steep climb up to Eastlake Avenue East for a couple of blocks, but soon you return to the waterfront. There are frequent street-end and pocket parks along this eastern shoreline where you can pause and soak in the atmosphere of life on the water.

Passing an old shipyard that still tends to larger watercraft, the route turns right and joins the South Lake Union Trail. This path can be clogged with clusters of people strolling from nearby offices, so you might be tempted to swerve onto the adjacent Valley Street. Just beware of the South Lake Union Trolley streetcar tracks that can catch bicycle tires and catapult bicyclists over the handlebars to the hard concrete.

Directly across the lake from the Gas Works Park, the 12-acre Lake Union Park is worth a visit for anyone interested in the Pacific Northwest's maritime history. Vintage ferryboats, tugboats, and sailboats moored here are open for walk-throughs and scheduled cruises on Lake Union. One vessel, the SS *Virginia V*, is among the few survivors of the famed Mosquito Fleet comprising hundreds of vessels that carried passengers and supplies across the Puget Sound during the nineteenth and early twentieth centuries.

This also is home to the Center for Wooden Boats, a foundation dedicated to preserving wooden boats, their culture, and the craftsmanship required to build and maintain them. Dozens of restored wooden rowboats, sailboats, and powerboats are on display at the docks at the eastern end of the park. Visitors can take a short cruise or watch artisans working on the latest projects—anything from a simple dugout canoe to a sailboat.

Keeping to the historical theme is the Museum of History and Industry (MOHAI), housed in the armory of the naval base that once inhabited this site. Relocated from the University of Washington campus in 2012, the museum houses archival documents and photographs from the Puget Sound region and hosts exhibits of life and culture here.

Arriving here on a hot summer day, you'll find relief in the water spouting from fountain walkways or enjoy watching hobbyists sailing handmade boats in a cement pond.

Leaving Lake Union Park behind, you will turn right onto South Lake Union Trail as it heads north along the west side of the lake. The trail turns into a route through a series of parking lots for more businesses that serve the maritime trade and marinas that house yachts and floating homes.

The Ship Canal Trail begins as you pass beneath the Fremont Bridge. Also a rail trail, this path follows alongside the Fremont Cut of the Ship Canal that first linked Lake Union with the Puget Sound in the 1930s. Cycling on the south side of the canal, you can observe a steady stream of watercraft powering past.

A recumbent cyclist rides along the Fremont Cut on the Ship Canal Trail.

Turn left onto 13th Avenue West just before the Ballard Bridge to merge with 15th Avenue West and cross the Ship Canal to Ballard. The Ballard Bridge carries 15th Avenue West into Ballard over Salmon Bay. I'd recommend using the walkway for crossing the bridge. Exit the bridge to the right at the first opportunity at Ballard Way and head downhill along an unnamed street to Northwest 45th Street. Follow this street for a couple of blocks until you pick up the Burke-Gilman Trail in front of a shopping center at 11th Avenue Northwest.

Now you'll find yourself across the channel from the Ship Canal Trail and heading in the opposite direction. The second bridge you pass under is the Aurora Bridge for SR 99. If you're interested in a side trip, head north a couple of blocks under this bridge to find the Fremont Troll at North 36th Street. The colossal statue beneath the bridge depicts the head and torso of a giant emerging from the ground crushing a Volkswagen in one hand.

This is just one of the oddities you'll find in the neighborhood that calls itself the People's Republic of Fremont. The boutiques and street life indicate an artistic flair. It comes to full bloom during the Fremont Fair's Summer Solstice Parade, which features the Painted Cyclists—more than a hundred men and women on bicycles wearing little more than a layer of body paint and a

Floating Homes

There are 500 houseboats in the Seattle area, and most are moored along the Lake Union and adjoining Portage Bay shorelines. Actually, the owners prefer the term "floating homes." They're essentially houses built on rafts that are permanently moored to a dock. Because they don't move around, they're not literally boats.

These homes come in many sizes, although most are multiple stories tall to maximize the living space on a small platform. The largest on Lake Union at 2,720 square feet is also the most famous. It's the houseboat—I mean "floating home"—featured in *Sleepless in Seattle*. Located at the end of a west shoreline pier just north of Boatworld Marinas, it's hidden from the South Lake Union Trail but clearly visible from the water. It was listed for sale in 2008 for $2.5 million.

The scenes of Tom Hanks enjoying the nautical views from his balcony give a pleasurable impression of life on floating homes, but they're not for everyone. Residents must put up with noisy motorboats and seaplanes, nosy kayakers, the occasional whiff of rotting fish, and droppings left on the deck by visiting otters.

smile. With that thought in mind, return to the Burke-Gilman Trail from your side trip. Your ride ends soon at Gas Works Park.

MILES & DIRECTIONS

0.0 Cross North Northlake Way from parking lot; ride begins with a right turn onto Burke-Gilman Trail.

0.9 Turn left at sign for University Bridge, follow path across crosswalk, and turn right at Northeast 40th Street.

1.0 Turn right onto University Bridge and cross the bridge using the bike lane.

1.4 Turn right onto Fuhrman Avenue East after crossing the bridge. Go down a short hill and the street turns to the left and becomes Fairview Avenue East.

1.9 Turn left on East Hamlin Street and proceed uphill for 2 blocks.

2.0 Turn right onto Eastlake Avenue East, go 1 block, then turn right onto East Edgar Street. After coasting downhill for 2 blocks, turn left onto Yale Avenue East.

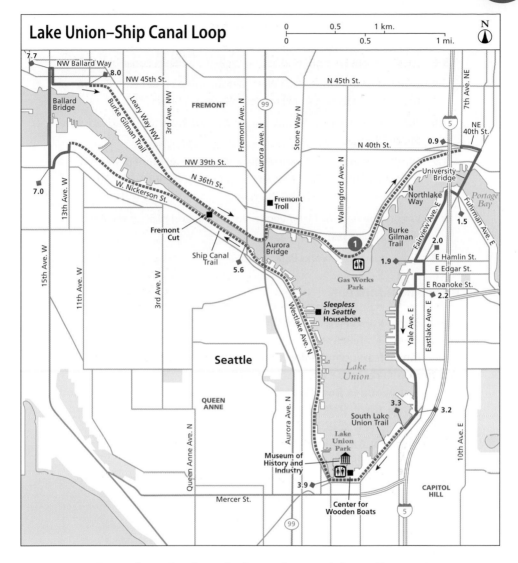

Lake Union–Ship Canal Loop

2.2 Turn right on East Roanoke Street, then turn left onto Fairview Avenue at the bottom of the hill.

3.2 Bear right and take the bike lane on Fairview Avenue; do not take the pedestrian trail on the right as it heads down steps to the waterfront.

3.3 Veer right onto multipurpose path that becomes the South Lake Union Trail.

3.8 Entrance to Lake Union Park.

3.9 Follow path to the right as it follows Westlake Avenue North. It follows a route over sidewalks and off-street parking lots for maritime businesses.

5.6 Pass beneath Fremont Bridge and pick up the Ship Canal Trail.

6.9 Turn left onto 13th Avenue West (before you pass beneath Ballard Bridge) and follow it uphill to West Nickerson Street.

7.0 Turn right onto the sidewalk of 15th Avenue Northwest and cross the Ballard Bridge.

7.7 Exit the bridge at Northwest Ballard Way, take an immediate hard right down the hill, and turn left at the T intersection with 45th Avenue Northwest. Follow the sharrows.

8.0 Veer to the right at 11th Avenue Northwest and pick up the Burke-Gilman Trail again.

10.4 Ride ends at Gas Works Park.

RIDE INFORMATION

Local Events and Attractions

Fremont Fair: A street festival in mid-June that includes the Summer Solstice Parade, which features more than 100 bicyclists in body paint—rain or shine. Visit fremontfair.org.

Lake Union Wooden Boat Festival: Classic wooden boats on display, food, crafts at Lake Union Park in late June or early July. Check with Center for Wooden Boats at cwb.org.

Fourth of July at Gas Works Park: Huge gathering during the day and good view of fireworks from Space Needle at night

Seattle Boat Show: Outdoor display of yachts on South Lake Union in late Jan or early Feb. Visit seattleboatshow.com.

Restrooms

Mile 0.0: Gas Works Park
Mile 3.8: Lake Union Park
Mile 10.4: Gas Works Park

Discovery Park Loop

This bike ride is completely within the confines of Discovery Park, the largest park in Seattle. Historically a military installation built to protect the southern Puget Sound, the area is becoming an urban wilderness. You'll pass old buildings that still command breathtaking views across the water, visit a saltwater beach, and spin through forests. Although the ride is relatively short at 5 miles, you'll want to budget more time for beachcombing, bird watching, sightseeing, and struggling up the road that climbs from the lighthouse.

Start: East parking lot at Discovery Park, located on the Magnolia Peninsula northwest of downtown

Length: 4.7 miles

Approximate riding time: 1 hour

Best bike: Road or hybrid

Terrain: The loop is relatively flat on the plateau, but experiences a steep descent and climb to and from the beach. Bicycles are only allowed on paved surfaces.

Traffic and hazards: The main thoroughfare—Discovery Park Boulevard—doesn't have shoulders, although there is a paved trail alongside. Traffic is heaviest between the park entrance and the visitor center at the south parking lot. You'll want a bicycle lock if you plan to spend time inside the visitor center or on the beach.

Things to see: Discovery Park Visitors Center, numerous abandoned military buildings, Puget Sound beaches, West Point Lighthouse, Daybreak Star Cultural Center, and views from the meadows across the sound to the Olympic Mountains. This is also a haven for birders.

Maps: *DeLorme Atlas & Gazetteer—Washington,* page 45; *Seattle Parks and Recreation—Discovery Park,* available at visitor center and online at seattle.gov/parks/trails_detail.asp?id=310

Getting there: From I-5, take the Mercer Street exit and head west, turn right onto Westlake Avenue North, and follow it as it becomes West Nickerson Street. After crossing 15th Avenue NW, turn left on West Emerson Place and right on Gilman Avenue Northwest. That street becomes West Government Way, which enters the park at 36th Avenue West. The name changes to Discovery Bay Boulevard. Turn left at the sign for the Discovery Bay Visitors Center in about 0.1 mile. GPS: N47 39.485' / W122 24.368'

THE RIDE

We can thank the federal government for preserving this point of land in 1900 as Fort Lawton, a military base created to protect the southern Puget Sound from naval invasion. It must have been a successful idea, as Seattle was never invaded.

The city of Seattle acquired more than 500 acres of the facility in 1973 to create Discovery Park, named for the ship of English explorer Captain George Vancouver. The city received the rest when Fort Lawton was decommissioned in 2011.

The bike ride starts at the entrance to the east parking lot at the visitor center, about 0.1 mile inside the park. There are a few displays inside the building and an information desk. Detailed maps are for sale here, and free ones are available at a kiosk outside.

Leaving the parking lot, turn left onto a paved trail running adjacent to Discovery Park Boulevard (remember, bicycles are allowed only on paved surfaces in the park). The first paved road on the left is California Avenue, and the entrance to the abandoned Fort Lawton Historic District. Rolling through here, the first building you encounter is the yellow frame administration building, which dates to 1902.

Gazing from its porch, down the meadow, and across the Puget Sound to the snow-covered Olympic Mountains, you might get the idea this wasn't such a bad location for deployment. The base didn't see much activity until World War II, when a building boom created space for 20,000 troops at a time to be deployed to war zones, and German and Italian prisoners of war were housed here. More troop deployment duties fell on the fort during the Korean War, and then it briefly saw duty as a Nike anti-missile base. Most of the base was declared surplus in 1964.

Bike Shop

BikeSport: 4550 9th Ave. NW, Ballard; (206) 706 4700; ilovemybike.com

Views across Puget Sound to the Olympic Peninsula dominate Seattle's largest park.

Follow the road to the left and you'll pass the old band barracks and post exchange/gymnasium. The route snakes through a meadow, making a U-shaped turn to the right. Many native grasses and flowering plants adorn this area on the bluff, which affords some of the best views of the Olympic Peninsula.

Keep an eye open for coveys of quail scampering across the old road here. Between this meadow, the seashore, and the forests, birdwatchers have identified some 270 species of birds, making the park a prime destination for birders. Bald eagles and other raptors are commonly seen here, and owls silently patrol the skies in the evening. Gulls, loons, and western grebes are among the birds that frequent the beach.

The park is a wildlife sanctuary, so you may spot furry critters like the occasional deer mouse or mountain beaver. It's unlikely you'll see anything bigger, although coyote and bears have been spotted here, and a cougar was trapped here and released in the Cascades in 2009.

When you return to Discovery Park Boulevard, turn left and start downhill. You quickly have to make a decision: If you are feeling strong and can tackle a Tour de France–worthy climb on the return, coast down this hill to the beach. If ascending 250 feet in less than a mile on the return trip isn't in your repertoire, then turn right at the first paved trail on your right.

Zooming downhill, you'll arrive at the end of the road out on West Point. You might want to lock up your bike before taking the 0.1-mile walk out to the West Point Lighthouse. Built in 1881, it's the oldest of a dozen such facilities that guide mariners on the Puget Sound and was the last to be automated—in 1985.

A steady parade of sailboats, powerboats, barges, and oceangoing container ships passes this 0.5-mile-long spit. A 300-foot bluff rises from the sandy South Beach, which is littered with bleached driftwood. The rocky North Beach on the other side of the spit reveals a world of tiny sea creatures to anyone willing to lift up small rocks to see what's underneath.

The return trip uphill is memorable and good training for anyone wanting to get in shape in a hurry. It's okay to walk, too. Pass the signs for the Hidden Valley and Loop foot trails before arriving at a paved path that heads left through the woods. Follow this trail through the second-growth forest. It curves to the right shortly before arriving at signs for a pond and the Daybreak Star Cultural Center a short distance away.

Although not on this bike route, a visit to the facility run by United Indians of All Tribes is worthwhile for anyone interested in Native American culture. The center hosts conferences and powwows throughout the year and houses a Native American art gallery.

The Daybreak center came into being after the only "invasion" of Fort Lawton in 1970. That's when some one hundred members of the United Indian People's Council breached the fort to claim land for a cultural center and were arrested. Supported by actress Jane Fonda and others, protesters set up a camp at the entrance for months until negotiations led to establishment of the cultural center (opened in 1977).

The paved trail ends in a parking lot and becomes a street—Texas Way. This road winds through the site of the Fort Lawton Army Reserve Center, which is slated for use as low-income housing. Texas Way also weaves around the military cemetery (entrance off Discovery Bay Boulevard), where a German POW and an Italian POW are among the 800 interred.

Arriving at Discovery Way Boulevard, turn right to return to the South Parking Lot and the end of the ride.

MILES & DIRECTIONS

0.0 The loop ride starts at the entrance to the east parking lot for Discovery Park Visitors Center (restrooms and drinking fountains). Turn left onto a paved trail adjacent to Discovery Park Boulevard as you leave the parking lot and begin climbing.

0.2 Turn left onto Washington Avenue, the first street on your left. You can ignore the sign restricting the road only to authorized motor vehicles.

0.4 Pause at the top of the hill for views of the Puget Sound and Olympic Mountains beyond. Immediately past the California Avenue intersection, leave Washington Avenue by heading to your right on an unnamed roadway; stay on the road as it loops to the left.

0.6 Veer slightly to the left through an intersection and pass an old gymnasium on your right. The road becomes Oregon Avenue.

0.9 At the next four-way intersection, make a hard right turn.

1.3 Turn left at the T intersection just past the rear of the gymnasium.

1.4 Turn left onto Discovery Park Boulevard and head downhill.

2.1 Pass the entrance to West Point Treatment Plant on the right; continue on Discovery Park Boulevard.

2.4 Park your bicycle at the end of the road and walk about 0.1 mile to the West Point Lighthouse. You'll head back up the Discovery Park Boulevard hill when you return.

2.7 Restrooms are on your left, as well as the junction with Hidden Valley foot trail.

3.1 Turn left on an unnamed paved trail that heads through a wooded area.

Discovery Park Loop

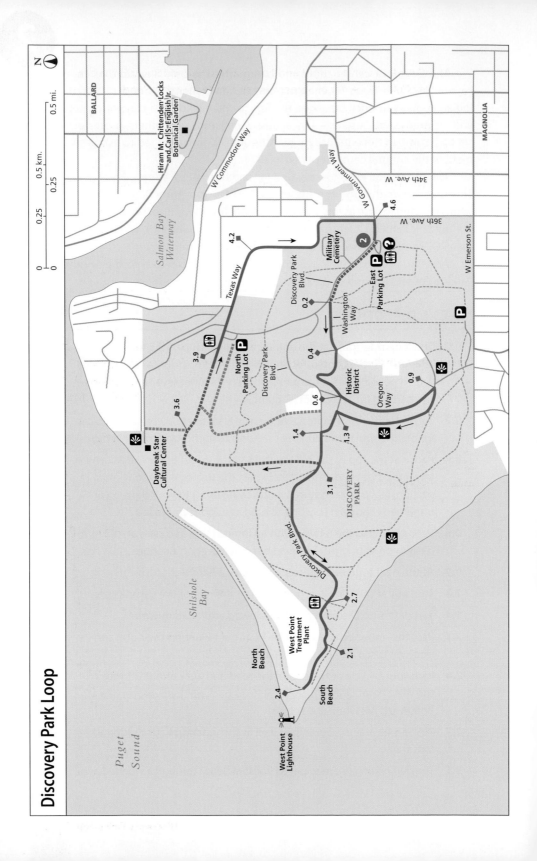

Puget Sound

Shilshole Bay

Salmon Bay Waterway

BALLARD

MAGNOLIA

Hiram M. Chittenden Locks and Carl S. English Jr. Botanical Garden

W Commodore Way

W Government Way

34th Ave. W

36th Ave. W

W Emerson St.

Military Cemetery

Discovery Park Blvd.

Washington Way

East Parking Lot

North Parking Lot

Discovery Park Blvd.

Texas Way

Daybreak Star Cultural Center

Historic District

Oregon Way

DISCOVERY PARK

West Point Treatment Plant

West Point Lighthouse

North Beach

South Beach

4.2

4.6

0.2

0.4

0.6

0.9

1.3

1.4

3.1

2.7

2.1

2.4

3.6

3.9

2

N

0   0.25   0.5 km.

0   0.25   0.5 mi.

3.6 Follow trail curve to right and pass paved trails (on left) to Daybreak Star Cultural Center or Serpent Mound and Reflecting Ponds.

3.9 Restrooms are on the right as you pass through the north parking lot. Road becomes Texas Way and you'll also pass the car entrance to Daybreak Star Cultural Center on the left.

4.2 Texas Way curves right as you pass signs and buildings of the Fort Lawton Army Reserve Center and zigzags around the military cemetery on your right.

4.6 Turn right onto Discovery Park Boulevard and head back uphill.

4.7 Turn left to east parking lot. End of ride.

RIDE INFORMATION

Local Events and Attractions

Discovery Park: Ongoing science and environmental education classes, 3801 Discovery Park Blvd.; seattle.gov/parks/environment/discovery.htm

West Point Lighthouse: Open on occasional weekends in the summer. Call (206) 386-4236 for information, or visit lighthousefriends.com/light.asp?ID=33.

Daybreak Star Cultural Center: Seafair Powwow in July. Check website for dates and details; unitedindians.org.

Restrooms

Mile 0.0: Discovery Park Visitors Center
Mile 2.7: Hidden Valley Trail
Mile 3.9: Parking lot (portable toilet)

Magnolia Loop

This bike route is more than a tour past the houses of Seattle's second largest neighborhood. Bicyclists cross the locks to Ballard; ride a waterfront bike path to a popular Puget Sound beach; then return to witness stunning views of the Olympic Peninsula, the Puget Sound, and downtown Seattle from the viewpoints on the Magnolia bluffs.

Start: Smith Cove Park, Seattle

Length: 13.6 miles

Approximate riding time: 2 hours

Best bike: Road or hybrid

Terrain: Mostly flat, except for 1 long hill to Puget Sound overlook

Traffic and hazards: Most of route is on bike paths, bike lanes, or residential streets with light traffic.

Things to see: Smith Cove Cruise Ship Terminal, Hiram M. Chittenden Locks, Carl S. English Jr. Botanical Garden, Golden Gardens Park, Puget Sound and downtown Seattle overlooks; side trip to Fisherman's Terminal

Maps: *City of Seattle Bike Maps*, available in bike stores and online at seattle.gov/transportation/bikemaps.htm; *DeLorme Atlas & Gazetteer—Washington*, page 45

Getting there: By car: From the north take I-5 South to exit 172, heading west on North 85th Street. Turn left on 15th Avenue Northwest, passing through Ballard and over the Ballard Bridge. Turn right at West Garfield Street and take the right exit on 23rd Avenue West. Turn left into Smith Cove Park at West Marina Place and find parking on the left. From the south, take I-5 North to the left lane exit 167 to Seattle Center. Merge onto Mercer Street and turn right onto West Lake Avenue North, which becomes West Nickerson Street. Take the "exit only" lane onto West 15th Avenue and proceed south. Turn right at West Garfield Street, then take the right exit on 23rd Avenue West. Turn left into Smith Cove Park and find parking on the left. **By bus:** Metro bus routes 24 and 33 stop under West Garfield Street viaduct (Magnolia Bridge). Proceed west onto 23rd Avenue West to West Marina Place and turn left. GPS: N47 37.933' / W122 23.214'

THE RIDE

Many voyages begin or end around Seattle's Magnolia neighborhood. Swank cruise ships come and go at the Smith Cove Cruise Terminal in the southeast, everything from little dinghies to luxury yachts pass through the ship canal locks in the north, and massive container ships handling trade from Asia ply the Puget Sound to the west and south.

Thousands of salmon swim up fish ladders to return to their home waters to spawn while old salts at Fishermen's Terminal unload the day's catch. This 13-mile loop around the large Seattle neighborhood—with a run up to the beach at Golden Gardens Park for good measure—touches all of these nautical comings and goings.

The ride starts at Smith Cove Park, where you might arrive to marvel at a giant cruise ship docked at the Smith Cove Cruise Terminal at Pier 91. (It's also home to the Seattle Bicycle Expo every March.) The vacation cruise industry is the latest to use the docks, bringing nearly one million visitors to Seattle annually. Built in 1913, the facility's early imports included fresh silk from Asia that sped out on trains that followed today's routes of the Cedar River and John Wayne Pioneer rail trails. The Navy acquired the docks during World War II, and they returned to commercial shipping in the 1970s.

Heading north from the parking lot, the route follows the Elliott Bay Trail (Terminal 91 Bike Path), created by the Port of Seattle in the 1990s. (The trail makes a horseshoe around the slips and heads east to the downtown

Bike Shops

Alpine Hut: 2215 15th Ave. West, Seattle; (206) 284-3575; alpinehut.com

BikeSport: 4550 9th Ave. Northwest, Seattle; (206) 706-4700; ilovemybike.com

Dutch Bike Co. Seattle: 4741 Ballard Ave. Northwest, Seattle; (206) 789-1678; dutchbikeco.com

Sprocketts Recycled Bikes: 1600 W. Armory Way, Seattle; (206) 535-8765; sprockettsrecycledbicycles.com

A Pacific madrone shades a view of Seattle from an overlook on the Magnolia bluff.

Seattle waterfront.) The bike ride leaves the trail at 21st Avenue West. It heads up a short hill to Thorndyke Avenue West, an arterial that rolls along the eastern border of Magnolia. The name changes to 20th Avenue West and Gilman Avenue West before it becomes West Government Way.

As you cross West Emerson Place at Mile 1.8, you might consider a short side trip to Fishermen's Terminal. This is home port to many fishing vessels in the North Pacific fishing fleet, including some featured on the TV show *Deadliest Catch* about the Alaskan crabbing industry. You can grab a bite to eat here and tour a fishing vessel in port.

A right turn off West Government Way onto 32nd Street West leads to a path and a bridge that deposits you across the street from the entrance to Commodore Park overlooking the Hiram S. Chittenden Locks, also known as the Ballard Locks. Remember to dismount and walk your bicycle through the park and locks facility or face a $75 fine. Walking is a good idea here anyway, as this is a year-round tourist destination, and the bridges across the spillway dam and the two locks are narrow and congested.

Walking through the north gate to the Ballard Locks (you can climb back in the saddle again), cross a parking lot and turn left onto the Burke-Gilman

Trail. This 2-mile section was completed in 2008 and takes cyclists past the sprawling Shilshole Marina to Golden Gardens Park.

Designed as a "Sunday outing" destination in 1907 at the end of a street-car line, the 88-acre park features a long, sunny (weather permitting) beach on the Puget Sound with restrooms. If you're interested in a halfway break, there's a concession stand here and a beachside hot dog joint right outside the park.

Retrace your route back to the gate for the Ballard Locks, dismount, cross the bridges, and walk your bicycle up the sidewalk to West Commodore Way.

Hiram M. Chittenden Locks

Known officially as the Hiram M. Chittenden Locks, this Army Corps of Engineers facility is a favorite tourist destination in the Seattle area. Some 65,000 commercial and pleasure craft navigate the locks annually, and many people crowd the railings to watch the boats as they're raised or lowered as much as 22 feet.

When the Lake Washington Ship Canal opened up a passage between Puget Sound and Lakes Union and Washington in 1917, the locks were constructed to prevent lowering the lake-water level too much and mixing the sound's tidal salt water with the freshwater from the lakes. Any vessel making the voyage must pass through one of the locks, which are among the busiest in the nation.

A sideshow attraction is the arrival of thousands of salmon that swim through fish ladders at the locks from mid-June through September. Hatched in the freshwater rivers upstream, they swim out to live in the Pacific Ocean for four or five years before returning to spawn in those same streams. Averaging ten to fifteen pounds, the biggest are the Chinook salmon that splash around as they circle below the locks before heading up the fish ladder. Visitors can watch the Chinook and other salmon species working their way upstream at below-water-level windows on the south side of the dam.

After enjoying the spectacle of the passing boat (and salmon) parade and crossing the bridges over the locks, you might want to check out the Carl S. English Jr. Botanical Gardens on the north side of the boat channel. More than five hundred types of plants, both exotic species as well as those indigenous to the Pacific Northwest, are grown here. A free summer concert series is held on Saturday and Sunday on the grounds.

Displays and special tours of the locks, fish ladder, and gardens are available at the visitor center.

Directly across the street find 33rd Avenue West, begin a steep climb up to and across the pedestrian bridge, and return to 32nd Avenue West.

Continue straight and the route becomes West Government Way. In about a 0.5 mile you arrive at Discovery Park. Turn left onto 36th Avenue West. (To take a 5-mile side trip on Discovery Park Loop, enter the park here and ride up to the parking lot entrance on the left of Government Way.)

Turn right onto West Emerson Street and chug uphill to the highest elevation on the route. Turn left onto West Magnolia Way and enjoy the spectacular vistas of the Puget Sound and Olympic Peninsula from these bluffs. A little farther you'll spy views of the Seattle skyline with the iconic Space Needle and barges and freighters moving around Elliott Bay.

Magnolia got its name from the vegetation atop these cliffs. Legend has it that early explorer Captain George Vancouver named the area for the magnolias he saw growing on the cliffs from his ship, *Discovery*. What he saw were actually Pacific madrone, which still keep a toehold on these southern exposures.

Magnolia Way turns away from the overlooks for about 0.5 mile as it takes a horseshoe route around a steep ravine and passes Magnolia Park. There's one more chance to scan the horizon from the bluffs before the route turns left onto Thorndyke Avenue West. Heading downhill, look for a right turn into the industrial area along 21st Avenue West, and make another right turn onto the Elliott Bay Trail that takes you back to the parking lot at Smith Cove.

MILES & DIRECTIONS

0.0   Starting at the Smith Cove Park sign, head north (retracing the way you drove in) on Elliott Bay Trail, also known as Terminal 91 Bike Path. Pass under the West Garfield Street viaduct and veer to your left to remain on the trail.

0.8   Turn left onto 21st Avenue West (the bike path continues straight).

1.0   Veer right onto the bike lane on Thorndyke Avenue West.

1.2   Road becomes 20th Avenue West.

1.4   Road becomes Gilman Avenue West.

1.8   Pass West Emerson Place on your right. (A side trip to Fishermen's Terminal is 0.6 miles round-trip. If you're comfortable riding in traffic, turn right onto West Emerson Place, go about 4 blocks, and turn left into Fishermen's Terminal at 19th Avenue West. Retrace to return to the route.)

2.4   Road becomes West Government Way.

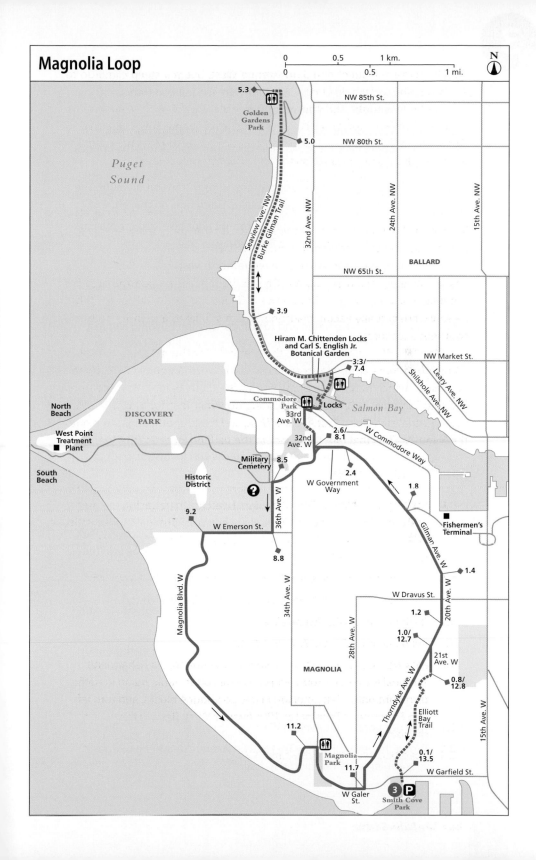

Magnolia Loop

0   0.5   1 km.
0   0.5   1 mi.

N

Puget
Sound

Golden Gardens Park
5.3
5.0

Seaview Ave. NW
Burke Gilman Trail

NW 85th St.
NW 80th St.

32nd Ave. NW
24th Ave. NW
15th Ave. NW

BALLARD
NW 65th St.

3.9

Hiram M. Chittenden Locks and Carl S. English Jr. Botanical Garden

3.3/
7.4

NW Market St.

Leary Ave. NW
Shilshole Ave. NW

Commodore Park
33rd Ave. W

Locks

Salmon Bay

North Beach

DISCOVERY PARK

West Point Treatment Plant

South Beach

Military Cemetery

8.5

32nd Ave. W

2.6/
8.1

W Commodore Way

2.4

1.8

Historic District

?

9.2

36th Ave. W

W Government Way

Fishermen's Terminal

W Emerson St.

8.8

34th Ave. W

Magnolia Blvd. W

1.4

W Dravus St.

Gilman Ave. W

1.2

1.0/
12.7

21st Ave. W

0.8/
12.8

28th Ave. W

20th Ave. W

15th Ave. W

MAGNOLIA

Thorndyke Ave. W

Elliott Bay Trail

11.2

Magnolia Park
11.7

0.1/
13.5

W Garfield St.

W Galer St.

3 P
Smith Cove Park

2.6 Turn right onto 32nd Avenue West. Follow a pedestrian trail that appears on the right, cross a bridge over the railroad tracks, and join 33rd Avenue West on the other side.

2.8 Cross West Commodore Way and turn right, heading downhill into Commodore Park. Bicyclists must dismount. Walk across the bridges for the dam and locks.

3.2 Pass Chittenden Locks visitor center and restrooms on the right. The entrance to Carl S. English Jr. Botanical Gardens is on the left.

3.3 Pass through the entrance gate, remount your bike, go across a parking lot, and turn left onto the Burke-Gilman Trail.

3.9 Take crosswalk over Seaview Avenue Northwest.

5.0 Burke-Gilman Trail ends at entrance to Golden Gardens Park. Use park road to enter.

5.3 Turn left for bike parking and to visit concession building and restrooms. Retrace your route through the parking lot and return to entrance to Burke-Gilman Trail.

7.4 Turn right into Hiram Chittenden Locks. Dismount and walk your bicycle through the park, cross the bridges over the locks, and walk uphill on the other side.

7.9 Cross West Commodore Way and ride up 33rd Avenue West to the pedestrian bridge over the railroad tracks and follow the path to 32nd Avenue West.

8.1 Continue straight as 32nd Avenue West turns into West Government Way.

8.5 Turn left onto 36th Avenue West. (If you're riding the Discovery Park Loop, continue straight into the park. The start of the loop is in the parking lot in the visitor center just up the hill.)

8.8 Turn right onto West Emerson Street.

9.2 Turn left onto Magnolia Boulevard West (this is the highest elevation of the loop).

11.2 Turn right onto West Howe Street and cross the short viaduct, and then turn right onto Magnolia Boulevard West, which becomes West Galer Street.

11.7 Turn left onto Thorndyke Avenue West.

12.7 Turn right onto 21st Avenue West.

12.8 Turn right onto Elliott Bay Trail as 21st Avenue dead-ends. Retrace your earlier route on Elliott Bay Trail.

13.5 Cross under West Garfield Street viaduct and veer right onto West Marina Place.

13.6 End of ride.

RIDE INFORMATION

Local Events and Attractions
Hiram M. Chittenden Locks: Locks information as well as dates for Sat and Sun afternoon concerts on the lawn; www.nws.usace.army.mil/Missions/Civil Works/LocksandDams/ChittendenLocks.aspx
Daily free naturalist tours of Hiram M. Chittenden Locks, June through mid-Oct; govlink.org/watersheds/8/action/salmon-seeson/ballard.aspx
Fishermen's Terminal: 3919 18th Ave. West, Seattle; www.portseattle.org/com mercial-marine/fishermens-terminal/pages/default.aspx
Seafood Fest: Downtown Ballard on a mid-July weekend features salmon barbecue, sidewalk sale, vendors, beer and wine garden, and lutefisk-eating contest; www.seafoodfest.org

Restaurants
Casual dining at several restaurants at the north entrance of the Hiram S. Chittenden Locks in Ballard, the Golden Gardens Park concession stand (seasonal), and Little Coney hot dogs in Shilshone Marina next to the park

Restrooms
Mile 2.8 Commodore Park
Mile 3.2 Hiram M. Chittenden Locks Visitor Center
Mile 5.3 Golden Gardens Park
Mile 7.4 Hiram M. Chittenden Locks Visitor Center
Mile 11.3 Magnolia Park

Space Needle–Fishermen's Wharf Loop

A good way to avoid the parking fees and congestion around the old site of the 1962 Seattle World's Fair is to visit by bicycle. The opening of the West Thomas Street Pedestrian and Bicycle Overpass in 2012 makes it easy to get to the Space Needle and other attractions from the bike trail in Myrtle Edwards Park. This loop throws in a trip through bike-centric Belltown and a stop at Fishermen's Wharf for more sightseeing possibilities.

Start: Parking lot for Elliott Bay Trail (Terminal 91 Bike Path) on 16th Avenue West

Length: 10.1 miles

Approximate riding time: 1 to 2 hours

Best bike: Road or hybrid

Terrain: Minor elevation gain to get to Seattle Center

Traffic and hazards: This route uses city streets marked with bike lanes; especially watch for car doors swinging open into your path, cars coming out of side streets, and motorists turning left in your path.

Things to see: Space Needle, International Fountain, Armory food court, Chihuly Garden and Glass, Experience Music Project, Monorail and Pacific Science Center at the Seattle Center, and Fishermen's Terminal

Maps: Seattle Bike Map, free in stores; Seattle Interactive Bike Map, seattle.gov/transportation/bikemapOnline.htm; *DeLorme Atlas & Gazetteer—Washington,* page 45

Getting there: By car: From the south, take I-5 North exit 166 and bear right onto East Olive Way. Turn left at Bellevue Avenue and left in 1 block onto East Denny Way. Take Denny Way through downtown to Western Avenue West, which merges to become Elliott Avenue West. Turn right at a large green sign over the street that says, "Terminals 86–91/ Magnolia Bridge/Amgen Court West/Exit Only." The ramp loops over the road; take the left fork marked "To Elliott Bay Trail." Turn right at the end of the ramp to follow signs to Elliott Bay Trail, go 1 block and turn right again, and then turn left onto 16th Avenue West. Back-in parking anywhere. From the north, pick up 15th Avenue Northwest, cross the Lake Washington Ship Canal in Ballard, and get in left-turn lane after the sign that says, "Terminals 86–91/Magnolia Bridge/Amgen Court West/Exit Only." The ramp loops over the road; take the left fork marked "To Elliott Bay Trail." Turn right at the end of the ramp to follow signs to Elliott Bay Trail, go 1 block and turn right again, and then turn left onto 16th Avenue West. Back-in parking anywhere. **By bus:** Metro bus routes 19, 24, 32, 33 and D Line serve the area at Elliott Avenue West and West Galer Street. GPS: N47 37.876' / W122 22.658'

THE RIDE

Visitors from around the world flocked to Seattle in 1962 to experience the futuristic attractions at the Seattle World's Fair, billed as the Century 21 Exposition.

Here we are in the twenty-first century and people still come to the former World's Fair grounds at the Seattle Center to visit some of those features, such as the Space Needle and Monorail, which have since become iconic images of the city.

Although it's located in a busy part of the city, improvements to bicycle paths and bike lanes in the vicinity make this spot easily accessible to bicyclists. Just remember to stay visible, follow the rules of the road, and be predictable when riding.

Bike Shops

Alpine Hut: 2215 15th Ave. West, Seattle; (206) 284-3575; alpinehut.com
Bicycle Pull Apart: Recycled bicycles, parts, and accessories, 2312 3rd Ave., Seattle; (206) 299-2674; bpaseattle.com
Elliott Bay Bicycles: Sales and repair, 2116 Western Ave., Seattle; (206) 441-8144; elliottbaybicycles.com
Velo Bike Shop: Sales and repair, 2151 6th Ave., Seattle; (206) 325-3292; velobikeshop.com

The Space Needle has become the iconic image for Seattle.

The route starts at a parking lot on the east side of Smith Cove, a frequent mooring for many of the cruise ships that regularly stop in Seattle. Pick up the Elliott Bay Trail (Terminal 91 Bike Path) that runs alongside the parking lot and head south toward the open water of Elliott Bay.

The trail curves left at the point that reveals the Seattle skyline and Alki Beach, as well as Bainbridge Island across Puget Sound. Although the trail is separated for pedestrians and bicyclists, joggers and walkers seem oblivious to the difference.

Pass beneath the West Thomas Street Pedestrian and Bicycle Overpass and enter from the far side. Built in 2012, the structure passes over a busy railroad yard and Elliott Avenue West for safe passage to the lower Queen Anne neighborhood. Bear slightly to the left onto Third Avenue West, and then right onto West Harrison Street.

In four or five short blocks you're at the plaza surrounding Key Arena. Opened in 1962 as the Washington State Pavilion for the World's Fair, the venue hosted The Beatles, Seattle's own Jimi Hendrix, and Elvis Presley in its early years, and was the home court for the Seattle SuperSonics basketball team from 1967 to 2008.

Ride around the plaza toward the right and then take West Thomas Street left to roll into the 74-acre Seattle Center. There's plenty to do for free here, although most activities require admission.

Straight ahead is the old Armory. Built in 1939 to house tanks, field artillery, and ammunition, the sturdy building has been through several rejuvenations and now features a food court and indoor dining. You'll also find food trucks that serve everything from burgers and hot dogs to falafel and tacos located around the grounds. There's variety in the music here too, as buskers open their instrument cases and perform for passersby.

More sounds can be heard at the International Fountain behind the Armory. Also built for the World's Fair, the fountain's water jets are synchronized to music. Children frolic in the fountain bowl on hot days, and the local contingent of the World Naked Bike Ride makes a stop here on its annual ride around town.

Of course Seattle's iconic Space Needle rises above it all. At 605 feet, it was the tallest structure west of the Mississippi River when it was built for the World's Fair and is a familiar sight from bike rides around the area. Today it is dwarfed by other buildings in town.

At the base are two recent additions to the Seattle Center campus. The architecture of the EMP Museum, which celebrates rock 'n' roll and popular culture, has been described as a melted guitar. Chihuly Garden and Glass features many of the glass sculptures of local artist Dale Chihuly.

Leave the center grounds by the walkway north of the Pacific Science Center (on your left). Turn left onto Second Avenue North, cross Denny Way, and bear left to stay in the left-hand bike lane of one-way Second Avenue.

The route heads through the trendy Belltown neighborhood, where nearly every street corner has a cafe and residents find everything they need within easy walking or biking distance. Looking to bring more urban-bicycling hipsters to the neighborhood, a 600-plus-unit high-rise apartment complex (Via6) offers bicycle parking, a bike club with a bike wash area, and easy access to a bike shop on the ground floor.

As you pass through Belltown you'll pick up Dexter Avenue North, which serves as a main bike commute thoroughfare. Remember to ride far enough away from parked cars here to avoid open doors.

The route rolls out of downtown toward Fremont, but turns onto the Ship Canal Trail just before crossing the Fremont Avenue Bridge. Proceed west along the waterway, admiring the parade of pleasure boats passing by.

Soon, you're riding behind the shipyards that service those vessels, among them the broad-shouldered ships of the Alaska fishing fleet. Several crabbing vessels from the Bering Sea featured on the *Deadliest Catch* television series get refitted here in the off-season.

At the end of the Ship Canal Trail is Fishermen's Terminal, which you can enter at the sign. There are restrooms in the building straight ahead, as well as an open-air pickup window for seafood lunch orders from Chinook's. A monument at the water's edge memorializes 500 local commercial fishermen who lost their lives on the high seas since the beginning of the twentieth century.

The route continues along the seawall for a look at the some six hundred vessels that call this home, then doubles back to West Emerson Place. From here, ride in the street and turn left onto the shoulder of Gilman Avenue West, which becomes 20th Avenue West.

The trail skirts the Interbay railroad yards as it picks up Elliott Bay Trail at a dead end. Follow it across the rail yard and back to the parking lot at Smith Cove.

MILES & DIRECTIONS

0.0 Facing the water, turn left from the parking lot and head south on Elliott Bay Trail (Terminal 91 Bike Path).

0.4 Pass by a fishing pier and restrooms on the right.

1.2 Turn right at the entrance to West Thomas Street Pedestrian and Bicycle Overpass. Follow it over the railroad yard and Elliott Avenue West. Bear left onto 3rd Avenue West after you cross and proceed uphill.

1.5 Turn right onto West Harrison Street.

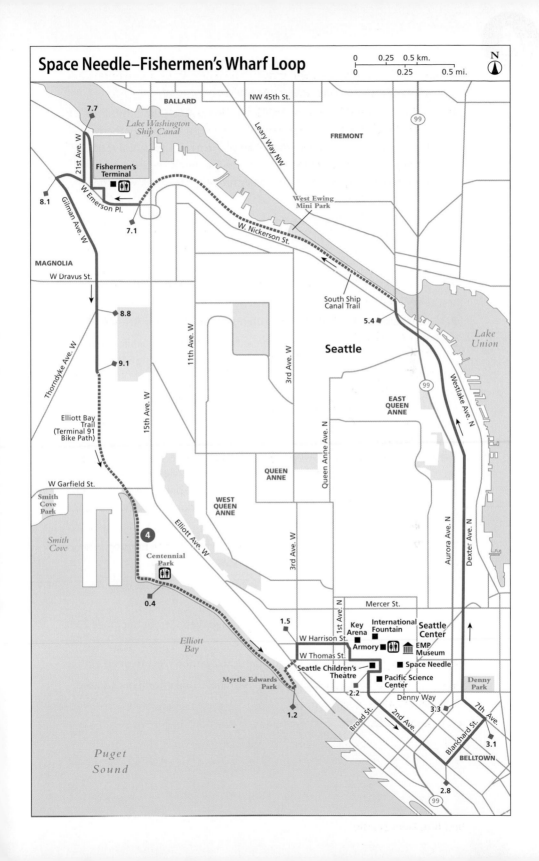

Space Needle–Fishermen's Wharf Loop

0   0.25   0.5 km.

0   0.25   0.5 mi.

N

NW 45th St.

BALLARD

7.7

Lake Washington
Ship Canal

Leary Way NW

FREMONT

99

21st Ave. W

Fishermen's
Terminal

W Emerson Pl.

8.1

Gilman Ave. W

7.1

West Ewing
Mini Park

W. Nickerson St.

MAGNOLIA

W Dravus St.

Thorndyke Ave. W

8.8

9.1

11th Ave. W

South Ship
Canal Trail

5.4

Seattle

Lake
Union

99

3rd Ave. W

Westlake Ave. N

Elliott Bay
Trail
(Terminal 91
Bike Path)

15th Ave. W

EAST
QUEEN
ANNE

Queen Anne Ave. N

W Garfield St.

Smith
Cove
Park

Smith
Cove

4

Centennial
Park

0.4

Elliott Ave. W

QUEEN
ANNE

WEST
QUEEN
ANNE

3rd Ave. W

Aurora Ave. N

Dexter Ave. N

Mercer St.

Denny
Park

Elliott
Bay

1.5

1st Ave. N

Key
Arena

International
Fountain

Seattle
Center

W Harrison St.

Armory

EMP
Museum

Space Needle

W Thomas St.

Myrtle Edwards
Park

Seattle Children's
Theatre

Pacific Science
Center

7th Ave.

1.2

2.2

Denny Way

3.3

3.1

Broad St.

2nd Ave.

Blanchard St.

BELLTOWN

Puget
Sound

2.8

99

1.7 Cross 1st Avenue West and enter plaza at Key Arena. Head right across the plaza and onto an unnamed access road.

1.8 Turn left onto Thomas Street and ride into Seattle Center grounds with the Seattle Children's Theatre on the right. (There are many places to ride around and visit while you're here. The actual route turns right onto the wide path past the Children's Theatre and turns right again at the Pacific Science Center. Leave the park with the Pacific Science Center on your left.)

2.2 Turn left onto 2nd Avenue North, cross Denny Way, and take the bike lane on the left side of one-way 2nd Avenue North.

2.8 Turn left onto Blanchard Street (one-way).

3.1 Turn left onto 7th Avenue, which becomes Dexter Avenue as it bears right.

3.3 Cross Denny Way; use bike lane on right side of Dexter Avenue.

5.4 Turn right to cross Westlake Avenue North at the crosswalk, turn right onto the sidewalk, and in 20 feet make a sharp left at sign that points downhill to Ship Canal Trail.

7.1 Take the right fork of Ship Canal Trail where it splits after crossing the railroad tracks. It comes up to street level and merges with the sidewalk on West Emerson Place.

7.3 Turn right into Fishermen's Terminal at 19th Avenue West. Fishermen's Terminal is straight ahead. Otherwise, turn left in 1 block onto West Nickerson Street, which runs through the parking lot, and then right onto 20th Avenue West, which allows a dockside view of the ships in the terminal.

7.7 Turn sharply left onto 21st Avenue West where the Fishermen's Terminal dockside road becomes West Commodore Way.

7.9 Turn right onto West Emerson Place and cross viaduct over railroad yard.

8.1 Turn left onto bike lane on Gilman Avenue West. Street becomes 20th Avenue West.

8.8 Bear left where road splits and take 20th Avenue West to dead end.

9.1 Turn left onto the Elliott Bay Trail (Terminal 91 Bike Trail) back to the parking lot.

10.1 End of ride.

RIDE INFORMATION

Local Events and Attractions

Northwest Folk Life Festival: Live music and vendors, Memorial Day weekend, Seattle Center grounds (admission); nwfolklife.org/festival

Bumbershoot: Live music and vendors, Labor Day weekend, Seattle Center grounds (admission); bumbershoot.org

Chihuly Garden and Glass: Glass exhibits; 305 Harrison St. (Seattle Center), Seattle; chihulygardenandglass.com

EMP Museum: Museum of rock 'n' roll, science fiction, and pop culture; 325 5th Ave. North (Seattle Center), Seattle; empmuseum.org

Pacific Science Center: Science displays and IMAX theaters; 200 2nd Ave. North (Seattle Center), Seattle; pacificsciencecenter.org

Space Needle: 605-foot tower with rotating restaurant; 400 Broad St. (Seattle Center), Seattle; spaceneedle.com

Fishermen's Terminal: Home port of the northern Pacific fishing fleet, 3919 18th Ave. West, Seattle; portseattle.org/Commercial-Marine/Fishermens -Terminal/Pages/default.aspx

Restaurants

The Armory: Food court with 14 vendors, 305 Harrison St. (Seattle Center), Seattle; seattlecenter.com/food

Fishermen's Terminal: 3919 18th Ave. West, Seattle; Chinook's at Salmon Bay, (206) 283-4665, anthonys.com/restaurants/detail/chinook-at-salmon-bay; Highliner Pub and Grill, (206) 216-1254, highlinerpub.net; The Bay Café, (206) 282-3435, baycafefishermansterminal.com

Restrooms

Mile 0.4: Centennial Park restrooms at the fishing pier
Mile 1.8: Inside the Armory at Seattle Center
Mile 7.3: Fishermen's Terminal

If you expect the North Lake Washington Loop to be a flat outing, prepare to be disappointed. Pound for pound, this bike loop around the northern half of the lake is among the toughest around. Sure, there are at least 11 miles of flatness along the venerable Burke-Gilman Trail. The other neighborhood streets and roads, however, deal with the past glaciers and stream erosion that carved the steep hillsides and ravines around the perimeter of the lake. It makes for a challenging, yet popular, bike route.

Start: Mercer Island Park and Ride, 8000 N. Mercer Way, Mercer Island

Length: 39.1 miles

Approximate riding time: 3.25 to 4.75 hours

Best bike: Road or hybrid

Terrain: Mostly hilly

Traffic and hazards: Light traffic on neighborhood streets in Seattle and Bellevue; heavier traffic through Kirkland on roads with wide shoulders or bike lanes; pedestrians on Burke-Gilman Trail

Things to see: Historic bikeways in Seattle, lakeside views, University of Washington, U District, Burke-Gilman Trail, beaches at waterfront parks, marsh habitat and critters

Maps: *DeLorme Atlas & Gazetteer—Washington,* page 46; Seattle Bicycle Map, available at bike stores or online at seattle.gov/transportation/bike maps.htm; King County Bicycle Map, kingcounty.gov/transportation/ kcdot/Roads/Bicycling.aspx

Getting there: By car: From the west, take I-90 to exit 7A, turn left onto 77th Avenue Southeast at end of ramp, turn right onto North Mercer Way, and turn left into the Metro Park and Ride garage. From the east, take I-90 to exit 7, go straight as the ramp becomes North Mercer Way, and turn right into the Metro Park and Ride garage. GPS: N47 35.323' / W122 13.897'. Also, parking is available at the Mercer Island Community Center, located on the street behind the park and ride at 8236 SE 24th St. **By bus:** Metro routes 201, 202, 203, 204, 205, 211, 213, 216, 550, and 554 provide service. GPS: N47 35.362' / W122 13.701'

THE RIDE

The ride starts on Mercer Island, a wealthy residential area that lies smack-dab in the middle of the second-largest natural lake in the state. The route heads west toward Seattle on the I-90 Bike Trail, part of the larger Mountains-to-Sound Trail.

Soon you're crossing Lake Washington just a few feet above the water on a bike path attached to a 2-mile floating bridge. Climbing up to the landing on the Seattle side, pause at a viewpoint that encompasses a giant sweep of the lake and, on clear days, snow-capped Mount Baker in the north and Mount Rainier to the south.

Climb a steep, short hill on South Irving Street on the north side of this park and turn right, following Lake Washington Loop bike-route signs toward Leschi Center. (A pedestrian tunnel on the west side of the viewing area goes to the "South of Downtown" area.)

The bike route wends through old Seattle neighborhoods for several miles on the historic corridor of Lake Washington Boulevard. Volunteers built 25 miles of bicycle paths between Seattle and Lake Washington in the 1890s, only to have many upgraded to boulevards for automobile use starting in 1909. Lake Washington Boulevard uses some of those old bike paths as it links a series of deeply forested parks, including Frink, Leschi, Lakeview, and the Arboretum parks north of the I-90 bridge.

After meandering among the hillside parks, the route dips down to the waterfront at Leschi Center, a longtime settlement for the original Native American inhabitants and the white homesteaders who followed.

Passing the waterfront Madrona Park and heading back uphill, don't be surprised to see tour buses parked at Denny Blaine Park. Listen in and you'll learn the park has a view of Microsoft founder Bill Gates's estate across Lake Washington in Medina. The park also is near the house where Kurt Cobain, lead singer of grunge band Nirvana, committed suicide in 1994. He's still revered locally, demonstrated by the graffiti and flowers on a bench in Viretta Park, which you just passed across the street.

Keep following the green Lake Washington Loop signs pointing toward the U District as the route abandons Lake Washington Boulevard to avoid heavy traffic in the Arboretum, a 230-acre plant lover's paradise. You'll take a collection of short streets, including an alley, as you wind your way past houses sporting a wide variety of architectural styles to the ornate Montlake Drawbridge over Lake Washington Ship Canal.

Cross the bridge on the sidewalk to get a good view of the canal dug in 1911 to create a boat passage between Lake Washington, Lake Union, and the Puget Sound.

Continue along the sidewalk on the eastside of Montlake Boulevard until you pass the University of Washington Husky Stadium and Edmundson Pavilion, and then take the short bicycle-pedestrian bridge to cross Montlake. Turn right to merge onto the Burke-Gilman Trail on the UW campus as it heads toward the University Village shopping district. (Look for changes in the bike route here during and after construction of the Sound Transit light rail station and the State Route 520 bridge across Lake Washington.)

The Burke-Gilman is a rail trail on the old right-of-way of the Seattle, Lake Shore, and Eastern Railway, which had been running through here for twenty years before the 1909 world's fair opened. The railway was abandoned in 1971 by subsequent owners Burlington Northern Railroad. The first section was reopened as a bike trail in 1978. Since then, the trail has grown to 19 miles from Golden Gardens Park on the Puget Sound to the town of Bothell at the northern tip of Lake Washington, the only interruption being a short distance in Ballard known as the "missing link."

The trail serves as a backbone for bike commuting and recreational riding in the area, a fact not lost on a bike shop whose front, and only, entrance opens onto the trail. The Burke-Gilman Trail, judged a Hall of Fame Trail by the

Bike Shops

Bicycle Center of Seattle: 4529 Sand Point Way Northeast, Seattle, (206) 523-8300; bicyclecenterofseattle.com

Counterbalance Bikes: Access directly from Burke-Gilman Trail at Northeast Blakely Street; 2943 NE Blakely St., Seattle; (206) 922-3555; counterbalancebicycles.com

The Polka Dot Jersey Bicycle Shop: 121 Lakeside Ave., Suite A, Seattle; (206)328-5400; thepolkadotjersey.com/home

Montlake Bicycle Shop: 2223 24th Ave. East, Seattle; (206) 329-7333; montlakebike.com

Gregg's Bellevue Cycle: 105 Bellevue Way Northeast, Bellevue; (425) 462-1900; greggscycles.com

A colorful mural tells the story of the Burke-Gilman Trail.

Rails-to-Trails Conservancy, shows its age in spots, but a long stretch in Lake Forest Park has been widened and resurfaced.

Log Boom Park in Kenmore is a good place to stop and have a snack before starting on the next leg of your journey. Watch for traffic on cross streets as you ride past float planes and a light industrial area on Lake Washington. Soon the route bypasses a trail underpass and turns right onto the shoulder of 68th Avenue Northeast as it crosses the Sammamish River and begins a 2-mile climb, the first of four notable climbs coming up.

Passing the entrance to mountain biking havens at St. Edward State Park and Big Finn Hill Park, bicyclists will fly downhill to Juanita Beach Park, a former resort dating to the 1920s. Look for an old boardwalk over an inlet after turning right onto 98th Avenue Northeast. The park is populated with frogs, turtles, and waterfowl. Signs describe the natural and human history of the Juanita area.

Merging back onto 98th Avenue, the road becomes Market Street, climbs another hill, and descends to the boat landing at Kirkland's Marina Park. This was historically the site of a ferry landing, and it is still a departure point for tourist jaunts across the lake. Kirkland's downtown surrounds it with tony boutiques, galleries, and cafes.

Traffic picks up as you head south on Lake Washington Boulevard Northeast's bike lane out of Kirkland. Just watch out for doors flying open on parked cars as you pass a string of popular waterfront parks. Another climb emerges as you labor uphill to cross SR 520 and enter the affluent Medina community, home to Gates, Amazon founder Jeff Bezos, and other tech mavens.

Lake views return as the route follows the jagged lakeside terrain in Bellevue. One of the quiet coves you'll pass is Meydenbauer Bay, named for founders of this little agricultural town that now boasts high-rises and booming commerce. It's hard to believe, but that embayment was home port to the country's last whaling fleet when it went out of business in the 1940s.

The route bypasses the historic downtown and soaring modern development to stay close to the lake, climbing hill after steep hill in lakeside neighborhoods. Don't blink after you turn onto 104th Avenue Southeast from Killarney Way or you'll miss the tiny town of Beaux Arts, founded as an artists' colony in 1908. At 299 residents in the 2010 Census and 128 acres (about one-tenth of a square mile) it's the smallest town in Washington state.

The bike route emerges from these shady waterfront residential communities at the I-90 bike path near Enatai Beach Park. Climb the path up to the bridge level and cross over to Mercer Island. The route is challenging to the end, as there's one last grade to climb to your finish at the Park and Ride lot.

Bridging the Lake

A new route across Lake Washington for bicyclists will be available when the replacement SR 520 bridge opens sometime in 2015 or beyond.

The old Governor Albert D. Rosellini Bridge–Evergreen Point (aka 520 Bridge) has been carrying cars between Seattle and the Eastside cities of Bellevue, Kirkland, and Redmond since 1963. Unlike the westbound I-90 bridge to the south, however, it was built without a bicycle/pedestrian lane.

That oversight will be rectified as a 14-foot-wide path for bicyclists and pedestrians will run along the north side of the westbound lanes of the bridge. The trail will feature five turnouts where bicyclists and pedestrians can pause and enjoy the views of mountains and water.

This crossing is something that bicycle commuters have wanted for a long time. Their choice has been to ride south to the I-90 bridge or to catch a bus with space available on a bike rack.

The new bridge and bike path will mean changes to the North Lake Washington Loop bike ride in the vicinity of Montlake on the west shore of Lake Washington and Medina on the eastern shore. Just look for green bicycle way-finding signs for direction.

MILES & DIRECTIONS

0.0 Starting at Mercer Island Park and Ride, turn right and follow the I-90 Trail (here it's the sidewalk).

0.3 Cross 76th Avenue Southeast and stay on the I-90 Trail.

0.9 Cross West Mercer Way and follow trail across the I-90 Bridge.

2.8 Bear right as you finish crossing the bridge (left goes to an overlook and tunnel toward SODO district), turn left onto very steep South Irving Street, then right onto Lake Washington Boulevard South.

3.5 Take the left fork after a four-way stop to remain on Lake Washington Boulevard South.

4.0 Left turn onto Lake Washington Boulevard in Leschi.

4.5 Pass by Madrona Park on the right.

5.2 Bear left to stay on Lake Washington Boulevard and follow signs to "U District" as the route loops through Lakeview Park.

5.5 Turn left onto East Harrison Street.

6.0 Turn right onto Martin Luther King Jr. Way East. Make a dogleg to the right to Madison Street East and pick up 28th Avenue East, which will become 26th Avenue East.

6.8 Turn left on East Galer Street and immediate right back onto 26th Avenue East. (East Interlaken Boulevard is another old bicycle route.) Cross Boyer Avenue East.

7.3 Turn left onto East Lynn Street, then turn right onto 25th Avenue East.

7.6 Cross East Roanoke Street and turn left into an unsigned alley (follow green Lake Washington Loop "U District" signs). Turn right onto 24th Avenue East, cross the SR 520 overpass, then pass straight through a set of street-end bollards.

7.8 Turn right onto East Hamlin Street, then the next two lefts onto East Shelby Street.

8.0 Turn right onto the Montlake Boulevard Northwest sidewalk and cross over the Lake Washington Ship Canal on the Montlake Bridge. Continue on sidewalk past Husky Stadium and Edmundson Pavilion. (Look for slight route changes after you cross the Montlake Bridge due to new bike traffic patterns created by the SR 520 bridge replacement.)

North Lake Washington Loop

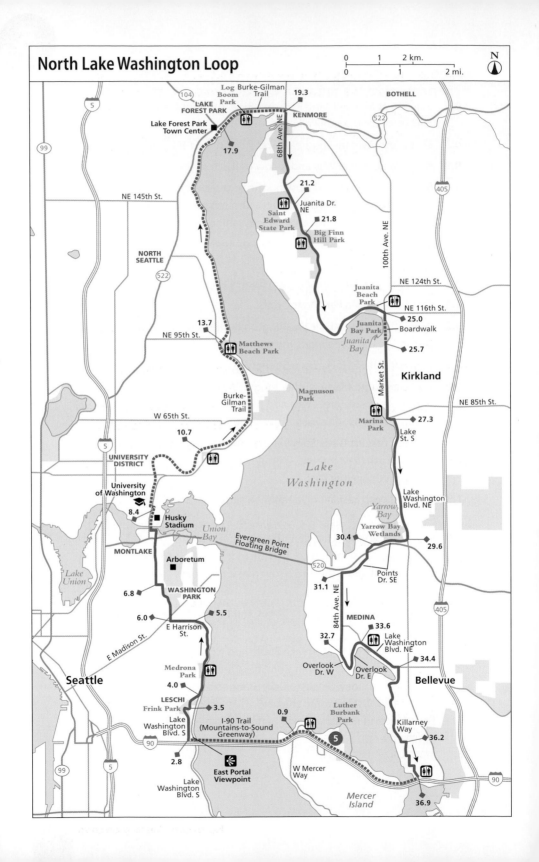

0   1   2 km.

0   1   2 mi.

N

104

Log Boom Park

Burke-Gilman Trail

LAKE FOREST PARK

19.3

BOTHELL

522

Lake Forest Park Town Center

17.9

68th Ave. NE

KENMORE

99

5

NE 145th St.

21.2

Juanita Dr. NE

405

Saint Edward State Park

21.8

Big Finn Hill Park

NORTH SEATTLE

522

100th Ave. NE

Juanita Beach Park

NE 124th St.

NE 116th St.

25.0

Boardwalk

13.7

NE 95th St.

Matthews Beach Park

Juanita Bay Park

Juanita Bay

25.7

Kirkland

Burke-Gilman Trail

Magnuson Park

Market St.

Lake Washington

NE 85th St.

W 65th St.

10.7

Marina Park

27.3

UNIVERSITY DISTRICT

Lake St. S

University of Washington

8.4

Husky Stadium

Union Bay

Evergreen Point Floating Bridge

Yarrow Bay

Lake Washington Blvd. NE

MONTLAKE

Arboretum

520

Yarrow Bay Wetlands

30.4

29.6

Lake Union

WASHINGTON PARK

6.8

Points Dr. SE

5.5

31.1

84th Ave. NE

6.0

E Harrison St.

MEDINA

33.6

E Madison St.

32.7

Lake Washington Blvd. NE

34.4

Medrona Park

Bellevue

4.0

Overlook Dr. W

Overlook Dr. E

LESCHI

Frink Park

3.5

Luther Burbank Park

Killarney Way

Seattle

I-90 Trail (Mountains-to-Sound Greenway)

0.9

36.2

5

Lake Washington Blvd. S

90

2.8

W Mercer Way

405

99

5

Lake Washington Blvd. S

East Portal Viewpoint

Mercer Island

36.9

90

8.4 Take the ramp up the bike-pedestrian bridge just past Edmundson Pavilion, cross Montlake, and turn right onto Burke-Gilman Trail.

9.5 Cross 25th Avenue Northeast.

9.8 Cross Union Bay Place Northeast (location of Counterbalance Bikes whose front door is right on the Burke-Gilman Trail; also offers rental bikes).

10.7 Cross 40th Street Northeast, followed by entrance to Burke-Gilman Playground Park on the right.

11.8 Cross Northeast 65th Street, which heads downhill to Magnuson Park on Sand Point Way.

13.7 Pass by Matthews Beach Park.

17.7 Cross Beach Drive Northeast at traffic signal.

17.9 Cross Ballenger Way Northeast (SR 104) at traffic signal. Honey Bear Bakery is across Bothell Way Northeast in the Lake Forest Park Town Center.

18.7 Arrive at Log Boom Park on the right. Watch for trucks at two busy road crossings.

19.3 Bear to the left of a trail underpass, then turn right onto 68th Avenue Northeast, which becomes Juanita Drive Northeast. A sidewalk on the Sammamish River Bridge is available to bicyclists.

21.2 Pass entrance to Saint Edward State Park and Bastyr University on the right.

21.8 Pass entrance to Big Finn Hill Park on the left.

24.8 Pass entrance to Juanita Beach Park on the right, then turn right at intersection onto 98th Avenue Northeast.

25.0 Turn right off road to access the Old Market Street Trail, which is a boardwalk across some wetlands.

25.7 After crossing the pier, reconnect with the bike lane on 98th Avenue Northeast (which becomes Market Street) as you climb the hill.

27.1 Go straight on Lakeshore Plaza Drive and enter Marina Park in downtown Kirkland. Bear left onto Kirkland Avenue to leave the park.

27.3 Turn right onto Lake Street South and follow sharrows through downtown. Pass by David E. Brink Park, Marsh Park, and Houghton Beach Park (restrooms) as road becomes Lake Washington Boulevard Northeast.

28.6 Cross Lakeview Drive.

29.6 Turn right onto Northeast Points Drive. Pass through bollards at top of hill. [After SR 520 is upgraded in this location in summer of 2014, bicyclists can cross Northeast Points Drive at the bottom of the hill, then turn right onto the new SR 520 bike trail.]

30.4 Turn left at 92nd Avenue Northeast, cross SR 520 overpass. (After completion of roadwork here, veer right off bike trail to traffic circle and take 92nd Avenue Northeast across SR 520.) Turn right onto Points Drive Northeast (becomes Northeast 28th Street).

31.1 Turn left onto 84th Avenue Northeast.

32.7 Turn left onto Overlake Drive West, which curves around Groat Point and becomes Overlake Drive East overlooking Meydenbauer Bay.

33.6 Bear right to rejoin Lake Washington Boulevard Northeast, which becomes Main Street.

34.4 Turn right onto 101st Avenue Southeast and turn left at bottom of hill onto 100th Avenue Southeast. Steep hill begins.

35.0 Turn right onto Southeast 7th Street, then left onto 99th Avenue Southeast. Road becomes 98th Avenue Southeast and then Killarney Way as it passes through the Beaux Arts neighborhood.

36.3 Turn right onto 104th Avenue Southeast, followed by a left onto Southeast 30th Street and a right onto 106th Avenue Southeast.

36.9 Turn left onto 108th Avenue Southeast at stop sign and make an immediate right onto bike path that runs alongside Southeast 34th Street. At top of climb make hairpin turn and use I-90 Trail to cross Lake Washington to Mercer Island.

37.9 Cross North Mercer Way and stay on I-90 Trail.

39.0 Arrive at Mercer Island Park and Ride Lot. End of ride.

RIDE INFORMATION

Local Events and Attractions
Seafair Weekend: Celebrates all things nautical in early August at Lake Washington, including hydroplane races as well as precision flight demonstrations such as the Navy's Blue Angels; seafair.com

Bellevue Festival of the Arts: Includes Downtown Arts Festival, Bellevue Arts Museum ArtsFair, and 6th Street Fair the last full weekend in July; bellevuefest .org/index.php

Kirkland Classic Car Show: Antique cars and hot rods on display throughout Marina Park and on closed downtown streets in late July; kirklandclassic carshow.com

Washington Park Arboretum: A 230-acre park displaying a wide variety of plants; Japanese Garden has admission fee but all other access is free; 2300 Arboretum Dr. East, Seattle; depts.washington.edu/uwbg/gardens/wpa.shtml
University of Washington: Sprawling campus dates back to 1895 and includes historic site of Alaska-Yukon-Pacific Exposition of 1909 and Husky Stadium on Montlake Boulevard Northeast; washington.edu

Restaurants
Honey Bear Bakery: Located in Third Place Books at Lake Forest Park Town Center; 17171 Bothell Way Northeast, Lake Forest Park; (206) 366-3330; honeybearbakery.com.

Restrooms
Mile 0.6: Feroglia Fields
Mile 4.5: Madrona Park
Mile 10.7: Burke-Gilman Playground Park
Mile 13.7: Matthews Beach Park
Mile 18.7: Log Boom Park
Mile 21.2: St. Edward State Park
Mile 21.8: Big Finn Hill Park
Mile 24.8: Juanita Beach Park
Mile 27.1: Marina Park
Mile 34.1: Clyde Beach Park
Mile 37.1: Enatai Beach Park

6

South Lake Washington Loop

This ride around the southern half of Lake Washington offers a steady diet of lakeside parks where cyclists can enjoy a shady picnic lunch or explore old-growth forests on foot. Although the route is mostly flat, a few climbs offer breathtaking views of Mount Rainier and the snow-capped Cascades and remind us that Ice Age glaciers carved out this 22-mile-long finger lake. Starting in the aviation hub in Renton, the route winds through Seattle, Mercer Island, Bellevue, and Newcastle.

Start: Gene Coulon Memorial Beach Park, 1201 Lake Washington Blvd. North, Renton

Length: 23.7 miles

Approximate riding time: 2.5 to 3 hours

Best bike: Road bike

Terrain: Flat at the beginning and end, with steep hills in the middle; all paved surfaces on trails, bike lanes, and city streets

Traffic and hazards: Heaviest traffic is on Rainier Avenue South, but with bike lanes. Street riding on Seward Park Avenue South and Lake Washington Boulevard South in Seattle can get heavy on weekends.

Things to see: Gene Coulon Memorial Beach Park, Renton Municipal Airport, Seward Park, Colman Park, East Portal Viewpoint, Enatai Beach Park, Newcastle Beach Park, Mercer Slough Nature Park

Maps: *DeLorme Atlas & Gazetteer—Washington,* page 46; Seattle Bicycle Map, available at bike stores or online at seattle.gov/transportation/bikemaps.htm; King County Bicycle Map, kingcounty.gov/transportation/kcdot/Roads/Bicycling.aspx

Getting there: Exit 5 west off I-405. Take Northeast Park Drive downhill to first light at Lake Washington Boulevard North, turn right, then turn left at stop sign into Gene Coulon Memorial Beach Park. GPS: N47 30.201' / W122 12.080'

THE RIDE

The ride starts at the City of Renton's Gene Coulon Memorial Beach Park, located at the southeast end of Lake Washington. The popular 57-acre park with boat launch, beach, and picnic areas sits on the site of historic coal and lumber shipping docks, pioneer industries on this side of the lake. Leaving the park, you're soon passing the hangars and tarmac of the sprawling Boeing facility, the city's major industry since World War II when "Rosie the Riveters" assembled warplanes. Since then, Boeing developed the first commercial jetliner here and still builds jets for passenger and military use.

As you pass the plant, the city's aviation history is preserved on the 0.75-mile shared-use Sam Chastain Trail. Some seventy bronze medallions embedded in the concrete commemorate aircraft built at the Boeing plant or flown out of the adjacent Renton Municipal Airport.

At the end of this path, you cross a narrow pedestrian bridge over the Cedar River and join a perimeter road around the airport. Passing the main entrance, you're greeted by the dashing appearance of Clayton Scott's statue. Pause here if you want to learn more about the life of this local barnstormer, who died at age 101 in 2006 after opening new passenger routes in the early days of aviation and test-flying Boeing aircraft.

For more aviation history, you can visit the Will Rogers–Wiley Post Memorial by taking a 0.2-mile detour from the left turn off West Perimeter Road. A stone marker at the south end of Lake Washington commemorates where, in 1935, beloved humorist Rogers and famous aviator Post took off in Post's Orion-Explorer for an around-the-world flight that ended in a fatal plane crash in the remote Alaska territory.

Bike Shops

g.h.y. bikes: 230 Main St. S., Renton; (425) 227-4825; ghybikes.com

Back to the route, you turn off West Perimeter Road to Rainier Avenue South where you pass lake-view neighborhoods settled by the Boeing Boomers in the 1950s. A right turn onto Seward Park Road South starts your first climb, where you'll catch occasional glimpses of Lake Washington. Keep your eyes peeled for the Seward Park signs as the route branches off to the right for a refreshing downhill run (test your brakes) to a final steep drop to the park.

Known also as the Bailey Peninsula, this thumb-shaped park that juts into the lake is a wonderful place for some exploration. A 2.4-mile flat bicycle/pedestrian path surrounds the 300-acre park. Continuing on curvy Lake Washington Boulevard South, you'll see what a landscape architect envisioned in 1903 as an "emerald necklace" of parks and open space along the lake. If you're lucky, you'll hit this 2.5-mile stretch during one of the 12 Bicycle

A cyclist heads across the 2-mile I-90 bridge.

Sundays scheduled every May through September when vehicular traffic is banned from the road. It is much less nerve-wracking to share the road with fellow cyclists than motorists who are also sightseeing. In August, the serenity is broken by the roar of racing hydroplanes for Seafair, Seattle's celebration of everything nautical. Stan Sayres Memorial Park, which you'll pass, is named for local car dealer and hydroplane builder/pilot who set the water speed record (160 mph) in the unlikely named *Slo-Mo-Shun IV* in 1950. That record, and the hydroplane's gold cup victory, has helped seal Seattle's love for this noisy sport.

At Colman Park, throw it in low gear and pedal up the switchbacks to the Mount Baker neighborhood where you'll see the snow-capped Cascades (and Mount Rainier to the south and Mount Baker in the north) from the viewpoint over the I-90 floating bridges.

Thanks to human error, the westbound floating span on the right sank in 1990 when the pontoons were left open during a storm. It has since been repaired and refloated. You're taking the bridge on the left, however, which carries the bike path for nearly two miles across Lake Washington to Mercer Island. It never sank.

Now you've entered the state's wealthiest enclave, with a $123,939 per capita annual income. You'll see some nice homes along the water, although your route keeps to the I-90 bike path that bisects the island. Also known as the Mountains to Sound Greenway Trail, the I-90 bike trail hops over another short bridge to Bellevue. The bike trail goes through the swampy Mercer Slough (pronounced "slew") on an elevated causeway, keeping your tires dry. The entire 320-acre area was underwater until about 1917 when engineers completed a channel between Lake Washington and Puget Sound and the lake level dropped 9 feet. The Pacific Science Center operates an environmental education center in this wild setting in urban Bellevue.

A right turn puts you back on Lake Washington Boulevard where it's a straight shot back to Renton. In the fall, you might encounter a little traffic at the Seattle Seahawks football training camp. As you approach Coulon Park, look over the lake to see the snow-capped Olympic Mountains in the distance. Then turn right into Coulon Park and left on the main service road back to the start.

MILES & DIRECTIONS

0.0   Ride out of the Gene Coulon Memorial Park south parking lot.

0.1   Turn right onto Lake Washington Boulevard North.

0.2   Turn right onto Park Avenue North, which becomes Logan Avenue North.

1.0   Veer right at North 6th Street onto Sam Chastain bike trail.

1.4   Cross narrow bridge over Cedar River and Cedar River Trail. Take immediate right onto unmarked street after bridge, then quickly turn left onto East Perimeter Road, following green BIKE ROUTE sign.

1.7   Statue to aviator Clayton Scott is on left as road name changes to West Perimeter Road, which bends to the right and heads north.

2.7   Turn left at stop sign, head up short driveway, then turn right onto Rainier Avenue South. (To see the Will Rogers–Wiley Post Memorial Seaplane Base and Monument, continue straight through stop sign, instead of turning left, for 0.2 miles. A small monument overlooks the south end of Lake Washington. Retrace your ride to return to the route, turning right at the stop sign.)

5.4   Turn right on Seward Park Avenue South.

7.2   Look for brown sign pointing right for Seward Park as Seward Park Avenue South veers right at V intersection.

7.7   Turn right at South Juneau Street, then continue down short hill to the entrance for Seward Park at Lake Washington Boulevard South. (An optional 2.5-mile bicycle/pedestrian trail encircles the peninsula park. It starts with a right turn at the bottom of the hill; turn left

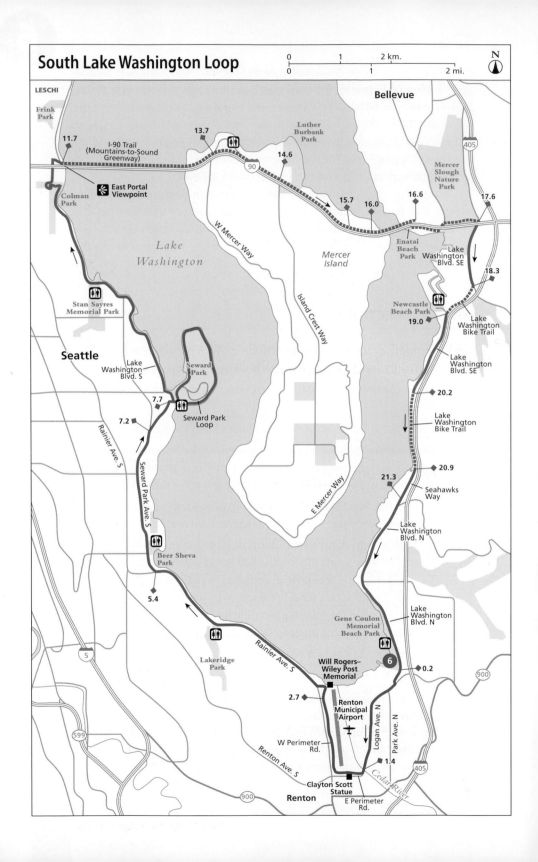

South Lake Washington Loop

0   1   2 km.
0   1   2 mi.

N

LESCHI

Bellevue

Frink
Park

11.7

I-90 Trail
(Mountains-to-Sound
Greenway)

13.7

14.6

Luther
Burbank
Park

90

Mercer
Slough
Nature
Park

405

East Portal
Viewpoint

Colman
Park

15.7   16.0

16.6

17.6

Lake
Washington

Lake
Washington

W Mercer Way

Mercer
Island

Enatai
Beach
Park

Lake
Washington
Blvd. SE

18.3

Stan Sayres
Memorial Park

Newcastle
Beach Park

Lake
Washington
Bike Trail

19.0

Seattle

Lake
Washington
Blvd. S

Seward
Park

Island Crest Way

Lake
Washington
Blvd. SE

20.2

7.7

7.2

Seward Park
Loop

Lake
Washington
Bike Trail

Rainier Ave. S

Seward Park Ave. S

E Mercer Way

20.9

21.3

Seahawks
Way

Lake
Washington
Blvd. N

Beer Sheva
Park

5.4

Lake
Washington
Blvd. N

5

Lakeridge
Park

Rainier Ave. S

Gene Coulon
Memorial
Beach Park

6

Will Rogers–
Wiley Post
Memorial

0.2

2.7

Renton
Municipal
Airport

Logan Ave. N

Park Ave. N

900

599

W Perimeter
Rd.

1.4

405

Renton Ave. S

Clayton Scott
Statue

Cedar River

900

Renton

E Perimeter
Rd.

when you reach the shoreline and continue counter-clockwise.) Turn left onto Lake Washington Boulevard South if you do not stop at the park. If you do enter the park, it will be a right turn onto Lake Washington Boulevard South.

10.9 Turn left into Colman Park (you remain on Lake Washington Boulevard South).

11.6 East Portal Viewpoint has commanding view of Lake Washington and Cascade Mountains.

11.7 Turn right at steep downhill South Irving Street, then turn right at I-90 Trail (also known as Mountains to Sound Greenway Trail) signs, ride past bollards, then turn left and follow the trail across the I-90 bridge. (A right turn takes bicyclists through the East Portal Bike Tunnel to Sam Smith Park and the SODO neighborhood of Seattle.)

13.7 Cross West Mercer Way and take the I-90 Trail as it heads uphill through the Park on the Lid.

14.3 Turn left across 76th Avenue Southeast on crosswalk and remain on the I-90 Trail, which runs along the north side of North Mercer Way.

Seward Park

Considering today's metropolitan sprawl, it's surprising that Seattle residents opposed buying the peninsula that was to become Seward Park at the turn of the nineteenth century because it was too remote.

Finally purchased by the city in 1911, the parkland came under public control before much of the timber could be removed. Huge stands of old-growth forest remain, especially in the so-called Magnificent Forest that comprises about two-thirds of the peninsula where the aged Douglas firs dominate. With many trees more than 250 years old, visitors get an idea of how the Seattle area looked before white settlement in the 1850s. Deer and mink no longer live here, but mountain beavers, raccoons, otters, owls, bald eagles, and pileated woodpeckers are just a few of the species that make the park their home.

The Seward Park Environmental and Audubon Center is housed in an old brick building at the entrance and contains information about the one hundred species of birds and mammals found here. Hiking trails crisscross the peninsula, and bicyclists can take a leisurely 2.4-mile ride around the perimeter. An 0.8-mile road inside the peninsula is the scene of weekly Thursday night bike racing from April through August.

California poppies bloom alongside I-90 Trail.

14.6 Pass the Mercer Island Park and Ride on I-90 Trail; watch out for pedestrians.

14.8 Cross Island Crest Way on crosswalk and remain on I-90 Trail.

15.7 Cross North Mercer Way on crosswalk and continue on I-90 Trail.

16.0 Cross East Mercer Way on crosswalk and continue on I-90 Trail, which crosses Lake Washington again.

16.6 Take a hairpin left turn at I-90 Trail kiosk, continue downhill, then follow trail as it goes beneath I-90 and continues uphill on the other side.

16.8 Enatai Beach Park is located across the street on right.

17.2 Ride beneath I-90 again and follow right-hand trail over a short pedestrian bridge over Mercer Slough and continue on I-90 Trail across the causeway.

17.6 At trail kiosk, turn right onto 118th Avenue Southeast. The street becomes Lake Washington Boulevard Southeast.

18.3 Veer right onto the crosswalks at entrance to Newport Shores neighborhood, slowing down for a tricky turn as you pick up the Lake Washington Bike Trail as it runs parallel to Lake Washington Boulevard Southeast.

19.0 Leave Lake Washington Bike Trail through an open gate and continue straight on Lake Washington Boulevard Southeast. (A right turn leads downhill to Newcastle Beach Park.) The road becomes 106th Avenue Southeast.

20.2 Continue straight onto Lake Washington Bike Trail as road turns to the right.

20.9 Turn left onto Seahawks Way as Lake Washington Bike Trail comes to an end. You'll pass the Seattle Seahawks training center on the right.

21.3 Turn right onto Lake Washington Boulevard North.

23.2 Turn right into Gene Coulon Memorial Beach Park, and immediately turn left for restrooms and restaurants (Kidd Valley and Ivar's) or to continue to the south parking lot.

23.7 Ride ends at the south parking lot.

RIDE INFORMATION

Local Events and Attractions

Seward Park: Features hiking trails, environmental education, and art gallery; 5895 Lake Washington Blvd. South, Seattle; (206) 684-4396; seattle.gov/parks/environment/seward.htm

Bicycle Sundays: Closes Lake Washington Boulevard in Seattle to vehicular traffic on 12 Sundays between May and Sept; seattle.gov/parks/bicyclesunday

Seafair Weekend: Celebrates all things nautical in early August, including hydroplane races and Blue Angels performances at Lake Washington; seafair.com

Restrooms

Mile 4.4: Lakeridge Park at Cornell Avenue and Rainier Avenue South
Mile 5.8: Beer Sheva Park on Seward Park Avenue South
Mile 7.7: Seward Park at Juneau Street and Lake Washington Boulevard South
Mile 9.6: Stan Sayres Park on Lake Washington Boulevard South
Mile 14.0: Feroglia Fields, I-90 bike path (0.2 mile east of West Mercer Way), Mercer Island
Mile 19.0: Newcastle Beach Park
Mile 23.2: Coulon Beach Park, Lake Washington Boulevard North, Renton

Seattle Waterfront to Alki Beach Round-Trip

This route visits every characteristic of Seattle's satisfyingly scenic waterfront on Elliott Bay: parkland, tourist attractions, cargo ship docks, and a seaside resort. While the riding is all flat, it can be hectic in the tourism and dock areas. A tunnel-boring project and replacement of a major thoroughfare mean that bicyclists who ride in this popular corridor must keep an eye open for bicycle route detours for years to come.

Start: Parking lot for Elliott Bay Trail (Terminal 91 Bike Path) on 16th Avenue West

Length: 21.4 miles

Approximate riding time: 2 to 3 hours

Best bike: Road or hybrid bike

Terrain: Flat

Traffic and hazards: On-street riding with traffic, high-use pedestrian areas, trail crossings in port area; recommended for off-peak traffic hours

Things to see: Views across Elliott Bay, Olympic Sculpture Park Garden, Seattle Aquarium, Waterfront Park and tourist shopping areas, Seattle Seahawks football stadium (Century Link Field) and Mariners baseball park (Safeco Field), cargo and container ships at Port of Seattle, and parks and sandy beaches on West Seattle's Alki Beach

Maps: Seattle Bike Map, free in stores; Seattle Interactive Bike Map, seattle.gov/transportation/bikemapOnline.htm; *DeLorme Atlas & Gazetteer—Washington*, page 45

Getting there: By car: From the south, take I-5 North exit 166 and bear right onto East Olive Way. Turn left at Bellevue Avenue and left in 1 block onto East Denny Way. Take Denny Way through downtown to Western Avenue West, which merges to become Elliott Avenue West. Turn right at a large green sign over the street that says, "Terminals 86–91/Magnolia Bridge/Amgen Court West/Exit Only." The ramp loops over the road; take the left fork marked "To Elliott Bay Trail." Turn right at the end of the ramp to follow signs to Elliott Bay Trail, go 1 block and turn right again, and then turn left onto 16th Avenue West. Back-in parking anywhere. From the north, pick up 15th Avenue Northwest, cross the Lake Washington Ship Canal in Ballard, and get in left-turn lane after the sign that says, "Terminals 86–91/Magnolia Bridge/Amgen Court West/Exit Only." Follow directions above from "The ramp loops over the road . . ." **By bus:** Metro bus routes 19, 24, 32, 33, and D Line serve the area at Elliott Avenue West and West Galer Street. GPS: N47 37.876' / W122 22.658'

THE RIDE

After the chronicler of the beat generation, Jack Kerouac, visited Seattle in 1958, he wrote in *Holiday* magazine, "Anybody who's been to Seattle and missed Alaskan Way, the old water front, has missed the point." The whole waterfront scene at that time hinted to Kerouac, "under the pure-cloud-mopped, sparkling skies of the Northwest, of great country to come." Today, Seattle's waterfront district on Elliott Bay has been transformed from a stretch of dark warehouses and pier sheds served by antique locomotives and box-cars into a booming tourist mecca. Urban bicyclists who navigate this and other sections of the Elliott Bay shoreline are treated to a wide range of sights and sounds that define the waterfront.

The ride starts on the Elliott Bay Trail (Terminal 91 Bike Path) at the Port of Seattle's Centennial Park. If it's summertime, you might see a huge cruise liner docked at the pier. Nearly 200 cruise ships visit Seattle annually, tying up here or at several other piers along the waterfront. In a recent year, the cruise ships alone brought more than 800,000 persons to Seattle's nautical doorstep.

A curve on Elliott Bay Trail brings you to a picturesque point with views of Alki Beach, Bainbridge Island, and the snow-capped Olympic Mountains across the water. Rounding the corner, you can see the Seattle skyline ahead of you with Mount Rainier in the distance. Here, you're passing through Centennial Park, and a little farther on you'll roll into the city of Seattle's Myrtle

Edwards Park. Both are served by the Elliott Bay Trail. The paved path is conveniently separated for bicyclists and pedestrians, but don't be surprised to find joggers, inline skaters, or dog walkers on the bike trail. At the far end of the park is a ramp up the hill into the Seattle Art Museum's Olympic Sculpture Park, opened in 2007. The former industrial site houses outdoor exhibits of large, contemporary sculpture and is free to the public.

A fountain marks the end of the trail at Alaskan Way. Most bicyclists take to the four-lane street here, as the sidewalk can be crowded with pedestrians. Elliott Bay Trail does resume on the north side of Alaskan Way in 1 block at Clay Street, but pedestrians also use that trail and there are frequent street crossings. It's best to stay in the right lane (out of the door zone) and stick to the street.

You're riding through the Central Waterfront District for the next couple of miles. It's marked by old piers either repurposed to the cruise-line trade or shops that serve visitors. Seattle's maritime industry was centered here until larger container ship facilities opened just south on Harbor Island in the 1960s. This is where trade with Japan thrived and a ship carrying gold from Alaska sparked the Klondike Gold Rush.

If the aroma of fresh seafood is making those energy bars in your jersey pocket less tantalizing, food is available here from cafes, walk-up restaurant windows, or street vendors. You won't get another chance like this until Alki Beach, 6 or 7 miles away. The Waterfront Park across from Pike Street is a good vantage point for a view of the harbor. If you carry a sturdy bike lock, you can visit the local fish, octopi, otters, and seals frolicking at the Seattle Aquarium.

Bike Shops

Alpine Hut: 2215 15th Ave. West, Seattle; (206) 284-3575; alpinehut.com
Back Alley Bike Repair: 314 1st Ave. South, Seattle; (206) 307-1179; backalleybikerepair.com
Cycle University, West Seattle: 3418 Harbor Ave. Southwest, Seattle; (206) 432-9982; cycleu.com
Elliott Bay Bicycles: 2116 Western Ave., Seattle; (206) 441-8144; elliottbaybicycles.com
The Bicycle Repair Shop: 928 Alaskan Way, Seattle; (206) 682-7057; thebicyclerepairshop.com

A bike lane emerges on Alaskan Way South after you pass the Washington State Ferry Terminals. You pass Century Link Field (home of the Seahawks and Sounders) and Safeco Field (home of the Mariners) on the left, and the road becomes East Marginal Way South and continues past a truck loading area for the port. Turn right at South Spokane Street where you pick up the West Seattle Bridge Trail. Although the trail switches from one side of the road to the other, way-finding signs embedded in the trail make it easy to find the route over the little-known drawbridge that sits hidden beneath

Beachgoers gather at the Statue of Liberty replica to watch the sunset at Alki Beach.

a viaduct that soars overhead. You'll get the best views of the container ships and tugboats that serve the maritime industry from viewpoints overlooking man-made Harbor Island in the Duwamish River.

Follow the signs for the Alki Trail after crossing the bridge and soon you'll be humming along next to a seawall with stunning views of the Seattle waterfront and skyline. The mix of old beach-style cottages next to new glass-front condominiums is reminiscent of more southerly beachfront destinations. Pass a few folks on inline skates and you may be convinced that you've been transported to southern California.

Alki Trail rolls along the waterfront for 2.5 miles nearly to Alki Point. Although there's a pedestrian lane, beachgoers and skaters meander all over the trail, so you're welcome to use the street, which is marked with a sharrow to remind motorists that bicyclists have the right to use the road. At the eastern end of Alki Trail is Jack Block Park, maintained by the Port of Seattle. If your whole point was to ride along the Alki shoreline, then this might be a better place to start. There is parking here. In 0.5 mile is Seacrest Park, the landing for the West Seattle Ferry.

The promised cafes and ice parlors pop up across the street from Alki Beach Park. As you pass the beach, keep an eye open for a granite monument that marks the site where the first settlers—the Denny Party—set ashore in November 1851. A local tribe led by Chief Seattle helped them survive the winter. The settlers moved across Elliott Bay to what's now the Pioneer Square

Hardhat Area

A massive project to bore a tunnel beneath downtown from the south end of the Central Waterfront District has been under way since 2012. Plans call for following that with the demolition of the old Alaskan Way Viaduct overhead as early as 2016.

Long-range plans call for a two-way cycle track—tucked between the road and pedestrian promenade—on the Elliott Bay side of Alaskan Way. Until then, keep an eye open for orange signs noting detours here until at least 2016.

As of this writing, the route crosses to the east side of Alaskan Way between Yesler Way and Jackson Street. It crosses back again to an Elliott Bay Trail detour that runs between the construction zone and a container ship facility.

If you'd like to skip the entire kerfuffle, slide into Pier 50 across from Yesler Way and take the Metro Transit Water Taxi across Elliott Bay to West Seattle. You'll need to buy a ticket or use your transit card and be able to carry your bike on board.

area of Seattle the following year. The Alki Trail ends just past the Southwest Stevens Street intersection. Although it's not on this route, you can continue around Alki Point and along the coast of Puget Sound to Lincoln Park and Fauntleroy Cove, site of the ferry to Vashon Island and Southworth.

Retrace your route to return to Seattle. After crossing the West Seattle Bridge, take a sharp left onto the sidewalk running next to East Marginal Way South. Pedestrians rarely use this wide sidewalk, and it gives bicyclists easy access back onto the trail at the south end of the Central Waterfront in about 1.5 miles. Follow the Alaskan Way, and detours, past the waterfront and return to your car.

MILES & DIRECTIONS

0.0 Turn left from the parking lot and head south on Elliot Bay Trail (Terminal 91 Bike Path).

0.4 Pass fishing pier and restrooms on the right.

1.2 Pass Thomas Street pedestrian overpass on the right.

1.4 Pass entrance ramp to Seattle Art Museum's Olympic Sculpture Park.

1.6 Pass fountain and enter right lane on Alaskan Way.

2.5 Pass Waterfront Park on the right at the foot of Union Street.

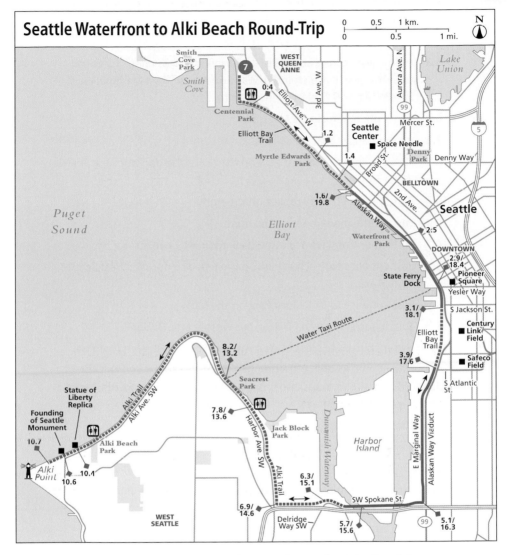

Seattle Waterfront to Alki Beach Round-Trip

2.9 Pass entrance to West Seattle Water Taxi on the right. Turn left at Yesler Way to follow detour, then right onto Alaskan Way.

3.1 Turn right onto Jackson Street and left onto Elliott Bay Trail.

3.9 Emerge from trail onto South Alaskan Way, which becomes East Marginal Way South.

5.1 Turn right onto West Seattle Bridge Trail (Alki Trail).

5.5 Follow directions embedded in path to cross 11th Avenue Southwest and Southwest Spokane Place on crosswalks.

5.7   Follow the trail around a loop to climb a grade to the level of drawbridge and cross it.

6.2   Take right fork to stay on Alki Trail; Duwamish Trail goes left.

6.3   Follow signs across a series of crosswalks to cross ramps for Southwest Marginal Place, Delridge Way Southwest, West Marginal Way Southwest, and Chelan Avenue Southwest.

6.9   Turn right to remain on Alki Trail.

7.8   Pass entrance to Jack Block Park on the right.

8.2   Pass entrance to Seacrest Park on the right; also dock for West Seattle Water Taxi.

10.4   Pass Statue of Liberty replica on the right.

10.6   Pass Seattle monument on the right.

10.7   Turn around and retrace route back to Smith Cove.

13.2   Pass entrance to Seacrest Park on the left; also dock for West Seattle Water Taxi.

13.6   Pass entrance to Jack Block Park on the left.

14.6   Turn left to stay on Alki Trail across West Seattle Bridge.

15.1   Use crosswalks to cross Chelan Avenue Southwest, West Marginal Way Southwest, and Southwest Spokane Street and follow signs.

15.6   Follow trail as it loops under bridge and continues on north side of South Spokane Street.

16.3   Turn left onto sidewalk adjacent to East Marginal Way South.

17.6   Follow sidewalk onto Elliott Bay Trail.

18.1   Turn right and then left onto Alaskan Way at South King Street.

18.4   Remain on Alaskan Way after crossing Yesler Way; the dock for the Seattle Water Taxi is on the left.

19.8   Turn left from Alaskan Way onto Elliott Bay Trail at fountain.

21.4   Arrive at parking lot. End of ride.

RIDE INFORMATION

Local Events and Attractions

Alki Beach Park: Stretches for 2.5 miles from Alki Point to mouth of Duwamish River; monument to first white settlers and a replica of Statue of Liberty; views of Seattle and Puget Sound islands and ships, ferries, and kayaks; 1702 Alki Ave. Southwest, Seattle; seattle.gov/parks/park_detail.asp?ID=445

A Ferris wheel dominates the tourist attractions for visitors to the Seattle waterfront.

Centennial Park: Operated by Port of Seattle; Elliott Bay Trail, Pier 86, Seattle; portseattle.org/Parks-Public-Access/Parks/Pages/Centennial-Park.aspx

Jack Block Park: Observation Tower, operated by Port of Seattle; 2130 Harbor Ave. Southwest, Seattle; portseattle.org/Parks-Public-Access/Parks/Pages/Jack-Block-Park.aspx

Myrtle Edwards Park: Operated by city of Seattle; 3130 Alaskan Way, Seattle; (206) 684-4075; seattle.gov/parks/park_detail.asp?ID=311

Seattle Aquarium: 1483 Alaskan Way, Pier 59, Seattle; (206) 386-4300; seattle aquarium.org (admission)

Seattle Art Museum's Olympic Sculpture Park: 2901 Western Ave., Seattle; (206) 654-3100; seattleartmuseum.org/visit/osp/ (free)

Waterfront Park: Views of Seattle shoreline from Piers 57, 58, and 59; fountain, benches; operated by city of Seattle; 1301 Alaskan Way, Seattle; (206) 684-4075

Restrooms
Mile 0.4: Centennial Park
Mile 7.8: Jack Block Park
Mile 10.1: Alki Beach Park
Mile 13.6: Jack Block Park
Mile 21.0: Centennial Park

Northside

Touring bicycles lean against a fence at the Nakashima Heritage Barn North Trailhead Park.

The Seattle metro area sprawls northward along the Puget Sound all the way into Snohomish County. Parts of eastern Snohomish County still retain a rural character, although there are pockets of development in the old farm country. The route of an old-time trolley line provides a no-traffic bicycle path from Seattle to Edmonds and beyond on the Interurban Trail, used by bike commuters and recreational riders alike. Farther east, another old railroad line provides the setting for the popular Centennial Trail that stretches between Snohomish and the Skagit County line.

The town of Snohomish, the southern terminus of the Centennial Trail, also is the beginning for a couple of other road rides that visit old mining, lumbering, and agricultural towns near the base of the Cascade foothills. For mountain bikers, a neglected forest has been cleaned up and now offers miles of single track with various degrees of difficulty.

Green Lake to Edmonds Loop

The last trolley passed through the station decades ago, but its route still lives in the Interurban Trail. This bike loop follows that old trolley line out of Seattle's Green Lake, but also visits the hillside communities of Innis Arden and Woodway before arriving at the Edmonds waterfront. It revisits the Interurban on the way back through Snohomish County and Shoreline before it reaches Seattle.

Start: Parking lot on West Green Lake Way North at the north end of Woodland Park, adjacent to Green Lake Park

Length: 24.5 miles

Approximate riding time: 3 to 4 hours

Best bike: Road or hybrid

Terrain: Gradual hills on paved roads and bicycle paths; one long steep hill leaving Edmonds. The trail is paved, but has numerous missing links.

Traffic and hazards: The route travels on some streets with traffic and crosses a couple of busy intersections. Otherwise, it uses residential streets and bike paths.

Things to see: Green Lake Park, Interurban Trail and Linden Avenue Cycle Track, Innis Arden neighborhood, ferry terminal, and downtown Edmonds

Maps: Snohomish County Interurban Trail maps, www1.co.snohomish .wa.us/Departments/Parks/Park_Information/Park_Directory/Regional _Parks/Interurban_Trail.htm; City of Seattle Bike Maps: Available in bike stores and at seattle.gov/transportation/bikemaps.htm; *DeLorme Atlas & Gazetteer—Washington,* pages 45 and 46

Getting there: **By car:** From I-5, take exit 170 onto Northeast 50th Street heading toward the Woodland Park Zoo (left turn onto Northeast 50th Street from northbound and right turn onto Northeast 50th Street from southbound). Go approximately 1 mile and turn right onto Green Lake Way North. Take the left fork at the Y intersection onto West Green Lake Way North and turn into the first parking lot on the left, which is across from the lake. **By bus:** Metro route 16 serves the east side of Green Lake; ride the Green Lake Trail to the parking lot on West Green Lake Way North. GPS: N47 40.272' / W122 20.621'

THE RIDE

This bicycle route borrows heavily from a defunct trolley line to find its way from the Green Lake Park area in Seattle to the waterfront in downtown Edmonds. The Green Lake to Edmonds Loop partly follows the path of the old Interurban Trolley that ran until 1939. Today that corridor comprises bike lanes on residential streets and several sections of the Interurban Trail, as well as Seattle's first European-style cycle track on Linden Avenue. The ride strays from the old Interurban to visit wooded hillside communities overlooking Puget Sound and the charming Edmonds waterfront. After leaving that half-way point, the route finds the Interurban corridor to return to the start.

The ride begins across the street from Green Lake Park, a magnet for people seeking outdoor pursuits in an urban setting. Many children have learned to ride their bikes on the 2.8-mile trail around the lake, and kayakers come here for recreation and competition. Early plans for the park almost didn't come to fruition, however, as housing reached the lake's edge before the city could acquire parkland in the early 1900s. A landscape architect hired by the city, John Olmsted, saved the day when he suggested that the lake level simply be lowered, thereby creating 100 dry acres around it in 1911.

Bike Shops

Gregg's Cycle: Green Lake, 7007 Woodlawn Ave. Northeast, Seattle; (206) 523-1822; greggscycles.com **Harvy's Bike Shop:** 19920 Hwy. 99, Suite C, Lynnwood; (425) 776-3746; harvysbikeshop.com

After leaving the park, the route picks up a north-south signed bicycle route on Fremont Avenue. The old Interurban tracks ran parallel between Fremont and Evanston Avenues, now the path of the Seattle City Light power lines. The Interurban trolleys ran between Seattle and Everett roughly from 1910 to 1939. Transportation returned to the Seattle portion of the line in the form of

Public art on the Interurban Trail depicts a deer sprouting antlers in a series of roadside signs.

bicycles in 2006 when the Interurban Trail was opened between North 110th and 128th streets. Bicycling along the route, you might be amused by a series of signs entitled "Flip Book," painted by a local artist who was inspired by the old-time Burma Shave signs. Each set tells a story, such as a fish swimming upstream, a volcano erupting, and a deer sprouting antlers.

The Interurban Trail ends at North 128th Street, and the route proceeds along Linden Avenue on Seattle's first cycle track, which opened in 2013. Common in some European countries, the cycle track is essentially a bike path on the street that's protected from moving traffic by either a curb or a line of parked cars. Bicyclists crossing North 130th Street have their own traffic signal.

Leaving the cycle track at North 143rd Street, the route heads over to Greenwood Avenue North. Proceed through this commercial district to Shoreline Community College and turn left at Northwest Innis Arden Way to begin a mostly downhill run to the Edmonds waterfront. The next few miles wind through some woodsy communities, starting with Innis Arden. Developed in the 1940s on the estate of the late aerospace magnate Bill Boeing, the neighborhood is ringed with forests that insulate it from higher-density surroundings in Shoreline. Houses are limited to four to the acre and their vistas of Puget Sound and the Olympic Mountains are protected by covenant.

After passing through a small business district in Richmond Beach, the route plunges into an even more forested community, the aptly named

Brackett's Landing on Edmonds waterfront is a great place to watch ferry boats come and go or to go beachcombing.

Woodway. You may think you're in the woods, but it's actually a town incorporated in 1958 to protect forest land. The original home lots had to be at least 2 acres, although some ⅓-acre and 1-acre lots are permitted now.

Emerging from the trees, you arrive in Edmonds on 3rd Avenue South. The first landmark you pass is the shady City Park. Turn left when you get to Main Street, and keep your eyes open for coffee and sandwich shops if you want a pick-me-up or bite to eat. The waterfront park at Brackett's Landing is a good place to find a bench to eat, see the ferries come and go, and watch scuba divers bobbing to the surface after they explore the underwater park. A lot of beach is exposed during low tides here. Monthly low tides can reveal starfish, sea anemones, mussels, crabs, and other critters.

Brackett's Landing gets its name from town founder George Brackett, who landed his canoe on this deserted beach at the edge of the forest in 1876. He started logging and opened a sawmill, and soon a community formed. Nearly enough people had moved to the area by 1890 to petition for a town. To ensure he had enough signatures, local legend says that two names on the petition can be attributed either to his two oxen or his bull and a cattle dog.

Since then, Edmonds has grown to the third-largest town in Snohomish County, although the downtown has retained its quaint charm with

Best Bike Rides Seattle

boutiques, restaurants, bakeries, and antique shops. You'll experience all that as you puff up Main Street and pass the fountain in the middle of the street at 5th Avenue North. The ascent continues on residential streets, some with excellent views of the Olympic Peninsula, until it arrives at the commercial sprawl along Aurora Avenue, SR 99. This major highway opened in 1932 and factored into the demise of the trolley line that closed seven years later.

The Interurban Trail in Snohomish County rolls along for nearly 19 miles from Everett to the King County line. More than half is off-road bike trail, while the rest is a marked route on bike lanes. This route picks up the Interurban Trail heading south at the end of 224th Street Southwest and follows it off- and on-road past Ballinger and Echo lakes. The trail continues through the Shoreline commercial district and avoids two busy intersections with two pedestrian overpasses.

The Interurban Trail arrives back at the Seattle city limits at North 145th Street. Signs help direct cyclists to join the Linden Avenue Cycle Track, which is on the left side as you head south. Exiting the cycle track at North 128th Street, follow the Interurban Trail and residential streets back to the parking lot at the north end of Woodland Park.

MILES & DIRECTIONS

0.0 Leave Seattle's Woodland Park parking lot at the southern end of Green Lake and turn left onto West Green Lake Way North.

0.2 Turn left onto North 63rd Street, follow underpass beneath Aurora Avenue, and emerge bearing right onto Woodland Place North, which becomes Linden Avenue North with a bike lane.

0.8 Bear left onto Linden Avenue North where road forks (Winona Avenue North goes right).

1.3 Turn left onto North 83rd Street, go 1 block, then turn right onto Fremont Avenue North.

2.7 Turn right onto North 110th Street and left onto the Interurban Trail.

3.7 Interurban Trail ends at North 128th Street. Proceed across the street onto the Linden Avenue North Cycletrack on the right side of the road. At North 130th Street, proceed through the special bike signal.

4.4 Turn left onto North 143rd Street from the Linden Avenue Cycletrack. This is a four-way stop.

4.7 Turn right onto Greenwood Avenue North.

4.9 Entering the left lane, bear left to continue on Greenwood Avenue North where the road splits (Westminster Way North bears right).

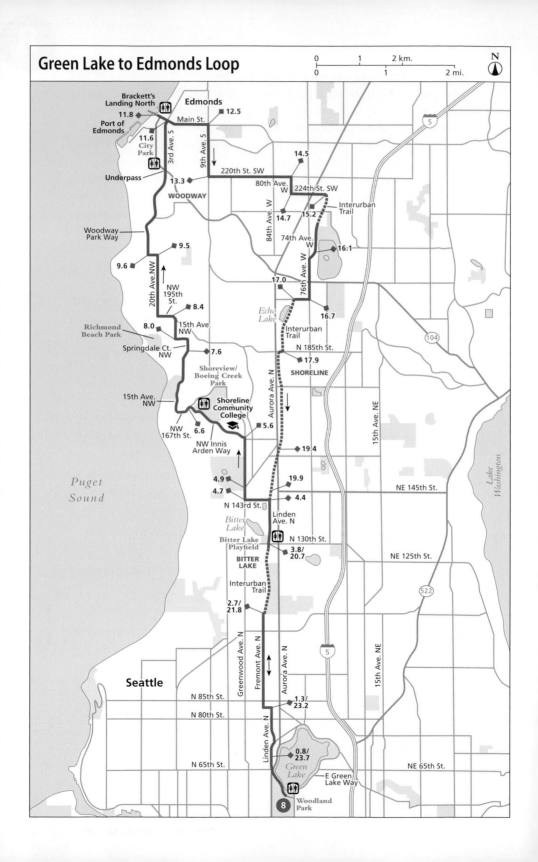

Green Lake to Edmonds Loop

0   1   2 km.

0   1   2 mi.

N

Brackett's Landing North 11.8
Edmonds 12.5
Port of Edmonds
11.6 **City Park**
Main St.
3rd Ave. S
9th Ave. S
Underpass
14.5
13.3
220th St. SW
80th Ave. W
224th St. SW
WOODWAY
Interurban Trail
84th Ave. W
14.7 15.2
Woodway Park Way
74th Ave. W
9.5
16:1
9.6
76th Ave. W
20th Ave. NW
NW 195th St.
17.0
8.4
16.7
Richmond Beach Park
15th Ave. NW
8.0
Echo Lake
Springdale Ct. NW
7.6
Interurban Trail
N 185th St.
Shoreview/ Boeing Creek Park
17.9
SHORELINE
15th Ave. NW
Shoreline Community College
5.6
NW 167th St.
6.6
19.4
NW Innis Arden Way
Aurora Ave. N
Puget Sound
4.9
19.9
4.7
4.4
NE 145th St.
15th Ave. NE
N 143rd St.
Bitter Lake
Linden Ave. N
Bitter Lake Playfield
N 130th St.
BITTER LAKE
3.8/ 20.7
NE 125th St.
Interurban Trail
2.7/ 21.8
522
Seattle
Greenwood Ave. N
Fremont Ave. N
Aurora Ave. N
5
15th Ave. NE
N 85th St.
1.3/ 23.2
N 80th St.
Linden Ave. N
N 65th St.
0.8/ 23.7
NE 65th St.
Green Lake
E Green Lake Way
8
Woodland Park
Lake Washington
104
5

5.6 Turn left onto Northwest Innis Arden Way.

6.6 Turn left at T intersection onto Northwest 167th Street. The road curves to the right and becomes 15th Avenue Northwest and then 14th Avenue Northwest.

7.6 Bear right onto Springdale Court Northwest.

7.8 Turn left at T intersection onto Northwest 188th Street (Ridgefield Road Northwest is a right turn).

8.0 Turn right onto 15th Avenue Northwest.

8.4 Turn left onto Northwest Richmond Beach Road, which becomes Northwest 195th Street.

8.6 Turn right onto 20th Avenue Northwest. It becomes Timber Lane after crossing Snohomish County line.

9.5 Turn left onto 238th Street Southwest.

9.6 Turn right onto 114th Avenue West, which becomes Woodway Park Road.

10.9 Route passes under SR 104 and becomes 3rd Avenue South.

11.6 Turn left onto Main Street.

11.8 Arrive at Edmonds Ferry Terminal (Edmonds Marine Walkway Park is on the right). Turn around to resume Green Lake–Edmonds Loop by heading uphill on Main Street.

12.5 Turn right onto 9th Avenue South.

13.3 Turn left onto 220th Street Southwest.

14.5 Turn right onto 80th Avenue West.

14.7 Turn left onto 224th Street Southwest (use caution at SR 99 intersection).

15.2 Turn right onto Interurban Trail. After crossing 228th Street Southwest, the trail ends at a gate and becomes 74th Avenue West.

16.1 Cross 236th Street Southwest and rejoin the Interurban Trail.

16.2 Turn left onto the bike lane on 76th Avenue West (the Interurban Trail dead-ends after crossing the street). The road becomes Meridian Avenue North after it crosses SR 104.

16.7 Turn right onto North 200th Street.

17.0 Turn left onto the Interurban Trail as you arrive at the Aurora Village Transit Center on Ashworth Avenue North.

17.9 Cross North 185th Street and turn right on the Interurban Trail.

19.3   Cross over SR 99 on pedestrian overpass.

19.4   Cross over North 155th Street on pedestrian overpass.

19.9   Use bike signal to cross North 145th Street and enter the Linden Avenue Cycletrack on left side of street.

20.8   Cycletrack ends at North 128th Street. Join the Interurban Trail.

21.8   Interurban Trail ends at North 110th Street. Turn right for half a block and then turn left on Fremont Avenue North.

23.1   Turn left on North 83rd Street.

23.2   Turn right onto Linden Avenue North.

23.7   Bear right to continue on Linden Avenue North (Winona Avenue North joins from left).

24.1   Remain straight at North 66th Street to join Woodland Place North (Linden Avenue veers right).

24.2   Bear left onto North 63rd Street to go under Aurora Avenue overpass.

24.3   Turn right onto West Green Lake Way North.

24.5   Turn right into second parking lot. End of ride.

RIDE INFORMATION

Local Events and Attractions
Milk Carton Derby at Green Lake: An opening event for the annual Seafair celebration in mid-July
Edmonds Classic Car Show: A car show on Main Street in early September

Restaurants
Richmond Beach Coffee Company: 1442 Richmond Beach Rd., Richmond Beach
Waterfront Coffee Company: 101 Main St., Edmonds

Restrooms
Mile 0.0: Green Lake Park across from parking lot
Mile 3.9: Bitter Lake Park, Seattle
Mile 6.3: Boeing Creek Park, Shoreline
Mile 11.1: City Park, Edmonds
Mile 11.8: Brackett's Landing Park, Edmonds
Mile 20.6: Bitter Lake Park, Seattle
Mile 24.5: Green Lake Park, Seattle

Snohomish–Monroe Loop (Three-River Loop)

This bike route passes through the bountiful farmland of the Snohomish Valley. It's an area with a rich agricultural history that thrives to this day at family dairies, Grange halls, and "u pick 'em" farms that dot the route. You'll also cross the three rivers—Snohomish, Snoqualmie, and Skykomish—that brought commerce to the region before the arrival of the railroad.

Start: Harvey Airfield, 9900 Airport Way, just south of Snohomish

Length: 25.9 miles

Approximate riding time: 2 to 3 hours

Best bike: Road and hybrid

Terrain: First half is flat; second half is hilly.

Traffic and hazards: Almost the entire route is on low-traffic roads with few bike lanes or shoulders; watch for rumble strips on the shoulder of SR 203 south of Monroe.

Things to see: Historic downtown Snoqualmie, scenic views of mountains and farmland, pick-it-yourself vegetable farms, old Grange hall, wildlife viewing areas in nature preserves

Maps: Snohomish County Bicycling, available at bicycle shops and (425) 353-RIDE; *DeLorme Atlas & Gazetteer—Washington,* page 46

Getting there: By car: Take SR 522 (also known as Lake City Way or Bothell Way) east out of Seattle. After passing I-405, exit onto SR 9 north to Snohomish in 2 miles. In 8.5 miles, turn right at the signal toward Airport Way and follow Airport Way to the left toward the airport in 1 mile. Park in the lot on the left side of the road where a coffee kiosk and restaurant are located. GPS: N47 54.425' / W122 05.945'

THE RIDE

It might be easy to forget that there's such a thing as hills as you pedal across the frying-pan flat agricultural valley between Snohomish and Monroe on this route. Be forewarned: There is hilly terrain on this bike loop, and it can snake-bite bicyclists who spend too much energy blasting past the farms on these low-traffic, rural roads early in the ride.

The bike route starts just south of downtown Snohomish at the Harvey Airfield, where you might see parachutists floating in for a landing from the adjacent sky-diving school.

Leaving the parking lot, head north on Airport Way and cross the Snohomish River, which drains the western slope of the Cascades between Stevens and Snoqualmie passes. Immediately you're in the old-time downtown district of Snohomish, a national historic landmark known as the Antique Capital of Washington. Watch for cars backing out of parking spaces as you pedal down First Street. At one time faced with extinction, this revitalized downtown core is now bustling with a touristy clientele drawn to shops and restaurants.

Less than a mile after starting, you cross the Centennial Trail, a rail trail that rolls north for 30 miles to the Skagit County line. In no time you're sliding off a bluff overlooking the river and onto the flat agricultural land of the Snohomish Valley. Glaciers scoured this area flat over thousands of years and the Skykomish, Snoqualmie, and Snohomish Rivers became the drainages for the glacial meltwater. While it made for flat bottomland that's good for farming and fun for bicycling, that grinding action also left steep hillsides like the ones you'll face later in the ride.

Bike Shop

Snohomish Bicycles: 1200 First St., Snohomish; (360) 862-8300; snohomishbicycles.com

The first climb, Lord Hill, starts about three miles into the ride as the road just skirts its base. The little bit of altitude, however, affords views to Mount Pilchuck soaring a mile above the valley floor. With your eyes you can follow US 2 across the valley below and trace it into the crease it follows into the Cascades on the way to Stevens Pass.

Coming downhill you arrive in Monroe, since 1907 home of the Monroe Correctional Facility that houses some 2,400 inmates. (Don't pick up any hitch-hikers as you ride through town.) The bike route turns onto Fryelands Boulevard, a residential area formerly the site of a 1,200-acre lettuce farm that kept a thousand people employed during the Great Depression. The first settlers arrived in the Monroe area at about the same time as they did in Snohomish. Logging, fishing, and agriculture buoyed the area's economy. When the

The Skykomish River meanders past gravel bars as it passes by Monroe.

railroad arrived in 1893, it passed too far from the original settlement near the river. The owner of the grocery relocated downtown by moving his building, which included the post office, closer to the railroad tracks.

The bike route crosses town to Al Borlin Park where the Skykomish River meanders over gravel bars in a wide floodplain. There are restrooms and a picnic shelter amid the towering Douglas firs and western cedar. Crossing the Skykomish River on a steel girder bridge equipped with a sidewalk, the route enters the flat farmlands of the Tualco district. The name is derived from a Native American term for "twin rivers," describing the Skykomish and Snoqualmie Rivers, which join nearby to form the Snohomish River.

Pastureland at the SR 203 roadside gives way to sprawling farm lots on Tualco Road. Crops grow nearly to the edges of the narrow roads here and massive hay barns dot the landscape. At least two farms feature pick-it-yourself harvesting of organically grown vegetables. A bright red building at the intersection of Tualco and Tualco Loop Roads is the Swiss Hall, which dates back to 1909 as the local Grange hall. It was sold to an organization of Swiss descendants in 1951.

Some of the land in this area is too wet to till, so it has been left as marshlands and oxbow lakes. Two state wildlife-viewing areas at Crescent Lake here are destinations for birders year-round. Tundra and trumpeter swans and other waterfowl flock here in the winter, and you're likely to see red-winged blackbirds and other birds flitting through the air or perched on reeds growing in the marsh in the summer.

The Snoqualmie River, which crashes 268 feet over a spectacular falls upstream, looks tame and docile at this river crossing just before it joins the Skykomish to form the Snohomish River. Pedaling across the bridge, there's hardly time for a deep breath before you leave the valley floor and ascend the valley wall that overlooks the river. After so much time on the flats, it might take a couple of minutes to acclimate to fighting gravity over the next mile. This is a rolling route up here, and there are glimpses of the valley floor through breaks in the trees along High Bridge, Elliott, and Connelly Roads. The route drops almost to the river level at the corner of Elliott and Connelly Roads, then begins another climb.

About halfway up this second climb you'll pass the Bob Heirman Wildlife Preserve at Thomas' Eddy. Three miles of hiking trails pass a couple of lakes and two hairpin bends of the Snohomish River, and hikers often report seeing ducks, geese, and swans. After summiting on Connelly Road, the route turns onto Springhetti Road, where you'll enjoy the welcome sight of the road curving down to the valley floor on its way back to the city of Snohomish and the end of the ride.

MILES & DIRECTIONS

0.0 Leave the parking lot for Harvey Airfield and turn left onto Airport Way Southeast, crossing the bridge.

0.3 Turn right onto First Street.

0.7 Cross Centennial Trail.

0.9 Turn right onto Lincoln Avenue Southeast (it becomes Old Snohomish–Monroe Road).

3.3 Pass 127th Avenue Southeast on the right; that's the road to Lord Hill Regional Park.

6.8 Turn left onto Fryelands Boulevard, go 1 block, and turn right onto Currie Road. It veers left and becomes 171st Avenue Southeast, then veers left again to become 155th Street Southeast, and then turns right to become 170th Avenue Southeast.

7.9 Turn right onto 154th Street Southeast.

8.5 Pass through four-way stop beneath SR 522. Road becomes Blueberry Lane.

9.1 Turn right onto North Kelsey Street.

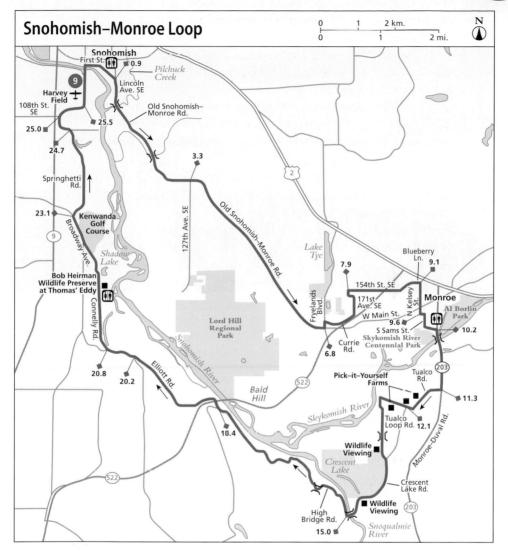

Snohomish–Monroe Loop

9.5   Cross West Main Street.

9.6   Take first left onto Pike Street, then first right onto South Sams Street. Follow Sams Street as it veers left and becomes Sumac Drive.

10.2 Cross SR 203 (South Lewis Street) and enter Al Borlin Park. Retrace your route out of Al Borlin Park and turn left onto SR 203 (South Lewis Street).

10.5 Cross Skykomish River Bridge.

11.3 Turn right onto Tualco Road.

A bicyclist in yellow raingear coasts downhill on Springhetti Road near Snohomish.

12.1 Go straight ahead on Tualco Loop Road at intersection.

13.3 Cross bridge over Riley Slough.

13.6 Pass state Department of Fish and Wildlife parking lot.

13.9 Rejoin Tualco Road; name changes to Crescent Lake Road.

15.0 Cross Snoqualmie River Bridge and turn right onto High Bridge Road.

15.9 Ride on bridge over ravine.

18.4 Bear right at intersection; High Bridge Road becomes Elliott Road.

20.2 Pass Fales Road on the left.

20.8 Turn right onto Connelly Road.

21.9 Pass parking for Bob Heirman Wildlife Preserve at Thomas' Eddy on the right.

22.7 Bear right; Connelly Road becomes Broadway Avenue.

23.1 Turn right onto Springhetti Road.

24.7 Turn left to stay on Springhetti Road.

25.0 Go straight through intersection and pick up Airport Way.

25.5 Turn left to stay on Airport Way.

25.9 Turn left into Harvey Airfield.

RIDE INFORMATION

Local Events and Attractions

Kla Ha Ya Days: Weeklong summertime festival throughout downtown Snohomish, mid-July

Evergreen State Fair: Last week of August; Evergreen State Fairground, 14405 179th Ave. Southeast, Monroe

Antique Tractor Pull and Threshing Bee: Vintage tractor displays and contests, mid-August, presented by Sky Valley Stock and Antique Tractor Club, Frohning farm on Crescent Lake Road in Tualco Valley, Monroe; skyvalley antiquetractor.com

Snoqualmie Historic Downtown District: "Antique Capital of Washington," First and Second Streets between Avenue D and Union Avenue; historicdown townsnohomish.org

Lord Hill Regional Park: 1,400-acre upland nature preserve with 6 miles of hiking and biking trails overlooking Snohomish River Valley; 12921 150th St. Southeast; www1.co.snohomish.wa.us/Departments/Parks/Park_Information/ Park_Directory/Regional_Parks/Lord_Hill.htm

Bob Heirman Wildlife Preserve at Thomas' Eddy: Waterfowl viewing, fishing, and hiking along two tight bends on the Snohomish River, 14913 Connelly Rd., Snohomish

Restaurants

Buzz Inn Restaurant: 9900 Airport Way, Snohomish; (360) 568-3970

Snoqualmie Bakery: Corner of First Street and Union Avenue, Snohomish; (360) 568-1682

Restrooms

Mile 0.5: First Avenue across from B Street, Snohomish

Mile 10.2: Al Borlin Park, east side of SR 203 (South Lewis Street)

Mile 21.9: Bob Heirman Wildlife Preserve at Thomas' Eddy (portable toilets)

Centennial Trail

The 30-mile Centennial Trail is a popular north-south rail trail that passes through agricultural and forest land in western Snohomish County. Full services for bicyclists are available in the towns of Snohomish and Arlington, and nearly a dozen trailheads allow easy access for riding shorter sections of the trail.

Start: Intersection of Maple and Pine Avenues in Snohomish

Length: 59.6 miles round-trip

Approximate riding time: 4 to 6 hours

Best bike: Road or hybrid

Terrain: No steep climbs, but 2 long uphill grades; paved trail, 10 to 12 feet wide

Traffic and hazards: Hikers and dog walkers, mainly concentrated around the major trailheads

Things to see: Historic downtowns of Snohomish and Arlington, Lake Cassidy, historic Nakashima Barn, Upper Marysville Valley overlook

Maps: *DeLorme Atlas & Gazetteer—Washington,* pages 32 and 46; Snohomish County Bicycling, available at bicycle shops and (425) 353-RIDE; Online Centennial Trail map, www.co.snohomish.wa.us/documents/Departments/Parks/maps/ctcompletereduced.pdf

Getting there: By car: From Woodinville, take exit 23 east off I-405 North to SR 522. Take SR 9 exit north toward Snohomish, go 9 miles, and take the Snohomish exit onto Second Street. Stay on Second Street for nearly a mile and turn left onto Maple Avenue. Go 0.6 miles to the intersection with Pine Avenue. Find parking on the shoulder of Maple Avenue. GPS: N47 55.264' / W122 05.112'

THE RIDE

The Centennial Trail takes its name from the one hundredth anniversary of Washington State, when the first 7-mile section of the abandoned Burlington Northern Railroad route through Snohomish County was opened to the public as a rail trail.

The goal of creating a first-class trail hasn't ended there, however. The Centennial Trail Commission of Snohomish County continues to support efforts by cities and the county to fill in missing gaps and increase its overall length. The current Centennial Trail rolls for 30 miles between downtown Snohomish and the historic Nakashima Heritage Barn North Trailhead on the Skagit County line. It is ten to twelve feet wide and paved for its entire length. A half million bicyclists, hikers, joggers, and dog walkers use the trail annually. Long-range plans call for extending the trail north to the Canadian border and south into King County, where it would connect to the rail-trail network there.

The trail runs on the abandoned rail line of the Seattle, Lake Shore & Eastern Railroad that dates back to 1889 and eventually became the Burlington Northern. It carried the usual mail and passengers, as well as freight—predominantly timber from the dense northwest forests destined for sawmills. Many of the towns along the trail are former railroad stops.

This bike route is a round-trip ride from Snohomish to the terminus at the Skagit County line and back again. There are at least half a dozen trailheads with parking lots and restrooms along the way, however, so riders can easily choose shorter options rather

Bike Shops

Arlington Velo Sport Bicycle Shop: 401 N. Olympic Ave., Arlington; (360) 629-6415; arlingtonvelosport.com
Snohomish Bicycles: 1200 1st St., Snohomish; (360) 862-8300; snohomishbicycles.com

than riding the entire length. To get started, consider shorter round-trip rides from Snohomish to Machias (9.4 miles), Pilchuck trailhead to Lake Cassidy (18.8 miles), or Legion Memorial Park in Arlington to Nakashima Heritage Barn Park Trailhead (16.4 miles).

The full round-trip ride starts at the traditional trailhead in Snohomish on Maple Avenue, just past its junction with Pine Avenue. This used to be the southern terminus of the trail, and the city created on-street parking for visitors. The trail now ends several blocks farther south on First Street, where you can turn right and visit many antiques shops and restaurants housed in restored Victorian-era buildings. Maple at Pine, however, is still the most convenient location for starting a ride.

Bicyclists gather at the Arlington Trailhead at Legion Memorial Park.

Heading north, it seems as if you're out of town in no time. The trail enters a narrow, agricultural valley with views of the scenic Pilchuck River on your right and occasional glimpses of snowy Cascade mountain peaks farther to the east. You'll find many excuses to pause at river overlooks here, and in the autumn you might catch sight of salmon swimming upstream to spawn.

The replica train depot at Mile 4.7 in Machias is another place to dawdle, as bicyclists tend to stop here to use the facilities and trade stories. Heading north, you'll lose sight of the Pilchuck River and may notice the slight uphill grade on your way to the outskirts of Lake Stevens. The trail passes through the outskirts of the town, which got its start in the lumber industry and later became a resort destination for Seattle residents.

The trail leaves the agricultural countryside behind after Lake Stevens and climbs into a forest. There are many wetlands throughout this area, and you'll catch a whiff of skunk cabbage that blooms here in the spring. At the high point of the trail sits Lake Cassidy. An inviting dock juts into the 125-acre lake, and the small rest area is another gathering spot for bicyclists. A steady downhill run into Arlington starts just after the lake, although many pause along the ridge to enjoy the views of farm country around North Marysville to the west, as well as the Olympic Mountains on the horizon.

The trail meets the valley floor at 168th Street Northwest, and it follows noisy 67th Avenue Northeast all the way into Arlington. Be sure to activate the crosswalk signals before crossing these busy roads around Arlington, the largest town on the route. Illustrated historic signs installed along the Centennial Trail tell different chapters in the story of Arlington—as a major Navy airfield during World War II; as the winner of a railroad depot over the adjoining town of Haller City (preserved today only in the name of a park); and as a logging town that earned the title "Shingle Capital of the World" by milling cedar from the surrounding virgin forests. Cyclists riding the trail also gather at the replica train station that serves as a public restroom in Legion Memorial Park. Across Olympic Avenue, old town Arlington storefronts offer a wide variety of food, including vegan.

Less than a mile up the trail you'll find breathtaking views of the countryside from the trestle over the confluence of the North and South Forks of the Stillaquamish River. Just beyond you'll find a shiny steel archway erected to mark the junction of the paved Centennial Trail with the future White Horse Trail. That right-of-way heads for 27 miles to Darrington, although all but 6 miles are closed because of rugged and unsafe conditions. The trail crosses busy Route 9 at Bryant, then continues in a nearly straight line to the Skagit County line, about 4 miles away. Passing through second-growth forest, the trail crosses another stunning bridge over Pilchuck Creek (no relation to Pilchuck River).

The trail ends at the Nakashima Heritage Barn North Trailhead. The bright red vintage 1908 barn marks the site of a sprawling dairy farm owned by several families over the years until the county acquired it in the 1990s. It's named for the Nakashimas, a Japanese-American family that operated a thriving business there from 1937 until they were forced to sell out and move to internment camps in 1942.

This is the turn-around point on the ride, and you might resolve not to dilly-dally on the way back to make up some time. Good luck with that, however, as you'll notice things you didn't see heading the other direction, and there are always other cyclists at rest stops eager to visit.

MILES & DIRECTIONS

0.0 Turn left onto Centennial Trail where it crosses Pine Street.

1.5 Pass Pilchuck Trailhead on the left.

4.7 Pass Machias Station Trailhead on the right.

7.3 Pass 20th Street Trailhead (Lake Stevens) on the left.

8.3 Pass the Highway 92 Trailhead.

10.9 Pass the pier for Lake Cassidy on the left.

12.4 Cross 84th Street Northeast (activate the pedestrian crossing signal). Also the Getchell Trailhead is around the corner to the right on Westlund Road.

13.8 Pass road sign for Culpepper Hill.

14.9 Valley view of North Marysville, Stimson's Crossing, and Tulalip Indian Reservation.

16.8 Pass Armar Road Trailhead.

18.5 Cross 172nd Street Northeast (activate pedestrian crossing signal). The trail runs alongside 67th Avenue Northeast.

19.8 Use care crossing railroad tracks (swerve to cross at 90-degree angle).

20.5 Cross 204th Street Northeast (activate pedestrian crossing signal).

21.6 Arrive at Arlington Trailhead on left.

22.4 Cross bridge over confluence of North and South Forks of Stillaguamish River at Haller Park.

25.4 Cross 268th Street Northwest at Bryant Trailhead.

25.6 Cross Highway 9.

27.0 Cross bridge over Pilchuck Creek.

29.8 Arrive at Nakashima Heritage Barn North Trailhead. Retrace your route.

34.0 Pass Bryant Trailhead.

37.2 Cross bridge over confluence of North and South Forks of Stillaguamish River

38.0 Arrive at Arlington Trailhead.

39.1 Cross 204th Street.

39.8 Use care crossing railroad tracks.

41.0 Cross 172nd Street Northeast.

42.8 Arrive at Armar Road Trailhead.

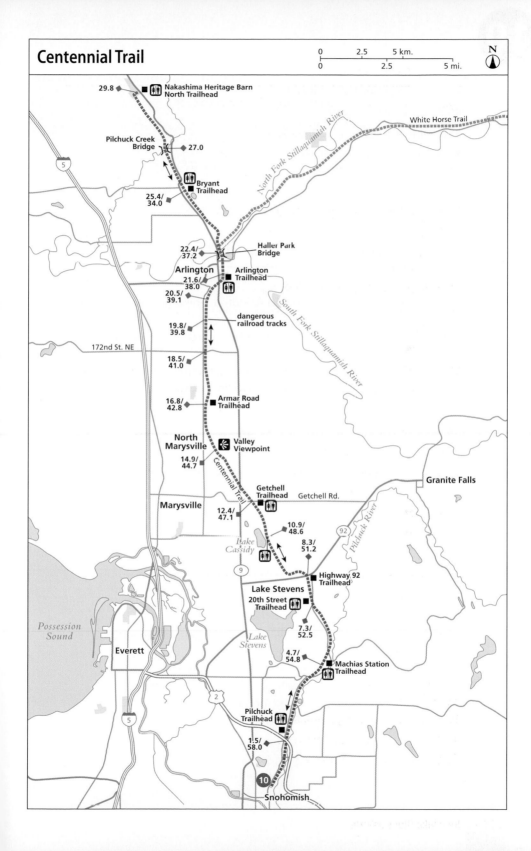

Centennial Trail

0   2.5   5 km.
0   2.5   5 mi.

N

29.8 ■ Nakashima Heritage Barn
        North Trailhead

Pilchuck Creek
Bridge ■ 27.0

Bryant
Trailhead

25.4/
34.0

North Fork Stillaguamish River

White Horse Trail

22.4/
37.2 ■ Haller Park
        Bridge

Arlington ■ Arlington
              Trailhead
21.6/
38.0
20.5/
39.1

19.8/
39.8 ■ dangerous
         railroad tracks

172nd St. NE

18.5/
41.0

16.8/
42.8 ■ Armar Road
         Trailhead

South Fork Stillaguamish River

North
Marysville ■ Valley
              Viewpoint

14.9/
44.7

Granite Falls

Marysville

Getchell
Trailhead   Getchell Rd.

12.4/
47.1

10.9/
48.6

Lake
Cassidy

8.3/
51.2

92   Pilchuck River

9

Lake Stevens

20th Street
Trailhead

Highway 92
Trailhead

Possession
Sound

Everett

7.3/
52.5

Lake
Stevens

4.7/
54.8 ■ Machias Station
         Trailhead

2

Pilchuck
Trailhead

1.5/
58.0

5

Centennial Trail

10

Snohomish

44.7 Pass valley viewpoint.

47.1 Arrive at Getchell Trailhead.

48.6 Arrive at Lake Cassidy .

51.2 Arrive at Highway 92 Trailhead.

52.5 Pass 20th Street Trailhead (Lake Stevens).

54.8 Pass Machias Station Trailhead.

58.0 Pass Pilchuck Trailhead.

59.6 Return to Snohomish to end the ride.

RIDE INFORMATION

Local Events and Attractions

Art Show in the Park: Legion Park in Arlington, Arlington Arts Council, first weekend after Labor Day

Kla Ha Ya Days: Weeklong summertime festival throughout downtown Snohomish, mid-July

Centennial Trail History Tour: Learn more about history along the rail trail at centennialtrail.com

Restaurants

Beetlejuice and Java Cafe: 707 Pine St. (Pine and Maple Avenues trailhead), Snohomish; (360) 568-0588

Local Scoop: 434 N. Olympic Ave., Arlington; (360) 403-8282

Shire Cafe: Vegan and vegetarian, 117 E. Division St. (at North Olympic Avenue), Arlington; (360) 403-9020

Snoqualmie Bakery: Corner of First Street and Union Avenue, Snohomish; (360) 568-1682

Restrooms

Mile 1.5 and 58.0: Pilchuck Trailhead (portable toilets)

Mile 4.7 and 54.8: Machias Trailhead (restrooms)

Mile 7.3 and 52.5: 20th Street Trailhead (portable toilets)

Mile 10.9 and 48.6: Lake Cassidy (portable toilets)

Mile 12.4 and 47.1: Getchell Trailhead (portable toilets)

Mile 21.6 and 38.0: Arlington Trailhead in Legion Park (restrooms)

Mile 25.4 and 34.0: Bryant Trailhead (portable toilets)

Mile 29.8: Nakashima Heritage Barn North Trailhead (portable toilets)

Snohomish–Granite Falls Loop

Bicyclists will appreciate the rugged flavor of the Cascade foothills as they climb from the flat river valley around Snohomish to the rugged landscape that surrounds Granite Falls. The route follows lumpy, forested terrain dotted with lakes until it returns to a valley overlook. From there, the ride ends with a screaming descent back to the Centennial Trail.

Start: Trailhead for Centennial Trail at Pine and Maple Avenues, Snohomish

Length: 37.7 miles

Approximate riding time: 3 to 4.5 hours

Best bike: Road

Terrain: Flat along Centennial Trail, then hilly with a half-dozen challenging climbs

Traffic and hazards: Traffic is heavy on brief stretches of South Machias Road and SR 92.

Things to see: Granite Falls Museum, Mountain Loop Highway, scenic lakes and forests, views of Mount Pilchuck, Centennial Trail

Maps: *DeLorme Atlas & Gazetteer—Washington,* pages 46 and 32

Getting there: By car: From Woodinville, take exit 23 east off I-405 North to SR 522. Take SR 9 exit north toward Snohomish, go 9 miles, and take the Snohomish exit onto Second Street. Stay on Second Street for nearly a mile and turn left onto Maple Avenue. Go 0.6 miles to the intersection with Pine Avenue. Find parking on the shoulder of Maple Avenue. GPS: N47 55.264' / W122 05.112'

THE RIDE

At one time Granite Falls was a bustling point of departure for entrepreneurs seeking their fortunes in the mining and forest trades in the Cascade Range. It's still known as a starting point, although most of the adventurers today are pursuing outdoor recreation. This ride is an adventure in itself, as it faces repeated challenging climbs into Cascade foothills.

The bike loop starts at Pine and Maple Avenues in the city of Snohomish alongside the 30-mile-long Centennial Trail. The popular trail follows the path of the Seattle, Lake Shore, and Eastern Railway that started serving these communities in 1889. Later sold to the Northern Pacific and then the Burlington Northern railroad, it was abandoned in 1987. Two years later, at the time of Washington State's centennial celebration, the first section of trail opened. The paved trail is now open all the way to the Skagit County line.

Riding north along the Pilchuck River, you'll see some snow-capped mountains in the distance. The hook-shaped peak of mile-high Mount Pilchuck is the most prominent and keeps a watchful eye over your approach to Granite Falls. The route turns off the trail at Machias, obviously an old railroad town as the restroom building resembles a vintage railroad station. If you've passed through on the trail, you might be surprised that there's still a small town here. Watch for traffic when you leave this burg and turn onto South Machias Road, a busy thoroughfare without much of a shoulder. It's okay, though, as you'll leave the busy road in less than a half-mile for O.K. Mill Road, named after one of the shingle mills that dotted the area in the early 1900s.

Bike Shop

Snohomish Bicycles: 1200 First St., Snohomish; (360) 862-8300; snohomishbicycles.com

You'll cross the rocky Pilchuck River right after you turn onto O.K. Mill Road, and then begin a steady climb. The road becomes steeper and curvier after you turn onto Newberg Road. You'll have plenty of time to study the old farmsteads you pass as you pedal uphill. The summit reveals views of Mount Pilchuck between the trees and a rolling downhill run to Lake Bosworth, a fishing lake surrounded by vacation homes. The descent doesn't end, however, as you drop all the way to the Pilchuck River again, and then roll into town on the level Granite Falls–Pilchuck Road.

If you stop at the town museum on East Union Street on the way in, you'll learn that Granite Falls was a late bloomer, not getting its start for some twenty-five years after the founding of Snohomish. That's not surprising, as there was no easy way to get here except for following the Pilchuck River or

The reward for a long climb is a long, scenic view.

hacking through 10 miles of dense, old-growth forest from Machias. Once the early settlers pushed through a trail, it didn't take long for the community to grow. Boom times hit in 1889 when gold and silver were discovered deeper in the Cascades at Monte Cristo, and Granite Falls became a departure point for the mine fields. That didn't last long, however, as the ore was poor quality and huge snowfalls caused avalanches and flood damage and the area was abandoned in 1897. Several comeback attempts failed. The lumber industry sustained the town until the Great Depression, as did the outdoor tourism industry. The recreation industry got a boost in the 1930s with construction of the so-called Mountain Loop Highway that starts in Granite Falls. The highway—some pavement and some gravel—carries hikers, campers, fishermen, and hunters into the Cascades and passes within 4 miles of Monte Cristo.

If you're hungry, cafes and markets populate the main intersection in town, and a supermarket 1 block north of SR 92 also sports a cafe. To leave town, go east on SR 92 (East Stanley Street) and then south onto South Alder Avenue. Soon you're out of town and climbing into forests that shade the road. You'll cross a small version of the Pilchuck River here, closer to its source. It spills out of the Cascades and heads northwest toward Granite Falls, then makes a U-turn and follows the valley southwest along the Centennial Trail to join the Snohomish River. That's why you cross the river four times on this loop.

Take the left fork on North Lake Roesiger Road and reach the summit of the loop before plunging along the shoreline of the lake. You can catch a cool drink or snack at the Lake Roesiger Store, a friendly country store on this isolated section of road. Access to the lake and restrooms is about a half-mile farther down the road. Leaving the lake you're still flying downhill through farm country but it's too soon to rejoice. You cross the nondescript West Fork Woods Creek and begin a climb that doesn't give up for 2 miles. After a short drop and rise at Three Lakes, turn right onto Three Lakes Road for an awesome view clear across the Snohomish River Valley and Puget Sound to the Olympic Mountains. It's a very fast 3 miles downhill, and after crossing the Pilchuck River for the last time, turn left onto the Centennial Trail for a 1-mile ride back to the trailhead.

MILES & DIRECTIONS

0.0   Start at street parking on Maple Avenue just past the corner with Pine Avenue. Turn left onto the Centennial Trail, heading north.

4.8   Turn right onto Division Street at Machias Trailhead Park, and then turn left onto South Machias Road.

5.4   Turn right onto O.K. Mill Road. Cross the Pilchuck River.

7.1   Turn left onto Newberg Road.

10.6   Follow road at sharp right where it becomes 48th Street Northeast.

11.4   Turn right onto Lerch Road and follow it right at the next fork.

12.0   Turn left onto Bosworth Drive. There's a steep downhill coming up with a stop sign at bottom of hill.

12.7   Bear left onto Granite Falls–Pilchuck Road, also known as Robe Menzel Road.

13.4   Cross Pilchuck River Bridge.

15.7   Turn right at four-way stop onto East Stanley Street (SR 92).

16.1   Turn right onto South Alder Avenue.

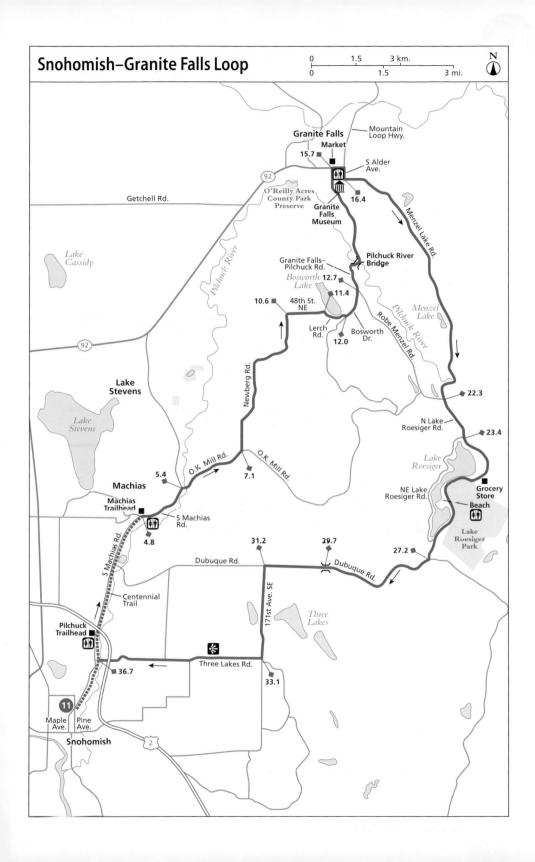

Snohomish–Granite Falls Loop

0   1.5   3 km.
0   1.5   3 mi.

N

Granite Falls
Market
15.7
Mountain Loop Hwy.
S Alder Ave.
16.4
92
Getchell Rd.
O'Reilly Acres County Park Preserve
Granite Falls Museum
Menzel Lake Rd.
Pilchuck River
Lake Cassidy
Granite Falls–Pilchuck Rd.
Pilchuck River Bridge
Bosworth Lake
12.7
11.4
10.6
48th St. NE
Lerch Rd.
Bosworth Dr.
12.0
Menzel Lake
Robe Menzel Rd.
Pilchuck River
92
Lake Stevens
Newberg Rd.
Lake Stevens
22.3
N Lake Roesiger Rd.
23.4
O.K. Mill Rd.
O.K. Mill Rd.
Lake Roesiger
5.4
7.1
Machias
Machias Trailhead
S Machias Rd.
NE Lake Roesiger Rd.
Grocery Store
Beach
4.8
31.2
29.7
Dubuque Rd.
Dubuque Rd.
27.2
Lake Roesiger Park
S Machias Rd.
Centennial Trail
171st Ave. SE
Three Lakes
Pilchuck Trailhead
36.7
33.1
Three Lakes Rd.
11
Maple Ave.
Pine Ave.
2
Snohomish

16.4 Turn left onto East Pioneer Street, which becomes Menzel Lake Road.

22.3 Pass by Carpenter Road on the right; road becomes North Lake Roesiger Road.

23.4 Take left fork to remain on North Lake Roesiger Road.

24.6 Grocery store on South Lake Roesiger Road and Monroe Camp Road.

25.2 Entrance for Lake Roesiger Park is on the right.

27.2 Turn right onto Dubuque Road.

29.7 Cross West Fork Woods Creek and face another climb.

31.2 Turn left onto 171st Avenue Southeast.

33.1 Turn right onto Three Lakes Road.

36.7 Turn left onto the Centennial Trail.

37.7 End of ride.

RIDE INFORMATION

Local Events and Attractions

Centennial Trail: A 30-mile rail trail linking Snohomish, Lake Stevens, and Arlington to the Skagit County line; www1.co.snohomish.wa.us/departments/parks/park_information/park_directory/regional_parks/centennial_trail.htm

Granite Falls Museum: Displays and photographs of early Granite Falls life; 109 E. Union St., Granite Falls; check for open days and times; gfhistory.org

Mountain Loop Highway: A 55-mile paved and gravel highway through western Cascades; check for road closures in winter and spring; starts at North Alder Avenue and SR 92 in Granite Falls; discovernw.org/Free_Publications/Mount_Baker_Snoqualmie_Mountain_Loop_Scenic_Byway.pdf

Railroad Days: Parades, entertainment, and street vendors; early October; granitefallswa.com/events-activities/rrday

Restaurants

Old Roesiger Store: Old timey, country store atmosphere, beer garden; 810 S. Roesiger Rd., Snohomish; facebook.com/LakeRoesigerStore

Beetlejuice and Java Cafe: 707 Pine St. (Pine and Maple Avenues trailhead), Snohomish; (360) 568-0588

Restrooms

Mile 1.5: Pilchuck Trailhead (portable toilets)

Mile 4.8: Machias Trailhead (restrooms)

Mile 15.6: Granite Falls (restrooms)

Mile 25.2: Lake Roesiger (restrooms)

Paradise Valley Conservation Area

There's enough variety for mountain bikers at the Paradise Valley Conservation Area to keep them coming back for more. Some trails, which evolved from old logging roads and skids, are smooth and flowy while others are a tangle of roots that weave through the second-growth forest just beyond the sprawling Seattle suburbs.

Start: Paradise Valley Conservation Area parking lot at Paradise Lake Road, Maltby

Length: 11 miles

Approximate riding time: 2 to 3 hours

Best bike: Mountain bike

Terrain: Fairly level with a couple of small climbs at the south end of the park. Some trails are smooth and fast, while others are twisty and technical; one advanced trail has man-made and natural structures. Trails drain well after rains and are rideable in a couple of days.

Traffic and hazards: Expect to encounter hikers, joggers, dog walkers, and equestrians.

Things to see: Hundred-year-old second-growth forest, wildflowers in season, wildlife

Maps: *DeLorme Atlas & Gazetteer—Washington,* page 46; Paradise Valley Conservation Area brochure (downloadable), www.co.snohomish.wa.us/documents/Departments/Parks/pvcabrochure.pdf

Getting there: By car: Take SR 522 east from I-405 and turn right onto Paradise Valley Road after about 5.2 miles. Turn right into Paradise Valley Conservation Area parking lot in less than 2 miles. GPS: N47 47.316' / W122 04.807'

THE RIDE

There's just no getting lost—or even confounded—on a mountain bike ride at Paradise Valley Conservation Area. The park in southern Snohomish County features 11 miles of dirt trails available for bikers in nearly 800 acres of dense, second-growth forest. Way-finding is easy because every trail at each junction is marked by a post bearing a waypoint number that corresponds to a number on the park map. Attached to each post are labels for the trail name, distance to the next trail, and whether horses, mountain bikes, or hikers are allowed. Further, there are no unmarked or "volunteer" trails to be found. This attention to detail doesn't detract from the riding experience in the park, unless you enjoy getting lost, in which case you can ignore the signs and plow ahead. Just be sure not to infringe on trails set aside for foot or horse traffic.

The trail system here always wasn't so organized. The Lloyd family homesteaded the property in 1887, logged it, and used some areas for pasture. In recent years they allowed some recreation on the property, but word-of-mouth spread and things got out of hand. When the county acquired the tract in 2000, inspectors found a hodgepodge of one hundred trails, some badly eroding. Hikers and mountain bikers, as well as equestrians and people driving motorbikes and all-terrain vehicles, used the old dirt logging roads and log skids as trails and made some of their own.

Because the public and private agencies raised funds for the purchase to protect the watershed of Bear Creek, a salmon-spawning stream, the county shut down the property for recreation. That didn't sit well with users, including what later became the Evergreen Mountain Bike Alliance. After some planning meetings, the parks department bought land for a thirty-seven-car parking lot and installed an entrance to a trail system. On Earth Day 2009, the conservation area was reopened with 13 miles of well-marked and maintained trails for hikers, mountain bikers, and equestrians; no motor vehicles allowed.

Mountain bikers have access to about 11 miles of trail, most of it single track. Although some depressions in the trails collect rainwater, all but the

Bike Shops

Eastside Ski and Sports: 15606 NE Woodinville-Duvall Rd., Woodinville; (425) 485-7547; eastsideskiandsport.com
Snohomish Bicycles: 1200 First St., Snohomish; (360) 862-8300; snohomishbicycles.com/
Woodinville Bicycle: 13210 NE 175th St., Woodinville; (425) 483-6626; woodinvillebicycle.com/

A crooked ladder bridge snakes around trees on Lloyd Trail.

most stubborn mud bogs dry out within four or five days of rain. The dirt trails wind through stands of Douglas fir and western hemlock, some estimated at one hundred years old. Elsewhere, more recently logged forestland is still covered in alder. In some areas, the forest floor is thick with sword ferns and salal. Slow down on spring rides to spot occasional trillium in shaded areas; your nose will alert you to skunk cabbage in wet areas. Don't be surprised to see Douglas squirrels or rabbits in the undergrowth and be aware that deer, raccoons, and mountain beavers make their homes here. The Lloyd family remembers cougar here over the years, and the parks department says the habitat also is ideal for coyote.

Gain entrance to the park and single track via an old logging road, the Mainline Trail. The trail begins wide but narrows after passing several trail junctions. It's not much wider than single track as it arrives at the Mountain Bike Park on a low hilltop at the south end. The Mainline Trail is the backbone for a couple of rides that link together trails with similar characteristics—Paradise Valley Smooth and Paradise Valley Rough.

PARADISE VALLEY SMOOTH (4.2 MILES)

This ride follows the smoother trails, where trail crews packed areas of exposed tree roots with dirt. Entering the park on the Mainline Trail, the route turns right onto the Cascara Trail. The trail weaves around trees, but the turns are fairly wide with some berms so riders can maintain their speed. The back section is almost straight, returning to the Mainline Trail.

The route then climbs up a low hilltop on the south side to the Mountain Bike Park. A glacial erratic boulder topped with dozens of stone cairns marks the entrance. At least three twisty trails take off from this hilltop that test riders' technique and agility. While the trail surface is smooth, the many sudden turns keep speeds low. Some sections have banked turns and others feel like a pump track. This is a place where bikers can ride repeatedly until they nail it.

PARADISE VALLEY ROUGH (5.0 MILES)

This route is more challenging than the "smooth" option. Trails are cluttered with exposed tree roots and turns are often up or down small rises and drops between trees. You'll encounter fallen logs to cross and a couple of ladder bridges over wetlands.

You'll first come upon tree roots and short ups and downs around trees on the weaving Red Alder Trail. It connects to the Two Trees and Ephemeral Trails. The latter can be wet as it takes some sharp turns around a wetland, but straightens out later before it meets up with the Two Trees Trail again.

At the next junction back on the Mainline Trail, advanced mountain bikers can take a run down the 0.5-mile-long one-way Cedar Run Trail with its natural and manmade structures. Others can take the Southern Traverse Trail, which crosses a seasonal muddy area on a ladder bridge.

The Lloyd Trail is an original mountain biking trace through the forest. It also crosses some rough rooty patches and some log piles, but also has some flowy sections. About midway you'll have to cross a crooked ladder bridge that bends around some trees and over the ferns.

And that's all there is to it—just follow the numbered wooden posts for a fun mountain biking adventure in a shady Pacific Northwest forest.

MILES & DIRECTIONS

(Waypoint numbers correspond to trail markers at the park and on the park map.)
Paradise Valley Smooth

0.0 Begin at Mainline Trail trailhead at northwest corner of the parking lot next to kiosk.

0.1 Turn right onto Cascara Trail (Waypoint 5).

0.6 Bear left to remain on Cascara Trail.

0.7 Take left fork onto 106th Drive Trail (Waypoint 7).

0.8 Turn right onto Mainline Trail (Waypoint 8).

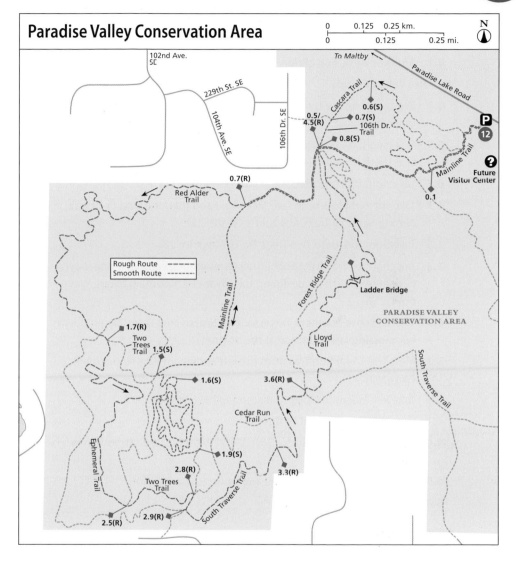

Paradise Valley Conservation Area

0   0.125   0.25 km.

0   0.125   0.25 mi.

N

102nd Ave. SE

229th St. SE

104th Ave. SE

106th Dr. SE

To Maltby

Paradise Lake Road

Cascara Trail

0.6(S)

0.5/
4.5(R)

0.7(S)

106th Dr.
Trail

0.8(S)

Mainline Trail

P
12

Future
Visitor Center

0.7(R)

Red Alder
Trail

0.1

Rough Route
Smooth Route

Mainline Trail

Forest Ridge Trail

Ladder Bridge

PARADISE VALLEY
CONSERVATION AREA

1.7(R)

Two
Trees
Trail   1.5(S)

Lloyd
Trail

South Traverse Trail

1.6(S)

3.6(R)

Cedar Run
Trail

Ephemeral Trail

1.9(S)

2.8(R)

3.3(R)

Two Trees
Trail

South Traverse Trail

2.5(R)   2.9(R)

1.5 Take left fork onto Mainline Trail (Waypoint 19).

1.6 After a short uphill, turn right into Mountain Bike Park at Waypoint 20, and then take the right fork for a smooth, flowy run around the "park" and back to Mainline Trail.

1.9 Turn left onto Mainline Trail (Waypoint 21).

2.1 Turn left into the Mountain Bike Park again at the Waypoint 20 fork and take one of the trails on the left. When you finish the loop, take the other trail.

3.0 Exit Mountain Bike Park and turn left on Mainline Trail (Waypoint 20.) Take right fork onto Mainline Trail (Waypoint 19). Watch your speed and other trail users on mostly downhill slope back to parking lot.

4.2 Arrive at kiosk. End of ride.

Paradise Valley Rough

0.0 Begin at Mainline Trail trailhead at northwest corner of the parking lot next to kiosk.

0.5 Go straight on Mainline Trail at junction with Lloyd's Trail on the left and 106th Drive Trail on the right (Waypoint 8).

0.7 Take right fork onto Red Alder Trail (Waypoint 9).

1.7 Take the right fork onto Two Trees Trail and then the next right fork onto Ephemeral Trail (Waypoints 10 and 25).

2.5 Take right fork onto Two Trees Trail (Waypoint 23).

2.8 Take right turn onto Mainline Trail (straight goes onto the one-way Cedar Run Trail that's designed for advanced mountain bikers, Waypoint 22).

2.9 Turn left onto Southern Traverse Trail (Waypoint 11) and begin downhill, crossing ladder bridge at the bottom.

3.3 Meet the Cedar Run Trail from the left and begin easy slope uphill (Waypoint 12).

3.6 Take left fork onto Lloyd Trail at top of hill (Waypoint 13).

4.1 Cross the curvy ladder bridge.

4.4 Take left fork to remain on Lloyd's Trail (right is Lloyd's Detour, Waypoint 18).

4.5 Turn right onto Mainline Trail and return to parking lot.

5.0 Arrive at kiosk. End of ride.

RIDE INFORMATION

Local Events and Attractions
Antiques stores and cafe in former high-school gymnasium in Maltby

Restaurants
Maltby Cafe: Serving breakfast and lunch, 8809 Maltby Rd., Snohomish; (425) 483-3123

Restrooms
Start: Two portable toilets in parking lot

Southside

A colorful mural in downtown Orting depicts a scene from the town's historic past.

The bike routes south of Seattle include rides in Pierce and southern King Counties. While heavily populated suburbs characterize the areas along the Puget Sound, the land gains a more rural flavor as you head east. Historic railroad and trolley lines are represented on the Green River–Interurban Loop, and the Cedar River and Foothills Trails. A former automobile road repurposed as a wilderness trail wends through dense forests in Mount Rainier National Park.

Mountain bikers will enjoy single track at Dash Point State Park; Taylor Mountain; the new trails in the Henry's Ridge, Black Diamond Natural Area, and Summit Ridge; and the ageless courses at Towers of Power. For roadies, a rural loop follows old farming roads to the Flaming Geyser State Park and passes a favorite bakery at the halfway point in the historic coal-mining town of Black Diamond.

Green River–Interurban Trails Loop

Early settlements south of Seattle relied on the Green River for transportation. Then an interurban railway fulfilled that role in the early twentieth century. Today, bicyclists follow those routes on flat, paved trails for recreation and commuting.

Start: Fort Dent Park, Tukwila

Length: 20.1 miles

Approximate riding time: 1.5 to 2.5 hours

Best bike: Road, hybrid

Terrain: Flat. Trail is paved and smooth; a couple of short stretches on low-traffic roads.

Traffic and hazards: Trail crossings in Kent; pedestrians

Things to see: Wildlife observation towers in Green River Natural Areas, historic mansion garden, riverside parks

Maps: *DeLorme Atlas & Gazetteer—Washington,* page 60; City of Kent Walking and Cycling Guide, ci.kent.wa.us/transportation/BikeWalk; King County Bike Map; kingcounty.gov/transportation/kcdot/Roads/Bicycling.aspx

Getting there: By car: From the north: From I-405 South, take exit 1 to Tukwila and get in the left lane. Cross the Interurban Avenue at the traffic signal and go straight onto Fort Dent Way. In a short distance turn left onto Starfire Way, cross a bridge, and find a place to park in the south end of the parking lot. From the south: From I-405 North, take exit 1 toward West Valley Highway and get in the left lane. Turn left onto West Valley Highway. Go north to the second traffic light and turn right onto Fort Dent Way. In a short distance turn left onto Starfire Way, cross a bridge, and find a place to park. By transit: Metro bus routes 150, 154, 161, and 280 stop just north of Fort Dent Way. GPS: N47 28.115' / W122 14.980'

THE RIDE

Recreational cyclists had been enjoying the flat, curvy ride along the Green River south of Seattle for years without realizing the true nature of that asphalt trail. That all changed one day in 2009 when heavy construction equipment arrived to deposit 4-foot-high sandbags that obliterated the trail for the next three years. Cyclists discovered that the Green River Trail was actually a trail atop a levee that protected thousands of residents and businesses in the towns of Tukwila and Kent from potential flooding. When engineers at the fifty-year-old Howard Hanson Reservoir upstream discovered cracks in the structure, they alerted downstream communities that they might need another three or four feet of protection in case the dam keepers had to release more water to relieve pressure.

The dangers passed without incident, however. The sandbags are gone and cyclists can once again ride along the serpentine Green River Trail. (Ongoing maintenance and construction along the levee may cause future trail closures and detours.) Now it's the first leg of this 21-mile loop that starts in Tukwila, meanders along a lazy stretch of river south to Kent, and returns via the arrow-straight Interurban Trail. The route starts at Fort Dent Park, originally the site of a Duwamish tribal village and later a military blockhouse to protect the area's settlers. The 54-acre park is home to the Starfire Sports Complex, which manages the soccer fields and provides ample parking.

This route begins at the south end of the parking lot. Follow the trail straight across a narrow deck on the Starfire Way bridge and turn left. (Bearing left immediately after the parking lot and following the trail under the bridge will take you north on the Green River Trail toward Cecil Moses Park, located 5 miles away.) The southbound Green River Trail wraps around a hotel complex and then passes beneath some highways. The river flows on your left on this

Bike Shops

Cycle Therapy: 708 Central Ave. South, Kent; (253) 854-7487; cycletherapybikeshop.com
REI Southcenter, Tukwila: 240 Andover Park West, Tukwila; (206) 248-1938; rei.com/stores/tukwila.html
Trek Bicycle Store of Southcenter: 331 Tukwila Pkwy., Seattle; (206) 575-1996; trekstorewashington.com
Tukwila Performance Bicycle: 351 Strander Blvd., South Center Plaza, Tukwila; (206) 575-6872; performancebike.com/webapp/wcs/stores/servlet/RetailStoreDetailView?catalogId=10551&langId=-1&storeId=10052&rsId=11594

first leg of the route that winds through business parks. Be on the lookout for pedestrians on lunchtime strolls as you ride around blind turns. Soon you'll enter a sprawling commercial zone. All the strip centers and big-box retail stores are focused on car traffic, however, so you safely pedal along the river in back of the businesses.

After crossing a bridge, you'll come across several pleasant riverfront parks, such as Briscoe Park. The next park, Three Friends Fishing Hole, memorializes three retired fishing buddies who died tragically in a small plane crash on a fly-fishing trip in Alaska. Dedicated in 2007, the 3-acre park features restrooms, a water fountain, and a wheelchair-accessible fishing pier. Soon, the warehouse environment gives way to a rural landscape. The Seattle Tacoma KOA Campground at the intersection of South 212th Street is a good destination for overnight bike trips from Seattle. Right next door is the 310-acre Green River Natural Resources Area, which got its start in the late 1960s as a giant lagoon system for treating human waste. By the 1990s it had been transformed into a more pleasing storm-water retention area and wildlife habitat that serves as a feeding, nesting, and brooding area for 165 species of birds that travel the Green River corridor. Fifty species of mammals also call it home. A trail system directs visitors to three observation towers that boast views of the wildlife-rich wetlands as well as Mount Rainier in the distance.

Earthworks Bike Tour

Riding along the Green River Trail, you might notice occasional markers for the Earthworks Tour. This is a signed bike route created by the Kent Arts Commission for self-guided tours to Land Reclamation as Sculpture sites.

The earthworks themselves are designed to reuse land in an artistic way. The Robert Morris Earthwork, for instance, is an abandoned sand and gravel pit transformed into a terraced park. The Herbert Bayer Earthwork incorporates a storm-water detention dam in a Bauhaus-inspired park setting. Lorna Jordan's Waterworks Park at the Renton treatment plant purifies storm water, enhances a wetland, and provides 8 acres of public space. The Green River Natural Resources Area is a sewage lagoon reclaimed as a wildlife habitat for 165 species of birds and more than 50 species of mammals.

The bike route uses the Green River Trail and Interurban Trails, as well as some side streets. Maps and cue sheets for three options of 12 to 20 miles can be found at the Kent Earthworks Bicycle Tour website at kentwa.gov/arts/earthworks.

Even sculptured bicyclists like to catch the slipstream of those in front.

Throughout this area the Green River Trail veers on and off of Russell Road, which carries the occasional car. After riding past the entrance to the natural resources area, look for the trail again on the right. It heads back to the riverbank and restrooms at Van Doren's Landing Park. Don't be alarmed by the barking; there's a kennel next door and all the dogs are behind fences. A pedestrian bridge south of the park offers access to rural riding along Frager Road South across the Green River, and the Puget Power Trail offers access to the Interurban Trail about a mile away.

Remaining on the Green River Trail, cyclists pass through Russell Woods Park to emerge alongside a riverside community nestled behind the levee. Watch on the left for an entrance to the Neely-Soames Historic Homestead, an 1880s-era mansion that features a heritage kitchen garden that's open year-round. (The Neely family moved to the Kent valley in 1854, building a home at the present site in 1885. Ruby Neely was born in the mansion in 1895 and lived there until she died in 1986.) Soon the Green River Trail is rolling along between the river and a golf course. Across the river are views of the surviving agricultural land that once covered the valley floor.

The Green River Trail ends at the Interurban Trail. A left turn heads north for an 8-mile return ride to Fort Dent Park. A right turn goes south for 8 miles past the Emerald Downs thoroughbred racetrack to the town of Pacific, just north of Puyallup. Future bike trail extensions in Pierce County will connect the Interurban Trail to trails heading to Tacoma in the west and the Foothills Trail heading east.

As straight as the Green River Trail is curvy, the Interurban uses the old roadbed of the Puget Sound Electric Railway that served towns between Seattle and Tacoma from 1902 to 1928. Bike commuters use this path in the mornings and evenings, and it's a regular corridor for long-distance bike travelers riding between Portland and Seattle. There are several busy road crossings in Kent where cyclists need to activate crossing signals, but most of the trail is a nonstop spin alongside the Burlington Northern Santa Fe Railroad and the industries it serves. Crossing under I-405, the trail winds around an amusement park and ends at the Green River Trail at Fort Dent.

MILES & DIRECTIONS

0.0 Begin at the trail at the south end of the Fort Dent Park parking lot. Take the ramp straight across the Starfire Way bridge, and follow the "River Trail" signs around a hotel complex.

0.5 Turn right at intersection with Interurban Trail.

0.7 Take left fork.

1.4 Pass a small park with restrooms on the right.

3.0 Turn left to cross bridge over Green River, then turn right.

3.9 Take left fork at Briscoe Park (right fork goes through the park).

5.1 Pass Three Friends Fishing Hole on left.

5.8 Take right fork to pass under road; pass Seattle Tacoma KOA Campground on the left after the underpass. Trail merges with Russell Road.

6.1 Pass Green River Natural Resources Area parking and observation towers.

6.4 Bear right onto Green River Trail.

6.6 Pass entrance to Van Doren's Landing Park on the left.

6.8 Green River Trail rejoins Russell Road.

7.0 Pass bridge over Green River to Frager Road on the right; pass Puget Power Trail on the left.

7.4 Turn right onto trail after the entrance to Russell Woods Park. The trail becomes the Green River Trail.

8.6 Join road briefly and continue on trail; watch out for bollards.

10.3 Pass bridge on the right.

11.2 Stay on Green River Trail as it merges with South 251st Street and then Hawley Road.

11.9 Go straight onto Green River Trail as road ends.

Green River–Interurban Trails Loop

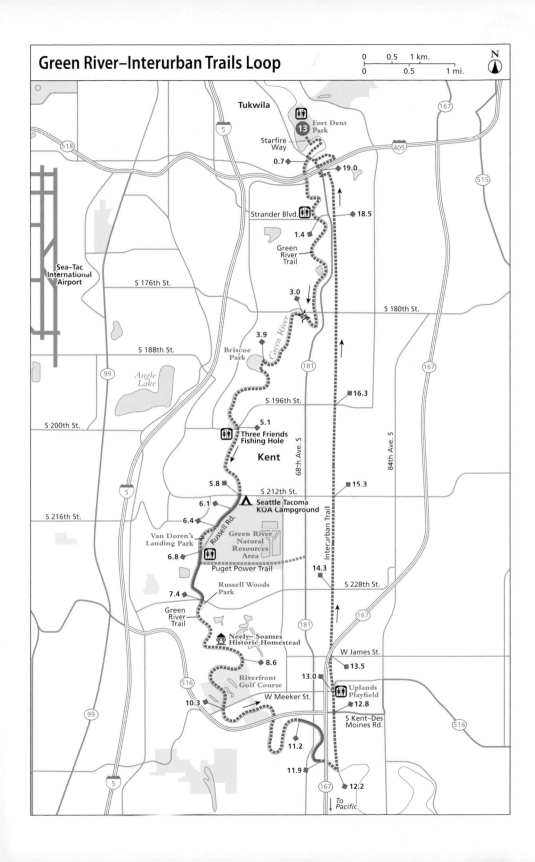

N

0   0.5   1 km.

0   0.5   1 mi.

Tukwila

13 Fort Dent Park

Starfire Way

0.7

19.0

5

518

405

515

Strander Blvd.

18.5

1.4

Green River Trail

Sea–Tac International Airport

S 176th St.

3.0

S 180th St.

181

3.9

Briscoe Park

Green River

99

Angle Lake

S 188th St.

16.3

S 196th St.

167

S 200th St.

5.1

Three Friends Fishing Hole

Kent

68th Ave. S

84th Ave. S

S 216th St.

S 200th St.

5

5.8

5.8

Interurban Trail

15.3

6.1

S 212th St.

Seattle Tacoma KOA Campground

6.4

Russell Rd.

Green River Natural Resources Area

Van Doren's Landing Park

6.8

Puget Power Trail

14.3

S 228th St.

Russell Woods Park

7.4

Green River Trail

Neely–Soames Historic Homestead

167

8.6

Riverfront Golf Course

W James St.

13.5

13.0

181

516

Uplands Playfield

12.8

10.3

W Meeker St.

S Kent–Des Moines Rd.

516

99

11.2

11.9

12.2

5

167

To Pacific

12.2 Turn left onto Interurban Trail (right turn goes south to town of Pacific).

12.8 Cross South Kent–Des Moines Road.

13.0 Cross West Meeker Street and pass Uplands Playfield.

13.5 Cross West James Street.

14.3 Cross South 228th Street.

15.3 Cross South 212th Street.

16.3 Continue under overpass.

18.5 Pass by Strander Boulevard on the left.

19.0 Follow Interurban Trail as it passes beneath I-405 and Southwest Grady Way and runs next to the Family Fun Center parking lot.

19.5 Turn right to follow Interurban Trail over bridge and turn right onto Green River Trail at junction.

20.1 Follow trail to trailhead. End of ride.

RIDE INFORMATION

Local Events and Attractions

Kent Farmers Market: Open-air market from 9 a.m. to 2 p.m. Saturday, June through September, Town Square Plaza at Second Avenue and Smith Street in downtown Kent

Green River Natural Resources Area: ci.kent.wa.us/GRNRA

Kent Cornucopia Days: Family festival in downtown Kent in mid-July; kcdays.com

Neely Soames Homestead: 1885 historic home with heritage kitchen gardens open year-round; 5311 S. 127th Place, Kent, or Mile 8.3 on Green River–Interurban Loop; ci.kent.wa.us/content.aspx?id=10928

Restrooms

Mile 0.0: Starfire administration building, Fort Dent Park (restrooms and drinking fountain)

Mile 1.4: Small park (restrooms)

Mile 5.1: Three Friends Fishing Hole (restrooms and drinking fountain)

Mile 6.6: Van Doren's Landing Park (restrooms and drinking fountain)

Mile 13.0: Uplands Playfield (portable toilets and drinking fountain)

Black Diamond–Green River Gorge Loop

This loop ride around southern King County starts out as a level meander on an old farm-to-market road in the Green River Valley. Soon enough it clambers into historic hardscrabble coal country where the Green River roars through a deep gorge and a surviving town of coal's boom-bust cycle is anticipating modern residential sprawl.

Start: Park and Ride lot, east side of Auburn

Length: 34.5 miles

Approximate riding time: 2.5 to 4 hours

Best bike: Road

Terrain: The first quarter of the route is a flat ride, but it becomes hilly the rest of the way. There are three long climbs and many short ones.

Traffic and hazards: Traffic is generally light along most of the route. There are wide shoulders on SR 169 and Southeast Auburn–Black Diamond Road where traffic is heavier. Leaving Black Diamond, there is a 1-mile stretch with no shoulder.

Things to see: Flaming Geyser State Park, Green River Gorge Bridge, Franklin ghost town, town of Black Diamond

Maps: *DeLorme Atlas & Gazetteer—Washington,* page 60; King County Bicycle Map, kingcounty.gov/transportation/kcdot/Roads/Bicycling.aspx

Getting there: By car: Take southbound I-5 to exit 142A onto SR 18 East. Go about 4 miles to the exit for Auburn–Black Diamond Road. This also is marked the exit for Flaming Geyser State Park. Turn left onto Southeast Auburn-Black Diamond Road at the bottom of the off ramp, go under the highway, and turn left into a gravel Park and Ride lot. **By Sounder Train:** From the Auburn Station, go north 1 block to Main Street. Turn right onto West Main Street, which becomes East Main Street. Turn right onto R Street Southeast, which becomes Southeast Auburn–Black Diamond Road. Look for the Park and Ride in 1.5 miles. GPS: N47 18.028' / W122 10.913'

THE RIDE

Although the Black Diamond–Green River Gorge Loop starts out at a noisy freeway interchange, it quickly leaves that behind to travel a historic road that's changed little in the past one hundred years.

As you leave the Park and Ride lot, you'll cross the placid Green River and turn right onto Southeast Green Valley Road. This farm-to-market road served an agricultural community that was so close-knit that, as recently as 1970, a sign at this end listed all the families and how far up the road they lived.

The road dates back to the 1880s and some buildings survive from that era. You'll see the first on your right as you turn onto Southeast Green Valley Road. The ornate Neely Mansion, listed on the National Register of Historic Places, was built in 1894 by a man who came to the Pacific Northwest as a child on the Oregon Trail. Farther ahead you'll see barns and farmhouses that date to the early 1900s to 1920s. Agriculture is still very much alive here. You'll pass crop farms, dairies, and pastures with cattle, horses, and llamas as you

Bike Shops

Bike Masters & Boards: 27203 216th Ave. Southeast, Suite 8, Maple Valley; (425) 584-7508; bikemasters.net
Cycle Therapy Bike Shop: 708 Central Ave. South, Kent; (253)-854-7487; cycletherapybikeshop.com

head down the winding road. If you're interested in a tasty treat, at least two farms offer berry-picking in season and another offers fresh honey.

After about eight miles, the valley gets narrower and the previously quiet Green River shows some whitewater. Turn right into Flaming Geyser State Park, cross over the bridge, and turn right onto a park road toward the geyser and restrooms. The old geyser ain't what it used to be. Discovered in 1911 when an exploratory drill hit a pocket of methane gas, the geyser used to emit a flame 4 to 6 feet high, sometimes erupting to 15 feet. Today the methane bubbles out of a pipe in the ground and can produce a 1 or 2-inch flame. The park is still popular, however, for tubing in the summer and salmon-spotting in the fall.

Returning to Southeast Green River Road, the day's first long climb to the top of the bluffs north of the river wakes up the legs. This steady 2-mile climb emerges from the woods into a roller-coaster ride to the former community of Kummer, marked by the "lonely red schoolhouse" on the right. Turning right onto the shoulder of SR 169, the road heads down a steep hill to a bridge over the Green River Gorge. Although it's tempting to stop here, I'd recommend putting your momentum to work on the ascent. A better view of the river gorge is coming.

The Green River rages through a gorge that's spanned by a one-hundred-year-old bridge.

Turn left onto Enumclaw-Franklin Road Southeast and pass a sign that reads ROUGH ROAD AHEAD. 'Nuff said. The roadside has been logged and mined in the past, and the road has its share of potholes and other damage. On the bright side, traffic is light as almost no one submits his or her car to this abuse. Take the left fork onto Green River Gorge Road and careen down a winding road to a one-lane bridge spanning the awesome 150-foot-deep Green River Gorge. The river runs unchecked through this gorge for 12 miles. Those who have run the river in rafts say this bend is one of the most stunning. Evergreens rise from the narrow shoreline and bushes and ferns sprout from cracks in the rock layers. A waterfall cascades down the rock face to the river below.

Earlier attempts to dam the gorge were blocked in the 1960s, and the state has acquired 80 percent of the riverfront for conservation areas and parks. One exception is the now-closed Green River Gorge Resort located right before the bridge. Crossing the bridge and passing the gate to the ghost town of Franklin on the left, you begin a steady 2.5-mile climb as you skirt Black Diamond Hill. This road is much better than the "rough road," however, and at about mile 23.0 begins a 2-mile downhill run to Black Diamond.

The little town dates back to 1882 and is named for the company that first discovered and mined coal here. The company owned the town, which grew to about 3,500 by 1900, and handled all of its economic and community affairs. After the mine closed, the company sold off parcels in the 1930s.

Black Diamond–Green River Gorge Loop

If residents couldn't buy their homes, the company sold them to someone else. Black Diamond's population is still about 4,000 but is poised to rise dramatically to 15,000 to 20,000 in the next fifteen to twenty years with dense housing developments surrounding the town. One impact for bicyclists will be more cars using these rural roads; traffic on Southeast Green Valley Road, for instance, is expected to increase 300 to 400 percent.

The gastronomic highlight for bicyclists riding these still-quiet roads is the Black Diamond Bakery at the bottom of Baker Street and to the left on Railroad Avenue. The owners have installed bicycle racks in the parking spaces out front to encourage bicyclists not to block the entrance with their rides. Cyclists can sit down with a sandwich and cool drink in the cafe, but most prefer to buy a sweet, gooey concoction at the bakery counter. Leaving

Franklin Ghost Town

If you're wondering what ever happened to the "Franklin" of Enumclaw-Franklin Road, you can find the answer immediately after crossing the Green River Gorge Bridge. A gate on the left marks a public path up to the coal-mining ghost town of Franklin. If you have wider tires on your bike, you can ride the mile on a forest road.

All that's left of the town of 1,100 people that flourished from the 1880s to about 1920 are some moss-covered foundations, an open shaft covered by a grate, an old cemetery, and a few other artifacts. Old photos depict boarding houses, schools, company stores, and rows of identical homes dwarfed by smokestacks and coal bunkers. A coal train ran between Franklin and its sister city of Black Diamond.

The town was the site of a contentious labor strike in 1891, made worse when the owners brought in miners from Minnesota as strike breakers. The violence that erupted led to at least one death and the arrival of the Washington State Militia to quell the disturbances.

Tragedy struck again in 1894 when thirty-seven miners suffocated in a fire, suspected to be arson, in a mineshaft more than 1,000 feet below the surface. It was one of the worst mine disasters in Washington's history. In 1914, a cave-in claimed the life of a miner, but his partner miraculously survived for seven days in cold, muddy tunnels without food or light. It took him five months to recover from his injuries. Then he returned to the mines.

The owners shut down most of the mining at the end of World War I and disbanded the town. It's the same fate that many coal towns suffered in western Washington, except for Franklin's sister city of Black Diamond, which survives to this day.

the bakery, go left and ride past the Black Diamond Museum (open on weekends) housed in the old railway depot. The route passes the Black Diamond Cemetery on the left, heads out of town on Morgan Street, and turns left onto Roberts Drive. This is a narrow street, but it gets a good shoulder in less than a mile when it becomes Southeast Auburn–Black Diamond Road.

Along this final stretch you're riding on the ridge you saw to the north of Southeast Green Valley Road. Expect some short, sharp climbs after turning left onto Southeast Lake Holm Road, especially as you pass Lake Holm itself. The route off the ridge and back to the Park and Ride on Southeast Auburn–Black Diamond Road is a fun, twisty descent, although you'll want to ride the brakes all the way down.

MILES & DIRECTIONS

0.0 Turn right onto Southeast Auburn–Black Diamond Road.

0.2 Turn right on Southeast Green Valley Road.

1.8 Cross a bridge.

5.6 Pass the Metzler Park Natural Area on the right.

8.3 Turn right into entrance for Flaming Geyser State Park and ride across the bridge over the Green River.

8.7 Turn right at T intersection. Follow signs to Flaming Geyser.

9.6 Either lock your bike at gate marking 0.1-mile pedestrian trail to Flaming Geyser or walk with your bike. Retrace your route.

10.7 Turn left onto park entrance road and cross the Green River bridge.

11.1 Turn right onto Southeast Green Valley Road and begin a climb.

13.3 Pass the historic Kummer schoolhouse on the right.

13.9 Turn right onto Enumclaw–Black Diamond Road Southeast (SR 169).

16.4 Turn sharp left onto Enumclaw-Franklin Road Southeast.

20.2 Turn left at the fork onto Southeast Green River Gorge Road.

20.6 Cross one-lane Green River Gorge Bridge.

20.8 Pass entrance to historic Franklin Town Site on the left.

24.8 Turn right onto 3rd Avenue (SR 169), go 1 block, and turn left onto Baker Street.

25.0 Turn left at Black Diamond Museum onto Railroad Avenue.

25.1 Black Diamond Bakery is on your right. On departure, retrace your route 1 block and continue straight on Railroad Avenue, which becomes Morgan Street in 2 blocks.

Black Diamond–Green River Gorge Loop

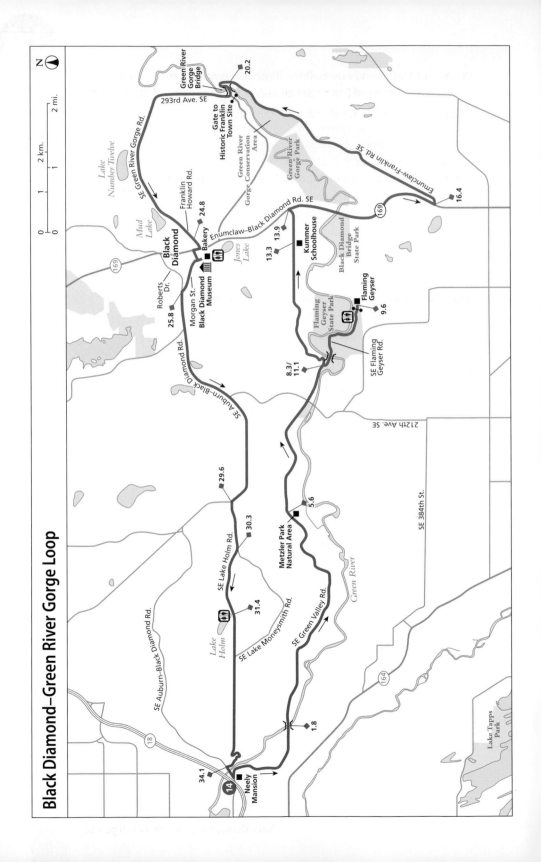

N

0   1   2 km.
0   1   2 mi.

Green River Gorge Bridge
20.2
293rd Ave. SE
Gate to Historic Franklin Town Site
SE Green River Gorge Rd.
Lake Number Twelve
Franklin Howard Rd.
Green River Gorge Conservation Area
Green River Gorge Park
Enumclaw–Franklin Rd. SE
16.4
169
Mud Lake
Bakery 24.8
Black Diamond
Enumclaw–Black Diamond Rd. SE
13.9
13.3
Kummer Schoolhouse
Black Diamond Bridge State Park
Roberts Dr.
25.8
Morgan St.
Black Diamond Museum
Jones Lake
Flaming Geyser State Park
Flaming Geyser 9.6
169
8.3/ 11.1
SE Flaming Geyser Rd.
212th Ave. SE
SE Auburn–Black Diamond Rd.
29.6
5.6
Metzler Park Natural Area
SE 384th St.
SE Lake Holm Rd.
30.3
31.4
Lake Holm
SE Lake Moneysmith Rd.
SE Green Valley Rd.
Green River
164
1.8
18
34.1
14
Neely Mansion
Lake Tapps Park

25.8 Turn left onto Roberts Drive, which becomes Southeast Auburn–Black Diamond Road after crossing Lake Sawyer Road on your right.

29.6 Turn left onto Southeast Lake Holm Road.

30.3 Bear right to stay on Southeast Lake Holm Road.

31.4 Pass Lake Holm on your right.

34.1 Turn left onto shoulder of Southeast Auburn–Black Diamond Road and cross Green River.

34.5 Turn left into Park and Ride lot. End of ride.

RIDE INFORMATION

Local Events and Attractions

Neely Mansion: Open for tours and special dates throughout the year; neelymansion.org

Flaming Geyser State Park: River tubing, hiking, and salmon watching; parks.wa.gov/

Green River Gorge Bridge: Built in 1914, spans the 150-foot-deep Green River Gorge near Black Diamond

Franklin ghost town: Access by a state easement through gate just west of Green River Gorge Bridge; foot tours offered by Black Diamond Museum

Black Diamond Museum: Displays and information on Black Diamond area history, open weekends and holidays, 32627 Railroad Ave., Black Diamond; blackdiamondmuseum.org

Restaurants

Black Diamond Bakery: Meals and baked goods, 32805 Railroad Ave., Black Diamond; blackdiamondbakery.com

Restrooms

Mile 9.6: Flaming Geyser State Park (portable toilets but no potable water)
Mile 25.1: Black Diamond Bakery (restroom)
Mile 31.4: Lake Holm (pit toilet)

Cedar River Trail

There's no mistaking that the Cedar River Trail is a rail-to-trail project—miles and miles of it are straight and flat. Many long-distance bicyclists incorporate it for rides in southern King County, but there's enough of interest in terms of scenery, wildlife, and history to make this a destination ride as well.

Start: Parking lot at Cedar River Trail Park, Houser Way South and Mill Avenue South, Renton

Length: 31.6 miles round-trip

Approximate riding time: 2 to 3.5 hours

Best bike: Road or hybrid

Terrain: The rail trail is mostly flat. The elevation gain heading east is negligible. The trail surface is paved for the first 11 miles and crushed rock for the next 5 miles. Two miles of the western Cedar River Trail between Lake Washington and this ride's trailhead aren't included in the ride because of numerous "dismount zones."

Traffic and hazards: Motor vehicles are not allowed on the trail. (A side route option does use an infrequently traveled rural road, and the shoulder of a busy highway.) The only hazards come at road crossings where bicyclists must watch for cars and trucks and ride between bollards installed in the trail. Bicyclists should also alert pedestrians before they pass.

Things to see: Renton Museum, salmon hatchery operations, scenic Cedar River views and natural areas, Cedar Grange pancake breakfast, Lake Wilderness

Maps: *DeLorme Atlas & Gazetteer—Washington,* pages 46 and 60; Regional Trails in King County, kingcounty.gov/operations/GIS/Maps/VMC/Recreation.aspx#6366BDAC031C4B179A0225581D55A339

Getting there: **By car:** From the north, take I-405 exit 4 and stay in right lane, which becomes Sunset Boulevard North. Pass through first traffic light and turn right on Bronson Way (SR 900) toward the City Center. Get into the left lane, go through traffic light at Park Avenue, and make the next left at Mill Avenue South. Go through the traffic light at Houser Avenue South and follow signs for Cedar River Trail. Parking is on the left. From the south, take I-405 exit 4 and stay left onto Bronson Way ramp. Turn right onto Bronson Way at bottom of the ramp. Go through the traffic signal at Sunset Boulevard North, merge into left lane, go through traffic light at Park Avenue, and turn at the next left onto Mill Avenue South. Go through the Houser Avenue South traffic signal and turn left, following the signs for Cedar River Trail. If the parking lot is full, try a lot at the corner of Mill Avenue and Houser Way or on-street parking. **By bus:** Metro routes 101, 148, 153 at Mill Avenue and Houser Way. GPS: N47 28.826' / W122 11.983'

THE RIDE

The Cedar River Trail makes a beeline on its way out of Renton across the valley toward the foothills of the Cascades. It's no wonder. This popular rail-to-trail path follows the route of the Chicago, Milwaukee, St. Paul, and Pacific Railroad, whose highballing silk trains historically rushed that precious commodity on the final leg of its transport from Asia to East Coast markets. That silk cargo dwindled by the time of the Great Depression, and the railway, eventually acquired by Burlington Northern Santa Fe, was abandoned in the early 1980s. The railroad right-of-way is public property today and is a paved trail 11 miles from here to Maple Valley and a crushed rock path for another 5 miles to its terminus in Landsburg.

Bike Shops

Center Cycles: 3950 Lind Ave. Southwest, Renton; (425) 228-3661; centercycle.com
G.H.Y. Bikes: 230 Main St., Renton; (425) 227-4825; ghybikes.com

If you are riding this trail in the late summer or fall, you're immediately reminded that thousands—some years more than tens of thousands—of bright red sockeye salmon return to the river to spawn every year. The Seattle Public Utilities Fish Hatchery in Landsburg sets up a temporary fish dam at this location in Renton to catch broodstock. Crowds gather here on sunny autumn weekends to watch salmon jump the weir. You'll see those that make

Trees on a park shoreline are reflected in Lake Wilderness.

it swimming upriver to spawn; later their carcasses wash ashore and attract seagulls and even bald eagles.

The first part of the trail can be congested with pedestrians and dog walkers heading to the off-leash dog park. Renton instituted a 10 mph speed limit all the way to the city limits at mile 3.0 (149th Avenue Southeast) after a tragic accident a few years ago involving a bicyclist and pedestrian. A violation carries a $101 fine, so watch your speed and give a bell or voice alert to pedestrians you are about to pass.

At first the trail passes through a mostly empty field hemmed in by Renton Hill on one side and the Cedar River levee on the other. If you visit the Renton Museum, you'll be shocked by vintage photos that show the massive Denny-Renton Clay & Coal Co. that once stood here. For a time, it was the largest maker of paving bricks in the world. Once employing as many as 350 people, it closed in 1992 with four employees. If you scan the levee as you roll past, you might see some of the old bricks and terra-cotta pipe jumbled among tree roots. In the late summer, however, you can't see the levee for the blackberry bushes. This luscious undergrowth along much of the trail provides a sumptuous berry smorgasbord that's free for the picking.

In a mile, you pass over the first of six old railroad trestles that span the Cedar River as it meanders back and forth across the narrow valley to Landsburg. These vantage points are worth a stop to enjoy the river, look for salmon in the fall, and scan the riverbanks—some of which are steep bluffs towering above. The river rises precipitously in rainy seasons and can flood if managers have to release too much water from the Chester Morris Dam upstream. Two underpasses—at Maple Valley Highway at mile 2.0 and 154 Place Southeast at mile 3.2—can flood, and the county has shored up several trail sections upstream where the river threatens to erode the trail.

After that first trestle, the trail loops under Maple Valley Highway and emerges alongside the Maplewood Golf Course on the other side. Farther up is Ron Regis Park, where there's always a soccer, softball, or cricket game under way. Crossing 149th Avenue Southeast you leave Renton and can pedal flat-out fast, being mindful of occasional pedestrians, of course. The Maple Valley Highway alongside the old railroad grade can be a noisy disturbance, but keep your attention to the forests and frequent wide-open river views on the left.

King County has been acquiring different parcels in the floodplain to the left as protected natural areas. You can visit the first at Cavanaugh Ponds,

Two Side Trips from Cedar River Trail

Jones Road: This option passes some of the old flavor of the Cedar River Valley as it rides along an old farm road on the other side of the river. At mile 3.2, take the underpass under 154th Place Southeast, then turn right onto the road instead of following the trail to the left. Cross the bridge on the road or sidewalk and turn right onto Southeast Jones Road, about a half-mile. The route rolls along an old farm road for about 3 miles between the base of a ridge on the left and the river on the right. It passes some small farm lots and sprawling horse pastures. Jones Road connects with Maple Valley Highway 3 miles after leaving the Cedar Trail. Turn right and backtrack west until you can get back on the trail in 0.7 miles, then turn right.

Green-to-Cedar Rivers Trail: This side trip visits the woodsy Lake Wilderness community. Turn right onto the crushed rock rail-to-trail path at mile 10.9 and pedal uphill. You'll pass through three short tunnels before you arrive at a kiosk (1.5 miles) that explains the paths through the arboretum. The scenic lake runs along the trail for another mile, which is a good place to turn around for a 5-mile side trip. The trail continues nearly another mile to the commercial Kent-Kangley Road area. This trail gets its name from future plans to run it south all the way through Black Diamond to the Green River at Flaming Geyser State Park.

which you reach by turning left at Riverbend Mobile Home Community. A gravel road leads to ponds where waterfowl live and a wide beach that's ideal for watching salmon swim past. Hawks and bald eagles may perch in trees overhead. Turning away from the natural side of the trail, you'll probably notice a long, two-story building across the road at mile 5.6. That's the former administrative office and shops for the Pacific Coast Coal Co., and the only intact structure left over from the coal boom that swept the Cedar River Valley until the late 1940s. It served a mine in the hill behind it.

The trail might get busy again as you get near to the trailhead in Maple Valley. There's a farm stand across the road in the summer, and the Cedar Grange holds pancake breakfasts the third Sunday morning of the month. There's also a market across the road, which is the last chance for food or water. The pavement ends in about a mile, but the crushed rock surface is fine for tires 28mm and wider.

As soon as you pass the turnoff for the Green-to-Cedar Rivers Trail, the traffic noise dies away and all you hear for the next 5 miles is the crunching rock beneath your tires and the rapids when you're close to the river. The valley narrows beyond here and forest comes right up to the trail. You'll pass small groves of fir and cedar when the trail veers away from the river. If no one else is on the trail, you might scare up some deer or elk as you pass. A thin strip of woods separates the trail from the river rapids as you near the end of the trail. When you reach the end of the trail at Hobart-Issaquah Road, you'll see where kayakers run the rapids.

Across the road is the watershed for the City of Seattle's drinking water supply, which is closed to the public. The railroad right-of-way runs through this property for 12 miles to the Snoqualmie Valley Trail and the John Wayne Pioneer Trail in the Cascade Mountains. Many dream of a future time when this might be open. To return to Renton, turn around and retrace your route.

MILES & DIRECTIONS

0.0 Leave parking lot and turn right onto trail.

0.2 The fenced-in dog park is a little beyond the portable toilet on the right side of the trail.

1.2 Continue over the trestle.

1.9 Cross 131st Avenue Southeast with the crosswalk light. Follow trail as it makes a horseshoe turn along Cedar River and crosses under Maple Valley Highway (SR 169).

2.7 Pass Ron Regis Park on the left.

3.0 Cross 149th Avenue Southeast (end of 10 mph zone).

Cedar River Trail

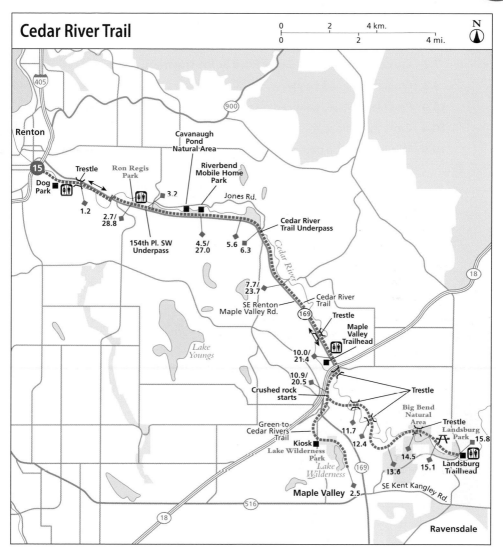

3.2 Follow path left as it goes beneath 154th Place SE and emerges on the other side. Continue on Cedar River Trail as it turns left. (See sidebar about the Jones Road side trip, which adds 2.2 miles. To return to Renton, turn left for a 13.6-mile lollipop loop ride.)

4.5 Pass the entrance to Riverbend Mobile Home Community. To visit Cavanaugh Pond Natural Area, turn left, ride about 100 feet to parking lot on the left, and ride down a gravel road to the ponds. Retrace your route to return to the trail.

5.6 Pass trail that leads to an overlook for Cedar River.

6.3 Ride under two overpasses; a footpath right after the second one leads to the Belmondo Reach Natural Area.

7.7 Cross Southeast Cedar Grove Road at the crosswalk.

9.3 Cross the railroad trestle.

10.0 Pass Maple Valley trailhead on your right.

10.4 Cross the railroad trestle.

10.9 This is where the pavement ends and the trail becomes crushed rock. Continue straight just beyond this point where the Green-to-Cedar Rivers Trail branches right. (See sidebar about the Green-to-Cedar Rivers Trail side trip.)

11.7 Cross the railroad trestle.

12.4 Cross the railroad trestle.

13.6 Cross Southeast 248th Street.

A rusty trestle over the Cedar River adds to the color of fall foliage.

14.5 Cross the railroad trestle.

15.1 Pass a picnic area on right and oxbow lake from Cedar River on left.

15.8 End of Cedar River Trail at parking lot on Landsburg Road Southeast. Turn around and return.

20.5 Pass the Green-to-Cedar Rivers Trail on the left.

21.4 Pass the Maple Valley Trailhead on the left.

23.7 Cross Southeast Cedar Grove Road on the crosswalk.

27.0 Pass the entrance to Riverbend Mobile Home Community on the right.

28.8 Pass the entrance to Ron Regis Park on the right.

31.6 End of Cedar River Trail ride; return to parking lot.

RIDE INFORMATION

Local Events and Attractions

Renton Museum: Permanent and temporary exhibits and large collection, 235 Mill Ave. South, Renton, (425) 255-2330; rentonwa.gov/rentonhistorymuseum

Renton River Days: Community festival in late July at Liberty Park, Bronson Way and Houser Way, Renton; rentonwa.gov/living/default.aspx?id=1138

Cedar Grange pancake breakfast: Third Sunday of the month, 25531 SE 218th, Maple Valley; wa-grange.org/localgrange.html

Lake Wilderness Arboretum: Open year-round, free to public; mile 1.5 of Green-to-Cedar Rivers Trail or 22520 SE 248th Maple Valley; lakewilderness arboretum.org

Lake Wilderness Park: Maple Valley city park with restrooms and water; enter through Lake Wilderness Arboretum on Green-to-Cedar Rivers Trail; maplevalleywa.gov/departments-and-services/parks-recreation/parks-and -trails/lake-wilderness-park

King County Cedar River Trail: kingcounty.gov/recreation/parks/trails/ regionaltrailssystem/cedarriver.aspx

City of Renton Cedar River Trail: rentonwa.gov/living/default.aspx?id=67

Restrooms

Mile 0.2/31.4: Portable toilet

Mile 0.9/30.6: Restroom and water; seasonal. Portable toilet in winter.

Mile 2.7/28.8: Ron Regis Park (portable toilets)

Mile 10.0/21.4: Maple Valley Trailhead, seasonal (portable toilets)

Mile 15.8: Parking lot on Landsburg Road Southeast, seasonal (portable toilets)

Foothills Trail Ride

This rail-trail bike ride goes through rustic countryside, but the Foothills Trail features all the necessities for happy bicycling. There are regularly spaced drinking water and restroom facilities, a bicycle shop and bakery at roughly the midpoint in Orting, and a trailside coffee stand at the turnaround in South Prairie.

Start: East Puyallup Trailhead, Pierce County

Length: 29.5 miles

Approximate riding time: 2 to 4 hours

Best bike: Road or hybrid

Terrain: Even railroad grade that gains about 375 feet in altitude between Meeker and South Prairie trailheads. The trail is 12 feet wide and paved.

Traffic and hazards: This is a heavily used trail in and around Orting with lots of families on bikes and pedestrians with strollers and dogs. Also use caution at road crossings in housing developments north of Orting.

Things to see: Flower bulb and crop farms, views of Mount Rainier, historic downtown Orting

Maps: *DeLorme Atlas & Gazetteer—Washington,* page 60; Pierce County Bicycle Map, available in bike shops and by calling (253) 798-7250

Getting there: By car: From I-405, take SR 167 South for about 20 miles to the SR 410 East exit toward Yakima. Go 2 miles and take the SR 162 East exit toward Orting. Go less than a mile, cross a bridge, and make the first right turn onto 80th Street East. Go about 0.75 mile to the East Puyallup Trailhead on the left. If the lot is full, there is an overflow parking lot in about 0.1 mile. GPS: N47 11.042' / W122 14.703'

THE RIDE

One look at the modern reincarnations of train station platforms at the East Puyallup Trailhead and you immediately realize that the Foothills Trail through northern Pierce County is a rail trail. This paved, 12-foot-wide trail follows a historic route of the Northern Pacific Railroad, which today has become the BNSF Railway. It starts at a point just east of Puyallup for a bicycle-friendly altitude gain of less than 400 feet over the 15 miles to South Prairie. At one time, this section was part of a railway that extended all the way from Tacoma to St. Paul. The owners abandoned this part in 1982, however, and a group that became the Foothills Rails-to-Trails Coalition began working with Pierce County two years later to create the trail, which is still a work in progress.

This route starts at the East Puyallup Trailhead (formerly Meeker), where there is parking, restrooms, drinking water, and a map describing the trail. Overflow parking is located another 0.1 mile down the road. As the trail heads out from the East Puyallup, it looks nothing like a typical straight-as-an-arrow rail trail. The path swings from one side of the right-of-way to the other, breaking up a little of the monotony for which rail trails are known. Hugging the western side of the Puyallup Valley, it passes miles of farm fields and a long Christmas tree farm, as well as chicken coops and vegetable patches in the backyards of some homes.

On clear days, you can catch views of snow-capped Mount Rainier looming over the valley. The Puyallup and Carbon Rivers spanned by old train trestles run chalk white most of the time as they carry away sediment from glaciers atop the 14,411-foot-high volcano.

You'll also see sirens mounted atop poles and occasional "evacuation route" signs. These are part of the Puyallup Valley's lahar warning system to alert residents of geologic activities on Mount Rainier that could trigger devastating mudflows in the valleys below. The last one swept through about five hundred years ago, and geologists say another could hit anytime in the next three hundred years—the blink of an eye in geologic time. Residents are told that they have forty-two minutes to get to high ground after the lahar sirens begin sounding, and the signs point to the quickest routes to find safety 80

Bike Shops

Bonney Lake Bicycle Shop of Sumner: 1406 Main St., Sumner; (253) 863-5145; bonneylakebicycleshop.net/
Trailside Cyclery: 207 Van Scoyoc Ave. Southwest, Orting; (360) 893-7333; facebook.com/pages/Trailside-Cyclery/294798420547331

Mount Rainier looms over the historic town of Orting, midway on the Foothills Trail.

feet or more above the valley floor. If you hear these sirens on your ride, curse your bad luck and head uphill instead of back to the car.

After crossing the Puyallup River, the trail leaves the agricultural zone and enters suburban sprawl north of Orting where riders must stop at many crossings with streets that connect with SR 162, which runs alongside the trail. Arriving in the Orting's historic downtown, the Foothills Trail passes through 3 blocks of parks—North Park, Central Park, and South Main Park—where you'll find restrooms and shade. The town dates back to the 1880s as a center of commerce for logging, farming, and coal-mining in the region. Colorful murals painted on buildings around downtown show scenes from Orting's past.

As you ride through Orting, you'll no doubt notice depictions of bright yellow daffodils on signs and even a statue between Central and South Main Parks. In April, the city hosts the Daffodil Festival, the Daffodil Classic bike ride, and the last stop in the four-city Daffodil Parade that's been an annual event since 1934. Why is Orting so daffodil crazy? Introduced about 1910, the daffodil flower-bulb industry replaced hop and berry-farming agriculture in the Puyallup Valley. Farmers here produced some sixty million daffodil bulbs annually by the late 1920s and at one time produced one-fourth of the nation's supply of fresh-cut daffodils.

The industry has all but disappeared from the valley, however, because of suburbanization and global market forces. The Van Lierop Bulb Farm, located across the street from the East Puyallup Trailhead, was one of the last daffodil farms in the valley. The owner, a descendant of a Dutch farmer who came to the United States to grow flowers, announced in 2013 that he was getting out of the business.

After passing through Orting, the trail appears to be heading straight toward Mount Rainier. It curves left as it heads to the northeast, crossing over the milky-white Carbon River on a railroad trestle. The trail is not without a river view, however, as it follows South Prairie Creek, a salmon spawning stream. Crop farming seems to have fallen away up this narrow valley to pastures for cows and buffalo, where there's a sign posted: DO NOT FEED ANIMALS.

There are several pleasant scenic overlooks with benches along the river here. Also there's a wetland habitat around mile 11 where a display tells about the bald eagles, osprey, and red-tailed hawks you might see here, as well as waterfowl such as wood ducks and great blue herons.

Soon you reach the small town of South Prairie. First there's a shelter, bike rack, and picnic table compliments of Trailside Espresso for bicyclists seeking

Expanding the Foothills Trail

Although the Foothills Trail ends at a dead end in the west and a chain-link fence in the east, there's plenty of work going on behind the scenes for extensions that would double the rail trail's length.

In the east, the Foothills Rails-to-Trails Coalition and Pierce County officials are trying to find funding to complete a connection to Buckley, which has its own 2-mile stretch of the Foothills Trail. In fact, four bridges for the trail have been built on abandoned railway owned by the county in an isolated area between South Prairie and Buckley. The coalition and county are working to gain access to this "missing link."

Also behind that chain-link fence, there's an old spur line headed south to serve the towns of Wilkeson, Carbonado, and Fairfax, now a ghost town. If acquisition and environmental issues can be resolved, this would open an off-road, non-motorized route almost to the doorstep of the Carbon River entrance to Mount Rainier National Park.

On the west side, trail enthusiasts want to connect the Foothills Trail to Puyallup's Riverwalk Trail, which is barely more than a mile away, and extend that to Tacoma. The next long-term goal would be to hook into the Interurban Trail that starts just across the border in King County and goes all the way to Seattle.

Glacial sediment gives the Carbon River a chalky appearance as it flows past the Foothills Trail.

a caffeinated pick-me-up or snack. Just past that is the South Prairie Trailhead, which is the turnaround point for this ride. The trail currently ends at a chain link fence about 0.2 miles from the trailhead.

The return ride to East Puyallup is slightly downhill, although not steep enough for coasting. You might notice that the pedaling is easier on the way back, another reason you'll have pleasant memories of your ride here.

MILES & DIRECTIONS

0.0 Turn left from the East Puyallup Trailhead onto the Foothills Trail.

0.6 Cross Pioneer Way East.

2.8 Take crosswalk to the right at Military Road East.

3.6 Pass Scholz Farms on the right; vegetable stand open Apr through Oct.

4.3 Pass the McMillin Trailhead on the left. Cross over the Puyallup River on an old train trestle.

5.5 Enter city limits of Orting. There are a half-dozen street crossings in the next 1.5 miles that all have stop signs or crossing lights for trail users. Caution: Watch out for bollards in the center of the trail at each intersection.

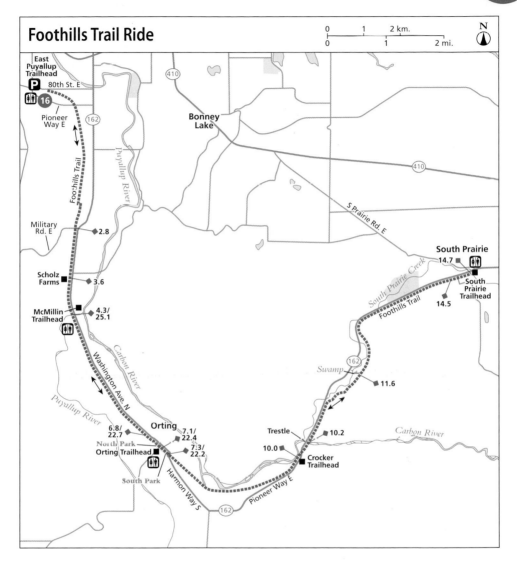

Foothills Trail Ride

6.8 Cross Whitesell Street Northwest and turn right to follow the Foothills Trail around a 1-block shopping district.

7.0 Enter North Park. Continue straight.

7.1 Enter Central Park; parking along Van Scoyoc Avenue East.

7.3 Leaving the South Main Park, cross Bridge Street South.

10.0 Pass Crocker Trailhead; parking on the right.

10.2 Cross trestle over Carbon River.

11.6 Cross bridge over wetlands.

14.5 Trailside coffee and ice-cream stand in South Prairie.

14.7 Trailhead parking on the left. Good turnaround spot; trail ends at bridge in 0.1 mile.

22.2 Use the crosswalk to cross Bridge Street South in Orting.

22.4 Pass restrooms at Central Park in Orting. Follow Foothills Trail to the right and turn left, crossing Calistoga Street East into North Park.

22.7 Follow Foothills Trail to the right, turn left to cross Whitesell Avenue (observe stop sign and bollards), then continue straight on Foothills Trail.

25.1 Pass the McMillin Trailhead.

29.5 Arrive at East Puyallup Trailhead. End of ride.

RIDE INFORMATION

Local Events and Attractions

Daffodil Festival: Started in 1934, the mid-April event features parades in Tacoma, Puyallup, Sumner, and Orting all at different times on the same day; thedaffodilfestival.org

Daffodil Days Classic bike ride: Mid-April bike ride with options of 40-, 60-, or 100-mile loops. Starts in Orting. Details at Tacoma Wheelmen's Bicycle Club; twbc.org.

Foothills Rails-to-Trail Coalition: piercecountytrails.org

Restaurants

Orting Bakery: Bakery products, sandwiches, beverages; 212 Washington Ave. South, Orting; (360) 893-2288

Trailside Espresso: Foothills Trail Mile 14.5 in South Prairie

Restrooms

Mile 0.0: East Puyallup Trailhead (restrooms and drinking water)
Mile 4.3: McMillan Trailhead (restrooms and drinking water)
Mile 7.1: Central Park, Orting (restrooms and drinking water)
Mile 14.7 South Prairie Trailhead (restrooms and drinking water)
Mile 22.4: Central Park, Orting (restrooms and drinking water)
Mile 25.1: McMillan Trailhead (restrooms and drinking water)
Mile 29.5: East Puyallup Trailhead (restrooms and drinking water)

Towers of Power

The Towers of Power trail system atop Renton Hill offers something for all levels of mountain bikers. Easy gravel roads and wide dirt trails connect six single-track runs that range from intermediate to advanced levels. These can be a good work-out. When you finish riding the entire course, you might be surprised at how few miles you've actually logged and find yourself returning to your favorite runs.

Start: Philip Arnold Park, Renton

Length: 6.6 miles

Approximate riding time: 1 to 2 hours

Best bike: Mountain bike

Terrain: Numerous steep climbs and descents on the trail. Newer trails (Silkworm and Bermsled) are smooth-packed dirt with berms on some curves; older trails have lots of roots, rocks, and short, tight turns. There's very little mud on the trails, even after wet weather.

Traffic and hazards: No vehicles on the trails. Silkworm, Bermsled, and Tapeworm should be ridden one direction (see descriptions), but Mr. DNA, Crop Circles, and Parasite are good either way. Watch for low branches. Silkworm has intermediate runs (blue arrow) that detour around some of the technical kickers and structures (black arrow).

Maps: Evergreen Mountain Bike Alliance, trails.evergreenmtb.org/wiki/Trail:Tapeworm_-_Towers_of_Power; *DeLorme Atlas & Gazetteer—Washington*, page 46

Getting there: By car: From the north, take I-405 southbound exit 4 and stay in right lane, which becomes Sunset Boulevard North. Pass through first traffic light and turn right on Bronson Way (SR 900) toward the City Center. Get into the left lane, go through traffic light at Park Avenue, and make the next left at Mill Avenue South. Go through the traffic light at Houser Avenue South and turn left onto South 3rd Street and then bear left onto Renton Avenue South. Continue uphill to a left turn onto South 7th Street. Bear right at the third cross street onto Beacon Way South and look for parking lot on right at Phillip Arnold Park. From the south, take I-405 northbound exit 4 and stay left onto Bronson Way ramp. Turn right onto Bronson Way at bottom of the ramp. Go through the traffic signal at Sunset Boulevard North, merge into left lane, go through traffic light at Park Avenue, and turn at the next left onto Mill Avenue South. Follow directions above from "Go through the traffic light at Houser Avenue South . . ." **By bus:** Metro route 148 at South Puget Sound Drive and Royal Hills Drive Southeast. Ride northwest on Beacon Avenue South about 0.8 miles to Philip Arnold Park. GPS: N47 28.374' / W122 11.727'

THE RIDE

The Towers of Power mountain-biking complex atop Renton Hill may look like a tangled hodgepodge of dirt tracks from the air. On the ground, however, bikers discover a series of carefully crafted dirt trails. They represent continuous volunteer labor since the late 1990s under the humming transmission lines around a Puget Sound Energy utility substation.

The landscape here isn't much to look at, although you can catch occasional glimpses of snowy Cascade mountaintops or vistas of Renton and surrounding environs. There's a patchwork of deciduous wood lots on the site, and wild blackberry bushes sprout in sunny open spaces. This place is all about pounding hard-packed dirt trails that weave between trees and around blackberry bushes. Bikers come here to attack on the steep ascents, feather their brakes on the descents, and test their abilities on making tight turns or jumping log piles. Some trails feature man-made ramps, bridges, and jumps for skilled riders, while offering detours to those less sure about their dexterity.

Six named trails make up the Towers of Power complex: Tapeworm, Mr. DNA, Crop Circles, Parasite, and the newer Silkworm and Bermsled. Gravel roads and easy dirt trails link them.

They say there are no right or wrong directions on these single tracks, although there are easier ways on some trails. The flowy turns and jumps on Silkworm work better when you start on the high side, and you might encounter fast-moving cyclists bombing downhill on Bermsled if you ride uphill. Tapeworm also has a suggested starting point.

Because the trails are narrow, it's important to leave the earphones in the car and listen for approaching riders; your eyes will likely be glued on the next turn. You might also consider wearing long sleeves, long pants, and long-fingered gloves in the summer when untended blackberry vines whip passing riders.

These are good trails for after-work weekday training rides. The reflectors nailed to trees guide cyclists rolling through here at night. Races are occasionally scheduled on Sunday afternoons, and non-competitors might want to avoid the trails during these times.

For the most part, the trails are unlabeled. A sign advertises the Silkworm, and the beginning of the Tapeworm is marked by an arch formed from an old knobby tire. Familiarize yourself with the gravel road that runs the length of the site and a couple of crossroads and trails to find your way around. The area isn't big enough to get lost, just momentarily confused. Other bikers are happy to share their knowledge of the grounds. There's no proper way to do all the rides. One suggestion is described in the Miles & Directions. When you visit, you'll likely discover many other ways to mix and match the trails.

Bike Shops

Center Cycles: 3950 Lind Ave. Southwest, Renton; (425) 228-3661; centercycle.com
g.h.y. bikes: 230 Main St. South, Renton; (425) 227-4825; ghybikes.com

A good warmup trail is the flowy Silkworm Loop, which is reached by a right turn onto a trail off the main gravel road. The connecting trail accesses Silkworm with a left turn at a sign posted in the trees. It's best to follow this 1-mile long trail from the top of the hill to take advantage of the berms on the downhill turns, which are wide and fast. The trail heads downhill twice. There are some man-made bridges, decks, and roller coasters on the descents. The trail splits in two places—the "black arrow" designates the more difficult path and the "blue arrow" the easier path.

Heading left from the main gravel road takes riders to Mr. DNA followed by Crop Circles. Both of these are older trails through the woods with some tight turns, which can be difficult when heading uphill. Mr. DNA is an unclosed 0.3-mile loop that returns to the connecting trail. Crop Circles, 0.4 miles, starts at the bottom of the hill and takes a winding route with many tight turns to the top and then an easy coast back to the bottom. A labyrinth section at this lower end that gave the trail its name no longer exists.

Bermsled can be reached from the gravel road that runs along the southern side of the trail complex. This is a fast 0.4-mile trail downhill that ends in a series of technical "black arrow" jumps and steep dirt piles. The entire length of trail is designed for catching some air, but beginners can roll over the kickers.

A man-made jump on Silkwood can be avoided by taking the "blue arrow" trail to the right.

The best-known trail here is the challenging Tapeworm, which winds back and forth between two wood lots separated by a clearing. The trail builders who concocted this maze followed the rules that the longest distance between two points is a twisting route around numerous trees, and every flat area should be avoided.

Tapeworm starts at a clearing in the woods, passing under an archway made by a knobby mountain bike tire and a sign that says "Begin." There are a few bridges and other man-made structures, but the unrelenting turns, roots, and rocks test a biker's skills. Once you ride it, it's easy to understand how they jammed 1.7 miles of trail onto 3 acres.

Lastly, there's Parasite on the north side of the trail complex, butting right up against the fence of Philip Arnold Park. This 0.8-mile single track is a lot like Tapeworm, except at about half the distance and on flatter terrain. There are a few log piles to negotiate, and none of the flowy curves on other trails.

If you have the energy, return to visit some of the trails by different routes or in a different order to change the experience.

MILES & DIRECTIONS

0.0 Turn right out of the parking lot at Philip Arnold Park. Pass around the barrier on Beacon Way South.

0.3 Pass a gate for a gravel road on the right side of the road. Go another 30 feet and turn right onto a path between two cement barriers into the woods. Follow the path uphill to the right and then downhill to the main gravel road and turn left.

0.4 Turn right at the trail crossing toward Silkworm.

0.5 Take the first left turn beneath the Silkworm trail sign on tree. Follow the trail through the woods. Be aware that "blue arrows" mark the less difficult sections and "black arrows" are most difficult.

1.3 Turn right onto connector trail that returns to the gravel road. (A left turn connects to back end of Parasite.)

1.4 Arrive at crossing for entrance gravel road and go straight across on the connector trail.

1.5 In quick succession, take the right fork at the first trail junction, the left fork at the second trail junction, and the right fork at the third trail. This is the beginning downhill run of Mr. DNA.

1.8 Turn right onto the connector trail and take it downhill to a gravel road.

1.9 Turn left onto path just before gravel road. This is the start of Crop Circles.

2.2 Crop Circles trail takes a sharp right turn.

2.4 Pass through a trail crossing and turn left onto a gravel road. Go 150 feet and turn left onto another gravel road. Take a path on the right into the woods just before the road gets to an open field. This is the start of Bermsled.

2.8 At the technical kickers and jumps at the base of Bermsled, look for a short path through the woods that connects to a dirt trail. Turn right on this dirt trail and go uphill.

3.0 Turn left onto a gravel road.

3.1 Turn left at intersection of two gravel roads.

3.2 Turn left at a dirt trail crossing. Go about 100 feet and turn right into the woods. Tapeworm begins under an archway in a clearing in these woods.

Towers of Power

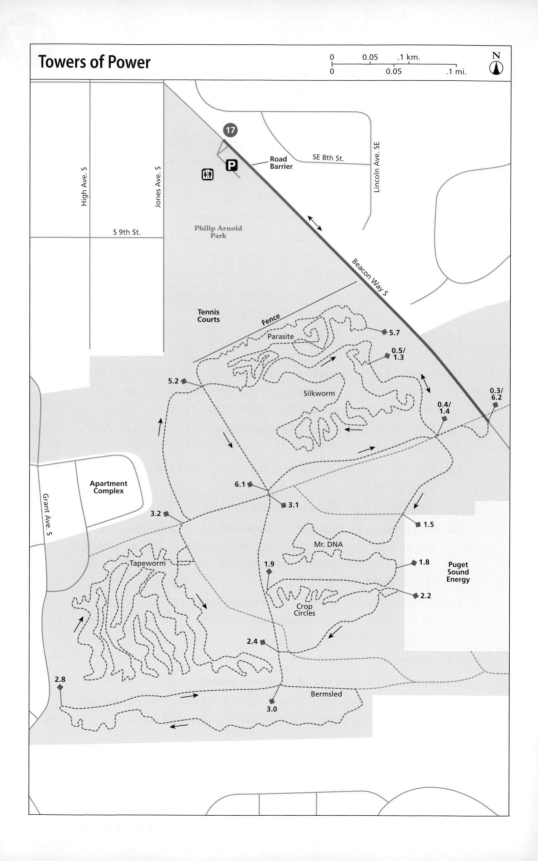

0   0.05   .1 km.
0   0.05   .1 mi.

N

17

High Ave. S

Jones Ave. S

S 9th St.

Philip Arnold Park

P

Road Barrier

SE 8th St.

Lincoln Ave. SE

Beacon Way S

Tennis Courts

Fence

Parasite

5.7

0.5/ 1.3

5.2

Silkworm

0.4/ 1.4

0.3/ 6.2

Grant Ave. S

Apartment Complex

6.1

3.1

3.2

1.5

Mr. DNA

1.8

Tapeworm

1.9

Crop Circles

2.2

Puget Sound Energy

2.4

2.8

3.0

Bermsled

5.0 End of Tapeworm. Continue to the connector trail and turn left. Cross the gravel road in about 100 feet and continue straight ahead on the trail.

5.2 Go straight through a trail crossing. Turn left on a trail in 170 feet (you may notice blue paint on tree trunks on either side of the trail). This is Parasite (straight ahead connects with the end of Silkworm).

5.7 Follow Parasite to the left at trail junction (right turn connects with Silkworm).

6.0 End of Parasite. Turn left onto connector trail.

6.1 Turn left onto dirt trail next to gravel road.

6.2 Turn right onto entrance path into woods, follow it between the barriers, and emerge onto Beacon Way South and turn left.

6.6 Return to parking lot at Phillip Arnold Park. End of ride.

RIDE INFORMATION

Local Events and Attractions

Renton Museum: Permanent and temporary exhibits and large collection, 235 Mill Ave. South, Renton; (425) 255-2330; rentonwa.gov/rentonhistorymuseum
Renton River Days: Community festival in late July at Liberty Park, Bronson Way and Houser Way, Renton; rentonwa.gov/living/default.aspx?id=1138

Restaurants

Dog and Pony Alehouse and Grill: 351 Park Ave. North, Renton; (425) 254-8080
Whistle Stop Ale House: 809 S. 4th St., Renton; (425) 277-3039

Restrooms

Mile 0.0: Phillip Arnold Park, Renton

Dash Point State Park Trails

Dash Point State Park might be better known for its scenic sandy beach on Puget Sound, but mountain bikers in communities south of Seattle are attracted to the single track in the forests up on the ridge. Spend a couple of minutes on the trails that wend around the tall evergreens and it's easy to forget you're in the midst of the booming town of Federal Way.

Start: Parking lot on Hoyt Road Southwest, Federal Way

Length: 10.4 miles

Approximate riding time: 1.5 to 2.5 hours

Best bike: Mountain bike

Terrain: Trails up to the ridge are very steep; more-difficult trails have short climbs and drops. Puddles can form on some trails in rainy weather; blackberry bushes and nettles encroach from trailside; otherwise well-maintained for mountain bikers.

Traffic and hazards: All off-road so no cars; watch for oncoming mountain bikers on narrow trails as well as hikers and off-leash dogs

Things to see: Mature second-growth forest, especially in ravines; 3,300-foot-long tidal shoreline for beach combing; overnight camping; lots of birds

Maps: *DeLorme Atlas & Gazetteer—Washington,* page 59; Dash Point State Park Trail Map, available at Dick's Bike Shop or online at philsbikeshop.com/dashpoint

Getting there: By car: Go south on I-5 to exit 143 onto westbound South 320th Street. Continue 4.5 miles to T intersection and turn left onto Hoyt Road Southwest (47th Avenue Southwest heads north to the beach entrance to Dash Point State Park). Turn right in 0.2 miles into Dash Point State Park day-use parking lot. Note: Washington State

Discover Pass is required for parking. **By bus:** Metro bus route 187 serves the Southwest 320th Street–Hoyt Road Southwest intersection. GPS: N47 18.711' / W122 23.548'

THE RIDE

As you motor past commercial strip development and suburban housing sprawl, it might be difficult to believe that some get-away-from-it-all mountain bike trails are available at the end of the road. That's the case at Dash Point State Park. The 398-acre park is bordered by the Puget Sound on one side and Federal Way on the other three. Well known for its 3,300-foot-long sandy beach, the park also has a mature forest up on the bluff where trails and single tracks lure mountain bikers.

State park rangers and local mountain bike advocates maintain these trails. Some, such as the Boundary and Ridge Trails, are suited for hikers as well as bikers, so follow trail etiquette and be careful about bombing around blind corners. Others, such as IMBA, Log Jam, and Technical Trails, are best suited for mountain biking and even sport the occasional bermed turn and skinny bridge over a wet spot. Most of the mountain-biking single track south of Boundary Trail is signed (look about 10 feet up the tree trunks) and graded for difficulty.

Bike Shop

Phil's Bike Shop: New and used bikes sales and repair; 2310 SW 336th St., Federal Way; (253) 661-3903; philsbikeshop.com/

The state acquired the land for Dash Point State Park from private owners in the 1940s, but nothing much happened there until it opened as a park in 1962. As the suburbs roll right up to the park boundary in places, the park's shoreline and forest habitat has come to support many species of birds as well as small mammals such as coyote, foxes, squirrels, skunks, raccoons, and rabbits . . . lots of rabbits.

A few years ago, the state park commission considered a "natural area" proposal for many of the trails that would have essentially banned biking on most park trails. The state backpedaled after hearing from the Evergreen Mountain Bike Alliance and local users, and now many more trails are open and a few new ones have been installed. The best place to get to those trails is the day-use parking lot on Hoyt Road. Make sure you hang your Discover Pass in the window.

There are essentially three mountain bike routes through the park that use different combinations of trails. They're ranked Easiest Route (2.8 miles), Intermediate Route (3.2 miles), and Advanced Route (4.4 miles). All three include a short, but not sweet, climb up to the Ridge Trail. The difficulty ratings speak to the overall technical aspects of the trails. All three use the same combination of trails to reach the Ridge Trail, so let's make the Easiest Route the base route.

Although the parking lot is on Hoyt Road, the trailhead there is named the 47th Avenue Trailhead. Slip into the woods behind the bulletin board and follow this wide trail. Take the first left onto Hoyt Road Trail and the next left onto Shannon's Shin (going straight on Hoyt connects to the campground, where you'll find water, restrooms, and a road downhill to the beach). Take the next right fork on Boundary Trail, which is a well-packed track that heads across the park to a four-way trail intersection.

A right turn heads down some steps to the beach; straight ahead dead-ends at a ravine with a missing bridge. The Easiest Route turns left onto the aptly named Heart Attack Hill trail. This unyielding steep trail is only 0.2 miles long. It connects with the Double Dip, which continues to ascend but offers two short downhill stretches before it arrives at Ridge Trail. Turn right onto Ridge Trail and right again onto Paul's Trail that connects with The Downhill as it descends. Watch for a couple of step-downs over roots before you reach the bottom and retrace your route back to the trailhead on Boundary, Shannon's Shin, and Hoyt Road trails.

The Intermediate follows the Easiest Route up to Ridge Trail, where you turn left and take the first left down a wooded ravine onto IMBA Trail, named no doubt for the International Mountain Biking Association. The berms for fast turns and the skinny bridges over potential muddy spots reflect a modern mountain-biking character for this trail. Take the right fork onto Log Jam Trail and maintain a rhythm downhill around curves and over a couple of fallen logs. As Log Jam ends, take the left fork to return to the Boundary Trail, where you can decide to either retrace your route back to the trailhead (right) or return to Heart Attack Hill (left) for another stab at the mountain biking area.

The Advanced Route reuses the Easiest Route to Ridge Trail, where you'll turn left and ride slightly uphill to a right fork onto Night Crawler followed by another right onto Technical Trail. This is the top of the wooded ridge, and you're likely to catch a refreshing breeze up here. These trails aren't flowy, however. They'll put you in a sweat as they twist and turn to follow the contour on the south side of the ridge and step up and down over big roots and rocks. Also look for a half-dozen narrow bridges up here.

Technical Trail ends at some dirt rollers for BMX riders. Bear right and you'll find yourself at the Funnel landmark, the base of an old water tank that once

One of the signs that marks trail names and degree of difficulty at Dash Point State Park.

sat up at the top of the ridge. Turn right and then the second left and you're heading down Paul's Trail again on your way back to the trailhead, probably relieved that the park staff decided to allow mountain biking on these trails.

MILES & DIRECTIONS

Easiest Route

0.0 Trailhead.

0.1 Take left fork on Hoyt Road Trail.

0.3 Take left fork on Shannon's Shin.

0.4 Take right fork on Boundary Trail.

0.9 Turn left onto Heart Attack Hill.

1.1 Take left fork onto Double Dip.

1.3 Take right fork to stay on Double Dip.

1.4 Turn right onto Ridge Trail.

1.5 Turn right onto Paul's Trail.

1.6 Take left fork onto The Downhill.

1.8 Take left fork onto Heart Attack Hill.

1.9 Turn right onto Boundary Trail.

2.3 Take left fork onto Shannon's Shin.

2.4 Take right turn onto Hoyt Road Trail.

2.6 Turn right onto trail to 47th Avenue Trailhead.

2.8 Arrive at 47th Avenue Trailhead. End of Easiest Route.

Intermediate Route

0.0 Follow Easiest Route to Ridge Trail.

1.4 Turn left onto Ridge Trail.

1.5 Turn left onto IMBA Trail.

1.7 Take right fork to Log Jam.

2.3 Take right fork to remain on Log Jam.

2.4 Take left fork (right goes to Highland Park Trailhead).

2.5 Turn right onto Boundary Trail.

2.7 Turn left onto Shannon's Shin.

2.8 Turn right onto Hoyt Road Trail.

3.0 Turn right onto trail to 47th Avenue Trailhead.

3.2 Arrive at trailhead. End of Intermediate Route.

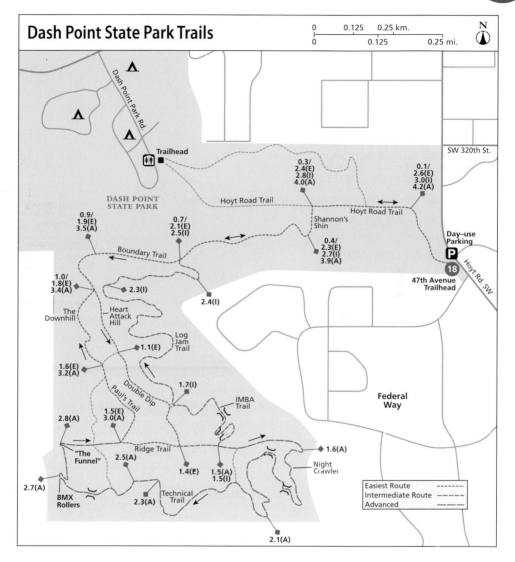

Dash Point State Park Trails

Advanced Route

0.0 Follow Easiest Route to Ridge Trail.

1.4 Turn left onto Ridge Trail.

1.5 Pass the IMBA Trail on the left.

1.6 Turn right onto Night Crawler.

2.1 Take right fork onto Technical Trail.

2.3 Take left fork to remain on Technical Trail.

2.5 Take left fork and remain on Technical Trail.

2.7 Bear to the right at dirt jump course.

2.8 Turn right onto Ridge Trail at The Funnel, the base of an old water tank.

3.0 Turn left onto Paul's Trail.

3.2 Take left fork onto The Downhill.

3.4 Take left fork onto Heart Attack Hill.

3.5 Turn right onto Boundary Trail.

3.9 Turn left onto Shannon's Shin.

4.0 Turn right onto Hoyt Road Trail.

4.2 Turn right onto trail to 47th Avenue Trailhead.

4.4 End of Advanced Route.

RIDE INFORMATION

Local Events and Attractions

Dash Point State Park: Offers 114 standard campsites, 27 utility campsites, 4 restrooms, and 6 showers; beachcombing with clams, crabs, and other critters visible at low tide; 5700 SW Dash Point Rd., Federal Way, Washington. Details, reservations at parks.wa.gov/.

Dash Point State Park 10K and Half-Marathon: Lots of runners on park trails, late March and early September; evergreentrailruns.com

Powells Wood Garden: Private garden featuring Pacific Northwest flora and fauna; open for special events; 430 S. Dash Point Rd., Federal Way. Details and calendar at powellswood.org

Restrooms

Mile 0.3: On Hoyt Road Trail; continue straight to campgrounds instead of turning left onto Shannon's Shin.

Henry's Ridge Open Space/ Black Diamond Natural Area/ Summit Ridge Mountain Bike Area

Here's an area where you can return many times and find pleasure no matter your mood. There is technical single track, flowy trails, and rocky and rooty paths. But the best part is that the land—once privately held and slated for development—is now controlled by landowners who welcome mountain bikers and encourage more use by the two-wheeled crowd.

Start: Henry's Ridge Open Space: On-street parking near the intersection of Southeast 281st Way and 253rd Place Southeast ("The Boulders") or near the intersection of Southeast Maple Ridge Drive and 253rd Place Southeast (Water Tower Park).

Black Diamond Natural Area: County parking lot on west side of SR 169, approximately 1.7 miles south of the intersection with Southeast Kent Kangley Road

Summit Ridge: Entrance gate for Real Life Church property on east side of SR 169, about 2.3 miles south of intersection with Southeast Kent Kangley Road. If no parking available, use Black Diamond Natural Area parking lot and ride 0.6 miles to Summit Ridge entrance or ride a utility road to freestyle jump area.

Length: 14.2 miles of mapped bike route; more than 30 miles of single track

Approximate riding time: 3 to 5 hours

Best bike: Mountain bike

Terrain: Mostly flat; climbs on Henry's Ridge Open Space and northern Black Diamond Natural Area. Trails are well maintained; those in Black Diamond Natural Area can be a little rough.

Traffic and hazards: Might encounter a few hikers or runners; hazards include the usual encounters with rocks and roots.

Things to see: Ravensdale Lake, mature evergreens along Ravensdale Creek, Black Diamond History Museum (off route), birds in the swamp

Maps: *DeLorme Atlas & Gazetteer—Washington,* page 60; Henry's Ridge Map, trails.evergreenmtb.org/wiki/File:Henry%27s_Ridge_Trail _Map_2008.jpg#file; Black Diamond Natural Area (Lake Sawyer) and Summit Ridge, trails.evergreenmtb.org/wiki/Trail:Lake_Sawyer

Getting there: By car: Drive south on I-5 from Seattle to I-405 north. Take exit 4 onto SR 169 (Maple Valley Highway) and drive about 14 miles to intersection of Southeast Kent Kangley Road. To Henry's Ridge: Continue south on SR 169 for 0.5 mile and turn left onto Southeast 276th Street (Southeast Maple Ridge Drive) and look for on-street parking in 0.7 miles in the vicinity of Water Tower Park. To Black Diamond Natural Area: Proceed 1.7 miles south on SR 169 past the Southeast Kent Kangley Road intersection to trailhead parking lots on right side of the road. To Summit Ridge: Proceed 2.3 miles south on SR 169 past the Southeast Kent Kangley Road intersection to entrance gate for Real Life Church. If no parking is available, park in the Black Diamond Natural Area parking lot. GPS: Henry's Ridge—N47 21.049' / W122 00.189'; Black Diamond Natural Area—N47 20.235' / W122 00.917'; Summit Ridge—N47 19.794' / W122 00.608'

THE RIDE

The common name for the Black Diamond mountain bike area refers to the old coal-mining town nearby, not the difficulty of the single track that wends through the woods just up the road on SR 169. The trail network offers biking for all skill levels. Whether you like flowy, technical, or basic bump-over-rocks-and-roots riding, it's all here. Originally an assortment of volunteer paths on private land, the three trail areas are either on public land or property owned by a church that's friendly to mountain bikers. Each area has acquired its own biking personality and character. What they have in common is how the county staff or church leaders worked with local mountain bikers.

Here are general descriptions of the three areas, with some suggested routes. Once you've tasted some of the trails below, you'll want to visit the many more miles of trails that cut through the woods and fields here.

HENRY'S RIDGE OPEN SPACE

The northernmost area is the Henry's Ridge Open Space, which surrounds the residential communities of Maple Ridge and Maple Wood. These communities weren't here a few years ago, and neither were the trails. To build urban densities in a rural area, the developers agreed to transfer 4 acres of open space to King County for every 1 acre of developed land. Mountain-bike groups expressed an interest in creating trails in the forest, and the county agreed as long as they could oversee the projects. The result is more than 200 acres set aside for single track.

A popular place to start a ride here is either "The Boulders" at the Southeast 281st Way and 253rd Place Southeast intersection, or Water Tower Park up the street at Southeast Maple Ridge Drive and 253rd Place Southeast. In either case, if the on-street parking gets too crowded, consider using the shopping center lots at the corner of SR 169 and Southeast Kent-Kangley Road, a location known locally as Four Corners.

A 4-mile loop that captures the character of the silky smooth single track on Henry's Ridge starts at the Water Tower Park. Passing a basketball court, the route disappears into the thick woods on the tight and twisty Iron Brigade Trail. In spite of the turns, it is possible to catch a rhythm by using the berms to sustain your momentum. The next trail in the loop, the Anaconda, is faster. It has turns but not to the extent as Iron Brigade. Those trails will drop you off on the Old Mike utility trail. Along the way, consider using the Viper Trail to return to the The Boulders.

Another loop combines new trails on Henry's Ridge with older trails in the adjoining Black Diamond Natural Area. Starting at The Boulders, head back up the Old Mike fire road to the Python on the right. This snaky downhill ride with berms ends at Snake, which takes you down to Beaver Tracks. This is an older trail with lots of big rocks and tree roots to negotiate as you pedal along Ravensdale Lake. Beaver Tracks is slow going through some mature second-growth forest right along Ravensdale Creek. A right turn onto the Route 66 utility trail returns to some fun single track in Henry's Ridge Open Space with a fairy-tale theme—Once Upon a Time, Bad Wolf, and Li'l Red.

BLACK DIAMOND NATURAL AREA

You'll find the oldest trails in this area, which stretches across SR 169 south of Henry's Ridge. Historically, most of the mountain biking trails in this area once known as Lake Sawyer were on private timber land. King County gained title to a huge swath of it in a complicated land swap that involved the owners, the city of Black Diamond, and the county. Although some of the original Lake Sawyer trails will be replaced with a master-planned housing development, the ones in the county-owned natural area will be preserved.

The terrain on both sides of SR 169 is mostly flat, but the trail can be rocky. Logging has taken its toll on the forest, so there can be scotch broom, blackberries, and stinging nettles growing up along the trail. Advocates keep a lot of it trimmed back, but some of the lesser-used trails can get overgrown. Some trails along a lake and Ravensdale Creek are home to big, beautiful Douglas firs and western red cedars.

There's a parking lot on the west side of SR 169 for trail users. A path out the back of the lot joins Main Line, which provides an easy, 1.5-mile get-acquainted loop route that finishes on Mistress at the edge of a swamp. The Black Lagoon Trail has a good picnic spot next to the swamp. Other trails, such as Ravensdale Creek and Jack Leg, pose more challenges along the edge of the scenic creek. As you head south on Red Dog and Jack Leg, you'll see predominately displayed No Trespassing signs posted at the natural-area boundary.

Bike Shops

Bike Masters & Boards: 23862 Southeast Kent-Kangley Road, Maple Valley; (425) 584-7508; bikemasters.net

On the east side of SR 169, the Master Link and Route 66 trails cross an open field under power lines and Northern Pacific Railroad tracks to reach Beaver Tracks and the trails on Henry's Ridge.

SUMMIT RIDGE

Mountain bikers can access miles of highly technical single track and freestyle runs on the Real Life Church property located on the east side of SR 169 just south of the Black Diamond Natural Area.

The church didn't intend to get wound up in mountain biking. It bought the property in 2007 for a future church site and gathering area. When they discovered the trails, jumps, ladders, and other mountain-bike trappings scattered around the woods, they considered taking a hard line with the trespassers. Cooler heads prevailed, however, remembering that community outreach was one of their missions. Now they encourage the trail building and regularly host mountain-biking events.

Summit Ridge has more than 9 miles of single track on the 25-acre church property. Users can park at the county parking lots on the west side of SR 169 or at two entrance gates farther south on the east side of the highway.

Although there are miles of trails from which to choose, you might want to sample a 4-mile loop that starts with the Deliverance trail to the left at the entrance. This is a biking test for those adept at sharp turns and obstacles, although most structures have detours. You'll be surprised to find any straight

This foliage creates a tunnel effect around the Railroad Grade trail at Black Diamond Natural Area.

sections in here. This joins the curvy Holy Roller trail that features a half-dozen rollers deeper in the forest and exits on the straighter Exodus trail.

MILES & DIRECTIONS

Henry's Ridge: Iron Brigade, Anaconda, and Viper Trails

0.0 Start at Water Tower Park and ride into the woods in back of the basketball court.

0.2 Take the left fork at trail junction to remain on Iron Brigade.

1.2 Take the left fork to remain on Iron Brigade (right fork returns to start).

1.7 Take the left fork to join Anaconda (right goes to neighborhood).

1.8 Take the left fork to stay on Anaconda.

3.0 Turn right onto Old Mike trail.

3.4 Turn left onto unnamed trail, then immediately left onto Viper trail.

3.8 Turn right onto access road at end of Viper, pass between The Boulders, then ride up 253rd Place Southeast to Water Tower Park.

4.1 End of ride.

Henry's Ridge: Old Mike, Python, Snake, and Beaver Tracks Trails

0.0 Starting at The Boulders, head 10 to 15 feet down the hill, and take the first unmarked trail on the left. This narrow track runs along the base of a hill at the edge of the forest.

0.3 Turn left onto Old Mike trail and head uphill.

0.5 Turn right onto Python.

1.2 As Python ends, turn right, then immediately turn left onto Snake.

1.4 Turn left to remain on Snake (left returns to sediment pond area below The Boulders on Bail to Ponds trail).

1.7 Turn right onto Beaver Tracks at junction.

2.3 Turn left at junction to continue on Beaver Tracks (right is another Bail to Ponds connector).

2.9 Turn right onto Route 66 trail (not marked) and head uphill (left goes across railroad tracks and under power lines to SR 169).

3.0 Turn right onto gravel access road.

3.1 Turn left onto Once Upon a Time after passing a sediment pond on the left.

3.4 Turn left at junction to remain on Once Upon a Time; then turn left at next junction and take Bad Wolf (right is Once Upon a Time).

Henry's Ridge / Black Diamond / Summit Ridge (North)

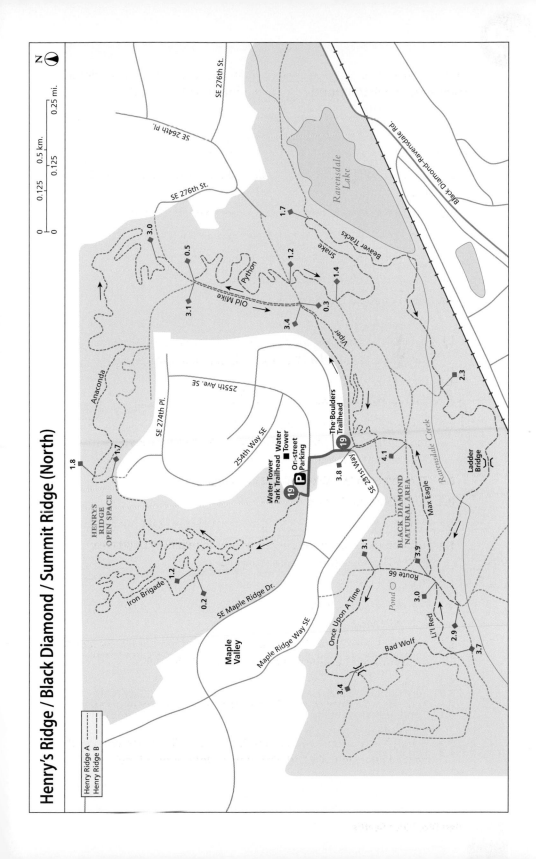

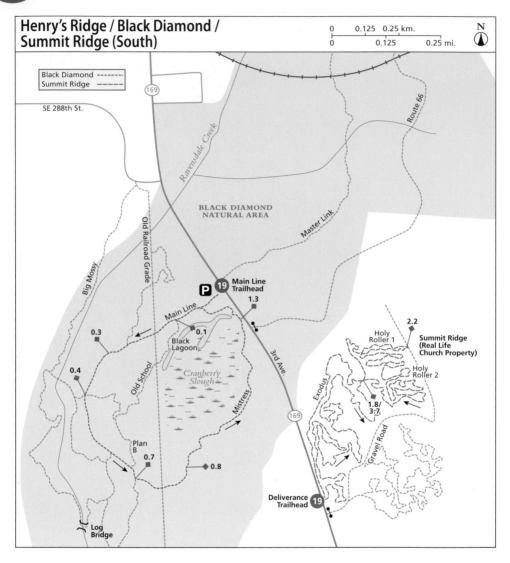

The map shows:

Henry's Ridge / Black Diamond / Summit Ridge (South)

3.7 Turn left onto Li'l Red at the junction. The trail follows an embankment and joins a utility road, heading left.

3.9 Turn right onto Max Eagle just after returning to the utility road.

4.1 Continue across utility road after Max Eagle ends; follow trail uphill with sediment pond on your right to return to The Boulders.

4.3 End of ride.

Black Diamond Natural Area: Main Line, Mistress, and Creature Trails

0.0 Start on path in back of trailhead parking lot on west side of SR 169. Take the right fork onto Main Line.

0.1 Take the right fork to bypass Black Lagoon Trail on the left. Cross over the abandoned railroad grade. Stay on Main Line as two smaller trails cross.

0.3 Turn left to stay on Main Line trail (Ravensdale Creek trail is on the right).

0.4 Cross Lake Sawyer Railroad trail. Pass Ripper and Red Dog trails, which go right, and Plan B, which goes left.

0.7 Take the first left fork after Plan B. Cross over the abandoned railroad grade. The trail becomes Mistress.

0.8 Take the next two left forks with unnamed junctions to stay on Mistress trail. Good views of the lake on the climb.

1.3 Take the left fork at junction to get onto Creature.

1.5 Ride ends at trailhead.

Summit Ridge: Deliverance, Holy Roller, Exodus Trails

0.0 Start just past entrance gate on SR 169 and turn left onto trail marked Deliverance.

1.8 Cross trails at left and right and go straight onto Holy Roller 1.

2.2 Turn sharply right at access road to pick up Holy Roller 2.

3.7 Go straight at crossroads to get onto Exodus trail. (Deliverance is left and Holy Roller 1 is right.)

4.3 Arrive at access road. End of ride.

RIDE INFORMATION

Local Events and Attractions

Black Diamond Museum: Displays and information on Black Diamond area history, open weekends and holidays; 32627 Railroad Ave., Black Diamond; blackdiamondmuseum.org

Restaurants

Black Diamond Bakery: Meals and baked goods; 32805 Railroad Ave., Black Diamond; blackdiamondbakery.com

Taylor Mountain Forest Loop

Taylor Mountain Forest has a mixed reputation among mountain bikers. Some find the dirt trails too muddy and too popular with equestrians. Others take the horses in stride, judge the trails fun to ride, and enjoy tooling along the old logging roads to explore the forest. You can make up your own mind after taking these two loops. One rolls along forest roads and trails to a summit view of Mount Rainier, while another uses mostly forest roads to visit a quiet beaver pond.

Start: Taylor Mountain Forest parking lot in Hobart

Length: 9.3 miles, plus 2 side-trip loops (1.8 and 3.9 miles)

Approximate riding time: 1.5 to 3 hours

Best bike: Mountain bike

Terrain: Hilly; with a steep climb in the first mile. About half and half crushed-rock logging roads and dirt trails. Muddy spots on some trails after rainy weather.

Traffic and hazards: Many of the trails are popular with equestrians. Remember to dismount and stand on the downhill side from horses. Also, break-ins reported in parking lot.

Things to see: Views of Mount Rainier and Tiger Mountain from Holder Knob, recovering second-growth Douglas fir and cedar forests, beaver pond. This is a wildlife corridor for deer, elk, and bear, among many other species.

Maps: *DeLorme Atlas & Gazetteer—Washington,* page 60; Taylor Mountain Forest Map—King County, your.kingcounty.gov/ftp/gis/web/vmc/recreation/BCT_TaylorMtn_brochure.pdf

Getting there: **By car:** Take eastbound I-90 to exit 17, Front Street, in Issaquah. Follow Front Street southward for about 9 miles (it becomes Issaquah-Hobart Road Southeast) to just past the interchange for SR 18. Look for parking lot entrance on the left side of road. GPS: N47 25.965' / W121 58.349'

THE RIDE

When the King County government bought about 1,800 acres of forestland on Taylor Mountain from a timber company in the late 1990s, there were only a few logging roads into the property and an old railroad grade. It's a different story today. Now mountain bikers, equestrians, and hikers roam freely over 30 miles of forest roads and trails, some open seasonally, others year-round. (**Note:** Some trails—including Elk Ridge, Sherwood, and Holder Creek—are closed Oct 15 to Apr 15.) Volunteer workers spent thousands of hours building dirt trails to connect roads or access scenic views, such as the view of Mount Rainier from Holder Knob.

While the roads are firmly packed dirt or crushed rock, the dirt trails can have muddy spots in the winter, dusty stretches in the summer, and be littered with horse poop. These rides explore about half the routes in the Taylor Mountain Forest, which is part of a huge wildlife corridor that stretches into the Cascades. Elk, deer, and black bear forage through the area, and smaller mammals such as coyotes, foxes, raccoons, and skunks make their homes here.

The Taylor Mountain Forest Loop starts with a mile-long climb from the parking lot on Issaquah-Hobart Road Southeast. Watch out for horse poop as you go around the gate that blocks the crushed-rock road from the lot. The climb is steep in places, so you can just throw it in your granny gear and grind it out.

At the summit, you'll see dirt trails to the left (to Holder Knob) and the right (Whisky Still). Sometimes the trail signs posted 8 or 9 feet up the trees have survived. Turn right and head down Whisky Still Trail, which sees plenty of equestrian use. In less than a mile you come to a junction with an old logging road in the woods. Turn right onto the road, then quickly go left onto Boot Trail, which continues downhill. Turn right onto Mountain Beaver Trail, which descends to the bridge over Carey

Bike Shops

Bicycle Center of Issaquah: 121 Front St. North, Issaquah; (425) 392-4588; bicyclecenter.biz
REI Issaquah: 735 NW Gilman Blvd., Issaquah; (425) 313-1660; rei.com/stores/issaquah.html

Bear Facts

As you venture deep into the forests of the Pacific Northwest on single track or even rail trails, there's an off-chance that you could encounter a black bear. The state Department of Fish and Wildlife estimates that there are 25,000 to 30,000 black bears living here. As development encroaches on bear habitat, they're squeezed into smaller areas of forestland.

You'll often see signs at trailheads to look out for black bears. In fact, you probably hear more about them rummaging through some neighborhood garbage cans than confronting mountain bikers on the trails. If they hear you coming, they'll make themselves scarce. That's why it's okay to make noise as you ride. Some bikers use bells that jingle-jangle as they bounce down the trail.

If you do encounter a bear, it's probably a surprise to both of you. Stop immediately and give the bear plenty of room to leave, especially if it's a mother with cubs. Biking with off-leash dogs is not a good idea in bear country.

Other hints from wildlife experts:

- Avoid direct eye contact, which could elicit a charge.
- Identify yourself as human by standing, talking, and waving your hands above your head.
- If you cannot move safely away and the bear doesn't budge, try to scare the bear by clapping or yelling.
- If the bear does attack, fight aggressively, perhaps by using your bicycle as a shield.
- As a last resort, curl into a ball to protect your stomach and play dead.

Creek, the lowest point on the route (except for the parking lot where you started) and the wettest.

Turn left onto Carey Creek Trail after crossing the bridge. This trail follows the creek for a little more than a mile with a rock crossing and another bridge. The trail is smooth, except for one rocky slope, and likely to be wet in a couple of places from springs or seepages off the ridge on your right, even in the driest months. Low shrubs brush your legs as you pedal up this trail. Turn left when you reach a gravel park maintenance road (a trailhead on Southeast 208th Street is on the right).

If you want to experience a more true-to-life Pacific Northwest mountain-biking experience, take a side trip on the Elk Ridge Trail (closed Oct 15 to Apr 15) to the right about 0.1 mile up the park maintenance road. This rough trail

Holder Knob offers a spectacular view of Mount Rainier.

winds through large second-growth Douglas fir into an otherwise closed-off portion of the Cedar River Watershed, which provides water for the City of Seattle. Here you'll encounter twisty turns, sharp climbs, exposed rocks, and slick tree roots. You might find several woodpeckers at work on some snags. There's even a muddy stream crossing about halfway. Pass two trails on the right, cross a gravel road, then head down the ridge.

Both routes arrive at a trail/road junction. (This is the beginning of the Beaver Pond Loop described below.) The Taylor Mountain Forest Loop takes the first gravel road on the left; the Elk Ridge side trip turns right onto the park maintenance road, then makes an immediate left onto the gravel road.

Turn left onto the first dirt trail (Boot Trail) off the gravel road and follow to another trail junction. Here we retrace our earlier route on Mountain Beaver and Whisky Still trails uphill to the main road.

Across the road is a dirt trail to the Holder Knob summit; to the right is a gravel road that takes a slightly less challenging route to the summit. In either case, it is a 200-foot climb to Holder Knob with spectacular views on clear days to Mount Rainier to the south and Tiger Mountain to the north.

Whenever you can tear yourself away from the summit, the Holder Ridge Trail heads downhill to Holder Creek and the parking lot. There are a couple of more scenic views heading down the trail, along with some switchbacks and one short climb after a stream crossing. Back into dense forest at the bottom of the ridge trail, look for a left turn into the parking lot.

BEAVER POND LOOP

At mile 4.9 on the Taylor Mountain Forest Loop, take the first gravel road on the right as you approach the trail/road junction. This begins a steady uphill ride through the Carey Creek valley and an old railroad corridor from the early logging days.

When the road ends after 1.2 miles, turn right onto a trail. This passes a swamp on the left and makes several creek crossings until it emerges onto a dirt road in a half-mile. Turn right and you're at the beaver pond. The peaceful pond fills a tight little valley that's home to bullfrogs and other amphibians. Don't be surprised to be greeted by a noisy kingfisher flitting between the trees.

To return, retrace your route on this dirt road and go straight instead of taking your previous trail on the left. Turn left onto the first dirt road, followed by a steep descent, and left again at another dirt road. (Going straight would connect to the seasonal Holder Creek Trail, which heads downstream to the Holder Ridge Trail and the parking lot.)

Still descending, pass into a dirt road junction in an open area and take the second left turn. Turn left onto a gravel road at a T intersection (right turn is a shortcut by road to the parking lot). You'll arrive back at the trail/road junction in 0.3 miles. Make the first right turn to rejoin the Taylor Mountain Forest Loop.

MILES & DIRECTIONS

Taylor Mountain Forest

0.0 Pass through gate at northeast end of parking lot and head up gravel road.

1.1 Turn right at top of climb onto dirt trail marked TRAIL; it's named Whisky Still Trail.

1.6 Turn right, and then turn left onto Boot Trail (marked with a sign) at a four-way intersection with an overgrown road.

1.8 Turn right onto Mountain Beaver Trail.

2.5 Cross bridge over Carey Creek then turn left onto Carey Creek Trail.

3.1 Cross creek on stones.

3.5 Cross creek on bridge.

3.7 Left turn onto gravel road; right turn goes to Southeast 208th Street trailhead.

3.8 Pass the Elk Trail on the right. (See Elk Trail side trip below.)

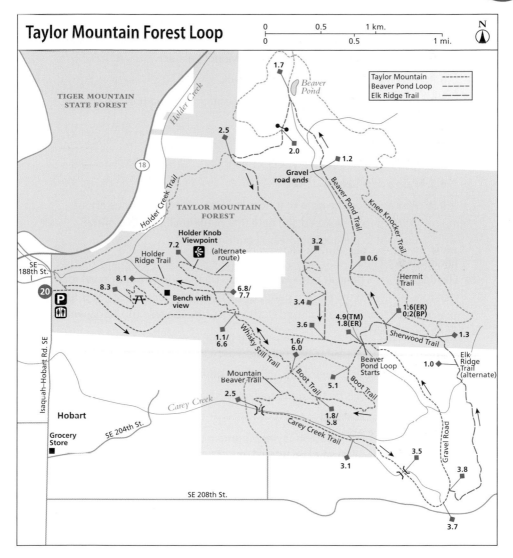

4.9 Arrive at junction of four gravel roads; turn onto the first gravel road to the left. (See Beaver Pond Loop side trip below.)

5.1 Turn left onto dirt path named Boot Trail.

5.8 Bear to the right at trail junction, remaining on Boot Trail.

6.0 At trail junction with overgrown road, head right onto road then turn left on dirt trail named Whisky Still.

6.6 Cross gravel road and continue up dirt trail to Holder Knob. (A gravel road just to the right of Holder Knob Trail is an easier, 0.6-mile ride to the summit. It becomes a dirt trail about halfway up; take a narrow path to left at summit for views of Mount Rainier.)

6.8 Pass the Holder Ridge Trail on the left.

7.2 Circling the Holder Knob, turn right onto narrow path to the summit. Retrace route down the knob.

7.7 Turn right onto Holder Ridge Trail.

8.1 Cross a creek.

8.3 Pass a park bench.

9.3 Pass a trail on the right that goes to Holder Creek. Continue about 100 feet to gravel road and gate that marks trailhead. End of trail. Proceed to parking lot toward your right.

Elk Ridge Trail

Elk Ridge Trail is a difficult but rewarding trail up the ridge from a gravel road that runs parallel to the eastern part of the Taylor Mountain Forest Loop. It's a seasonal trail that is usually closed Oct 15 to Apr 15. The side trip starts with a right turn at mile 3.8.

0.0 Leave gravel road with a right turn onto marked Elk Ridge Trail.

1.0 Creek crossing, very steep hill on the other side.

1.3 Pass two trails on the right; trail name changes to Sherwood Trail.

1.6 Cross a gravel road.

1.8 Arrive at gravel road on Taylor Mountain Loop. Take the second gravel road on right and rejoin Taylor Mountain Loop at mile 4.9.

Beaver Pond Loop

The Beaver Pond Loop uses gravel roads and trails to a pond behind a beaver dam up the flank of Taylor Mountain. It's open year-round, although the trail around the edge of the marsh can be wet year-round. The side trip starts with a right turn onto a gravel road as you arrive at the trail/road junction at mile 4.9.

0.0 As you arrive at the trail junction on Taylor Mountain Forest Loop, turn right on the first gravel road.

0.2 Cross Sherwood Trail.

0.6 Take the left fork on the gravel road.

1.2 Gravel road ends; take Beaver Pond Trail to the right.

1.7 Arrive at the beaver pond. Retrace your route for about 200 feet and stay on gravel road, passing Beaver Pond Trail on the left.

2.0 Take the left fork at gravel road junction; pass through a gate about 200 feet down the trail.

2.5 Turn left onto gravel road; Holder Creek Trail intersects (this is a seasonal trail closed Apr 15 to Oct 15).

3.2 Arrive at trail junction; take the second gravel road on the left.

3.4 Pass road on the right.

3.6 Turn left onto gravel road.

3.9 End of Beaver Pond Loop. Turn right onto gravel road, joining mile 4.9 of Taylor Mountain Forest Loop.

RIDE INFORMATION

Local Events and Attractions
Taylor Mountain Forest: King County, kingcounty.gov/recreation/parks/trails/backcountry/taylor_trails.aspx
West Tiger Mountain Natural Resource Conservation Area: dnr.wa.gov/AboutDNR/ManagedLands/Pages/amp_na_tiger.aspx

Food Store
Hobart Food Market: Groceries, drinks: 20250 276th Ave. Southeast, Maple Valley

Restrooms
Start: Portable toilet

21

Carbon River Road

The only off-road bicycling at Mount Rainier National Park is this abandoned and deteriorating road that has been permanently closed to motor vehicles. The route follows the meandering, milky-white Carbon River, which drains the lowest glacier in the park. Bicyclists can park their rides and take short strolls to an old copper mine or waterfall, or hike 3.5 miles to the glacier.

Start: Carbon River Ranger Station, Mount Rainier National Park

Length: 10.2 miles round-trip

Approximate riding time: 1 to 2 hours

Best bike: Mountain bike or hybrid bike

Terrain: Steady elevation gain of 600 feet; crushed rock trail and road with a couple of short cobblestone stretches

Traffic and hazards: No traffic; very difficult to ride over occasional cobblestones on the trail; check national park website for weather alerts

Things to see: Historic Fairfax Bridge, historic town of Wilkeson, hikes to old copper mine, Chenuis Falls, Carbon Glacier

Maps: Mount Rainier National Park Map, available at ranger stations; *DeLorme Atlas and Gazetteer—Washington,* page 60

Getting there: From Seattle, travel south on I-5, north on I-405, and south onto SR 167. Exit at SR 410 in Sumner and head east about 11 miles to a right turn on Munday Loss Road, then left onto SR 162, and right onto SR 165. Follow SR 165 through Wilkeson and Carbonado. About a mile past the high Fairfax Bridge over the Carbon River, take the left fork on Carbon River Road toward the Carbon River Ranger Station, about 8 miles away. Parking lot is at entrance. GPS: N46 59.699' / W121 54.926'

THE RIDE

The National Park Service built the 5-mile Carbon River Road in Mount Rainier National Park in 1921 so tourists could enjoy a pleasurable drive along the Carbon River. Mother Nature had other ideas. Creeks swollen by heavy rains occasionally washed out parts of the road, and the meandering course of glacier-fed Carbon River either spilled over its banks or gouged away the shoreline supporting the road.

After flooding washed away or swamped a mile of roadway with trees and rocks in a bad storm in 2006, the National Park Service pulled the plug on trying to resuscitate the road every few years and declared it a biking and hiking trail in 2011. Now it's the only trail accessible to bicyclists in the park.

The bike ride starts at the ranger station, which is about 14 miles south of Wilkeson, the picturesque old logging and coal-mining town that offers the last-chance food stop at Skeeks restaurant. A few miles later, the Fairfax Bridge also is a worthy distraction. Built in 1921, a one-lane steel lattice arch bridge soars 250 feet above the Carbon River. Entrance to the park is only $5 because you're on a bicycle (you don't pay at all if you have an annual, Access, or senior pass). A wilderness permit is required for staying overnight at Isput Campground at the end of the trail.

Passing through the gate, the trail is clearly the old, two-lane, packed gravel road that tourists used for decades to visit this side of the park and to hike to the Carbon Glacier. This is the wettest side of the park, getting upwards of 76 inches of precipitation a year. Sitka spruce, which don't grow anywhere else in the park, can be found here, along with western red cedars and aged Douglas firs. Thick moss hangs from tree branches, and ferns cover the ground.

Bike Shops

Enumclaw Ski and Mountain Sports: 240 Roosevelt Ave. East, Enumclaw; (360) 825-6510; skiandbicycle.com
Trailside Cyclery: 207 Van Scoyoc Ave. Southwest, Orting; (360) 893-7333; facebook.com/pages/Trailside-Cyclery/294798420547331

At 1.1 miles you'll pass the Old Mine Trailhead to a deserted mine to the right of the road. Washington Mining and Milling Co. staked out this copper mine in 1899 about a quarter-mile from the road. Long-closed, the entrance is blocked by a grate that offers a peek inside.

So far the gravel road has been smooth and easygoing, but just past here it loses its civilized look. It narrows into a 10-foot-wide packed gravel trail in places that meanders through the undergrowth. One of the first examples is a large tree that has fallen across the road. Instead of buzz-sawing a section out of the log, rangers packed dirt to form a gradual ramp that goes up and over the

A black-tailed deer forages in rocks strewn in the bed of the Carbon River.

log. Elsewhere, sections of road washed away by flowing water are replaced by wooden bridges. While most of this rerouting by trail is on crushed gravel, there are a few places where cobblestones are used to prevent the trail from eroding. Use caution and consider walking your bike over those sections.

The Green Lake hiking trail leaves the road at 3.2 miles for a 4-mile detour to a serene mountain lake. In another half-mile you come to a river overlook that's becoming overgrown after the disappearance of cars from this route. The water is milky colored, an indication that's its full of glacial flour created by the glacier scraping across rocks. A hiking trail to Chenuis Falls heads to the left here, across the Carbon River.

This hike, about a half-mile round-trip, gives visitors an idea of the river's nature. It flows in meandering ribbons through a wide, rocky channel. Temporary log bridges that span the rushing water are often washed out or must be relocated as the river changes course. In places, the debris carried downstream from the Carbon Glacier is actually piled higher than the road. The waterfall is a short climb up the opposite shore; listen for the gushing water and take the left fork when the trail branches.

After returning to your bicycle, follow the road upstream with the river on your left for a mile and a half. First you'll cross a wooden bridge over the new channel for Isput Creek, then the road bridge over the new channel. This is the entrance to the Isput Creek Campground, which the park service is transforming into a wilderness campground. A few parking spots may still be visible in the debris under the trees, but all this is slowly disappearing.

A No Biking sign at the far end of the campground marks the end of the bike route. The Wonderland Trail leaves here for a 3.5-mile hike to the base of the

Carbon River Road

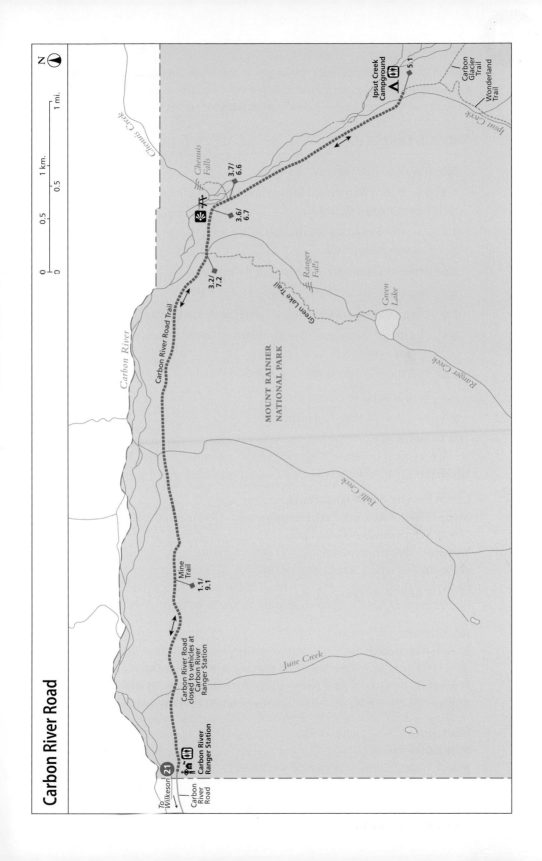

N

To Wilkeson

21

Carbon River Road

Carbon River Ranger Station

Carbon River Road closed to vehicles at Carbon River Ranger Station

Mine Trail
1.1/ 9.1

Carbon River Road Trail

Carbon River

Chenuis Creek

Chenuis Falls
3.7/ 6.6

3.6/ 6.7

3.2/ 7.2

Green Lake Trail

Ranger Falls

Green Lake

Ranger Creek

MOUNT RAINIER NATIONAL PARK

June Creek

Falls Creek

Ipsut Creek Campground
5.1

Ipsut Creek

Carbon Glacier Trail

Wonderland Trail

0   0.5   1 km.
0   0.5   1 mi.

Carbon Glacier. It's the deepest and largest in the lower forty-eight states. After exploring the campground and information signs, you return by the same route. It might seem a little easier as it descends about 600 feet to the parking lot.

MILES & DIRECTIONS

0.0 Bike ride starts at gate.

1.1 Pass trail to Washington Mining and Milling Co. copper mine on right; trail to mine is 0.25 miles.

3.2 Pass the Green Lake and Ranger Falls hiking trail on the right; the trail is a 4-mile round trip.

3.6 Arrive at Carbon River overlook and picnic area.

3.7 Pass trailhead for Chenuis Falls Trail on the left.

5.0 Cross two bridges and arrive at Ipsut Creek Campground.

5.1 End of trail for bicycles. The Wonderland Trail to Carbon Glacier begins here.

6.6 Pass Chenuis Falls Trail on the right.

7.2 Pass Green Lake Trail on the left.

9.1 Pass the Old Mine Trail on the left.

10.2 End of ride.

RIDE INFORMATION

Local Events and Attractions

Mount Rainier National Park Headquarters: 39000 SR 706 E, Ashford; (360) 569-2211; nps.gov/mora/index.htm

Wilkeson, WA: A historic logging and coal town with many old buildings. The Wilkeson Elementary School, Railroad Avenue off Route 165, is on the National Register of Historic Places. Also, the town sponsors the Annual National Hand-car Races every July. Check town website at townofwilkeson.com.

Restaurant

Skeeks Restaurant: This restaurant, pizza parlor, espresso stand, and ice cream store is the last chance to stock up on the way to the Carbon River entrance of Mount Rainier National Park. Many old photos of the town and artifacts are on display; 535 Church St., Wilkeson; facebook.com/SkeeksInWilkeson

Restrooms

Mile 0.0: Entrance
Mile 5.1: Ipsut Creek Campground (pit toilets)

Near Eastside

Paths in Saint Edward State Park are wider than most mountain bike trails.

The booming communities in the shadow of Microsoft and other high-tech companies are the setting for both flat and hilly rides on the Eastside. Road bicyclists seek out the scenic, rolling loop around Mercer Island for training and sightseeing, while a loop ride around Lake Sammamish includes a flat rail trail as well as a hilly return to the start at Marymoor Park.

More altitude change is in store for cyclists who challenge the summit of Cougar Mountain, which once served as a missile base overlooking the Seattle area. A dead flat ride along the Sammamish River links two rail trails—the Burke-Gilman and the East Lake Sammamish trails—and offers a detour into the Woodinville "Wine Country."

The Eastside provides close-by routes for mountain bikers as well. They can hone their skills on single track running through woods near a former seminary and adjoining county park, while a series of utility trails under power lines and over water pipelines creates a loop that builds stamina.

Mercer Island Loop

Here's a bike loop on low-traffic roads that's convenient to bicyclists in Seattle and the eastern suburbs. Amateur racers come here to improve their conditioning on the many hills, while recreational cyclists come to enjoy the scenery while they ride.

Start: Park on the Lid, Mercer Island

Length: 13.4 miles

Approximate riding time: 1 to 2 hours

Best bike: Road or hybrid

Terrain: Hilly

Traffic and hazards: Most of the route is on roads without shoulders. Traffic is light.

Things to see: Groveland Park, Clarke Beach Park, Luther Burbank Park, vistas of Seattle, Bellevue, and Renton shorelines

Maps: King County Bicycle Map, kingcounty.gov/transportation/kcdot/Roads/Bicycling.aspx; *DeLorme Atlas & Gazetteer—Washington,* page 46

Getting there: By car: From the west, take eastbound I-90 to exit 6, West Mercer Island Way. Turn left onto West Mercer Way, go 1 block, and turn left into parking lot for I-90 Lid Park. From the east, take westbound I-90 to exit 7, Island Crest. Continue straight on North Mercer Way after exit and turn left onto 76th Avenue Southeast. Cross over the expressway and turn right onto Southeast 24th Street. Go up and over a hill and turn right onto West Mercer Way. Turn left into the I-90 Lid Park. **By bus:** Metro Express bus route 550 stops at the Mercer Island Park and Ride; take the I-90 Trail west to the trailhead. GPS: N47 35.434' / W122 14.907'

THE RIDE

In the eyes of a bicyclist, Mercer Island's somewhat kidney-shaped appearance in the middle of Lake Washington is as inviting as a giant, outdoor velodrome. The island is encircled by roads that offer good bicycling opportunities for road warriors and recreational bicyclists alike.

Some cyclists regularly incorporate the hilly, non-stop 10-mile stretch between stop signs or traffic signals into their regular after-work training regimen. Others ride the scenic perimeter route to enjoy the shoreline views and get away from the hustle and bustle of urban bicycling. In either case, it's important to remember that some 22,000 people call this place home and use these roads as well. Fortunately, most of the island's population is located inland and these waterfront roads are used primarily by local motorists who are accustomed to bicyclists. Still, sharing the road and exhibiting good bicycle etiquette can go a long way toward curbing the calls for bicycling limitations that reach the Mercer Island City Council every few years.

Bike Shop

Veloce Velo Bicycles: 2750 77th Ave. Southeast, Mercer Island; (206) 236-0123; velocevelo.com

This bike ride starts at the Park on the Lid, located above the I-90 tunnel. It's easy to reach from the Seattle or Bellevue side of the island. It could become more costly to drive to the trailhead, however, if the Washington State Department of Transportation proceeds with plans to charge tolls on the I-90 bridges. Bicyclists could easily avoid these future tolls, and rack up a couple of more miles, by parking in Seattle or Bellevue and using the I-90 Trail to reach the island.

Pulling out of the parking lot, turn right onto West Mercer Way for a counter-clockwise tour of the island. Heading uphill to Southeast 24th Street, you'll pass the last stop sign for 10 miles. The road, which becomes East Mercer Way at the southern tip of the island, is narrow and winding with a nonexistent shoulder. Small, raised reflectors called Botts' dots border the right-hand side of the road, but there usually isn't more than a foot's distance between them and roadside hedges, trees, or ditches.

Mercer Island was named in 1860 for Thomas Mercer, an early Seattle pioneer who enjoyed exploring the island. Although a few settlers staked claims in the woods, the first community—East Seattle—sprouted on the northwestern tip of the island around a grand hotel built in 1889. As the population center grew, regular ferry service began and continued after the hotel burned down in 1908. With the opening of the floating bridge from Seattle in 1940,

Luther Burbank Park

A pleasant stop is Luther Burbank Park, a 77-acre park on 0.75 miles of Lake Washington shoreline at the northeast corner of Mercer Island. It was originally the Parental School, a reformatory for young miscreants from Seattle that opened in 1904. The brick dormitory, now parks department administrative offices, and a waterfront steam plant built in 1924 are still standing.

Boys and girls both attended the school, where the average length of stay was nine months. They received an education and health care here, also performing many tasks to keep the school running. As the school strived for self-sufficiency, farm work became a central element of its curriculum.

The name changed to Boys Parental School after the girls were sent to their own facility in the 1920s. Considering its emphasis on agriculture, the school was renamed the Luther Burbank School in 1931 for the noted horticulturist who created so many new varieties of crops and flowers through hybridization.

Ironically, one of the improved plant species Burbank created was the Himalayan blackberry. Today the pernicious plant with tasty berries is considered a noxious weed. Gardeners in parks throughout western Washington, including the Luther Burbank Park, often do battle with it to preserve native species. In August and September, foragers arrive with buckets in hand to harvest the berries from parks and roadsides.

ferry service to the island stopped and the commercial district moved inland for better access to the highway.

Soon you emerge into a forested residential area that borders the entire shoreline of the island, which is 5 miles long and 2 miles wide. The road generally remains 100 to 150 feet above water level, so in many cases you're looking across the roofs of houses to catch glimpses of the Seattle, Renton, and Bellevue shorelines across the lake. Architects did their best to incorporate the terrain into these expensive homes that are perched on steep slopes to gain expansive views of Lake Washington.

The Mercer Island Loop is a hilly route that can improve muscle strength and cardiovascular fitness. Although you reach the highest point in the ride at about mile 2.0, it's not downhill the rest of the way. The road dips in and out of countless wooded ravines that drain the hills in the center of the island.

If you want to sightsee, there are two waterfront parks with restrooms (in season) and beaches on the lower half of the island. Groveland Park is directly across from Seattle's Seward Park, and Clarke Beach Park boasts a warm southern exposure on sunny days and views of the Renton shoreline and the Seahawks football team's massive waterfront training facility. Both require arduous climbs, even dismounts, to return to the road.

Climbing a hill past Clarke Beach Park, the road on the eastern side of the island has a series of fun horseshoe turns as it snakes in and out of drainages. At mile 7.4 there's an access trail to Pioneer Park, a 113-acre park in the center of the island that has mountain-biking trails.

The stop-free section of the Mercer Island Loop ends when it arrives at the access roads for I-90 on the north side of the island. Cross the expressway and turn left onto the I-90 Trail. For this ride, we leave the trail by turning right at North Mercer Way.

Go straight at mile 11.8 after stopping at Southeast 24th Street. This intersection and Southeast 26th Street at the top of the hill are notorious ticketing spots for local police. At the top of the hill, go straight instead of turning left if you want to visit Luther Burbank Park (see sidebar).

The route follows some residential streets at the north end of the island before returning to West Mercer Way and the West I-90 Lid Park. Keep your eyes open for the Roanoke Inn at 72nd Avenue Southeast and North Mercer Way. Founded in 1914, the tavern is the only survivor of the days when ferries carried travelers here to the commercial center of the island. As you're less than a half-mile from the finish, this might be a worthwhile stop for refreshment. Just be prepared for the final climb.

MILES & DIRECTIONS

0.0 Turn right onto West Mercer Way from Park on the Lid.

0.1 Cross intersection with Southeast 24th Street.

3.5 Pass Deerford Road on your right (turn right to go to Groveland Park).

6.5 Pass entrance to Clarke Beach Park on your right (turn right to Clarke Beach Park).

7.4 Pass trail on left that provides access to Pioneer Park (mountain biking).

8.1 Pass trail on left that provides access to Parkwood Natural Area.

10.5 Cross entrance ramps to I-90 at traffic signal and continue on 100 Avenue Southeast.

10.6 Turn left onto I-90 Trail on the other side of the freeway.

10.8 Turn right at street crossing onto North Mercer Way and follow it parallel with bike trail.

11.8 Cross Southeast 26th Street and continue straight up the hill.

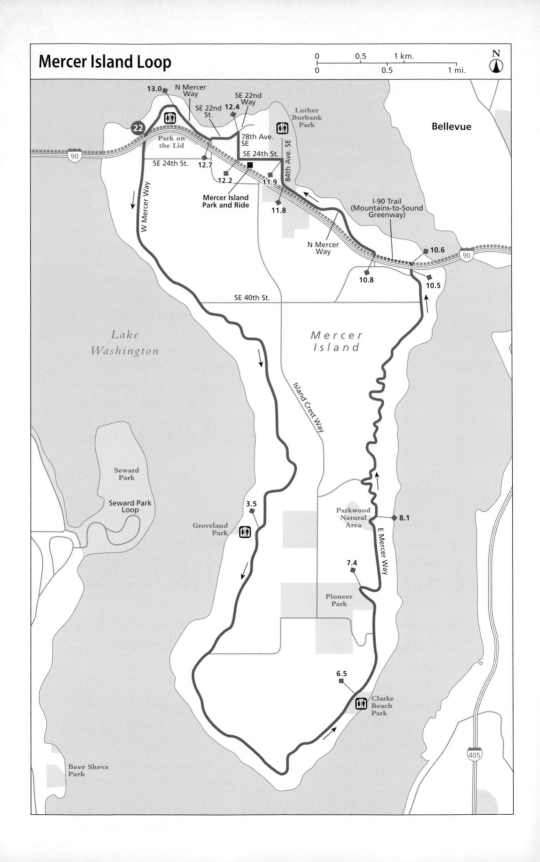

Mercer Island Loop

0   0.5   1 km.
0   0.5   1 mi.

N

13.0 N Mercer Way

SE 22nd Way

SE 22nd St. 12.4

Luther Burbank Park

Bellevue

22

Park on the Lid

78th Ave. SE

SE 24th St.

SE 24th St. 12.7

90

84th Ave. SE

12.2

11.9

Mercer Island Park and Ride

11.8

I-90 Trail (Mountains-to-Sound Greenway)

N Mercer Way

10.6

W Mercer Way

10.8   10.5

SE 40th St.

Lake Washington

Mercer Island

Island Crest Way

Seward Park

Seward Park Loop

3.5

Groveland Park

Parkwood Natural Area

8.1

E Mercer Way

7.4

Pioneer Park

6.5

Clarke Beach Park

Beer Sheva Park

405

A cyclist leans into one of many curves on East Mercer Way.

11.9 Turn left onto Southeast 24th Street (go straight to visit Luther Burbank Park, about 0.25 miles).

12.2 Turn right onto 78th Avenue Southeast.

12.4 Turn left onto Southeast 22nd Street.

12.7 Turn right onto North Mercer Way.

13.0 Turn right onto 72nd Avenue Southeast in front of Roanoke Inn. Road becomes West Mercer Way.

13.4 Turn right into West I-90 Lid Park parking lot. End of ride.

RIDE INFORMATION

Local Events and Attractions

Summer Celebration: Fireworks, picnicking at Luther Burbank Park, second full weekend in July

Luther Burbank Park: 2040 84th Ave. Southeast, Mercer Island; mercergov .org/page.asp?navid=1138

Mercer Island Community Center: 8236 SE 24th St., Mercer Island; (206) 275-7609; mercergov.org/page.asp?NavID=1951

Restaurants

Roanoke Inn: 1825 72nd Ave. Southeast, Mercer Island; (206) 232-0800; facebook.com/roanokeinntavern

Restrooms

Mile 0.0: West I-90 Lid Park (portable toilet)
Mile 3.5: Groveland Park (restrooms, seasonal)
Mile 6.5: Clarke Beach Park (restrooms, seasonal)
Mile 11.9: Luther Burbank Park (restrooms)

Cougar Mountain–May Valley Loop

This "sufferfest" in the eastside Seattle suburbs takes you to a high overlook on Cougar Mountain that at one time served as an anti-aircraft gun emplacement and a missile base. Otherwise, it's a flat ride along valley roads with a stop in the historic mining and lumber village of Issaquah.

Start: Lake Boren Park in Newcastle

Length: 23.7 miles

Approximate riding time: 1.5 to 3 hours

Best bike: Road or hybrid

Terrain: Gently rolling, almost flat, until you start the 3-mile, 1,300-foot climb up the switchbacks to the top of Cougar Mountain.

Traffic and hazards: There is steady traffic on parts of the route, although those sections have bike lanes or shoulders. The rural valley road along May Creek has no shoulder, although traffic is light. The biggest hazard is getting sweat in your eyes as you climb the road to the summit of Cougar Mountain.

Things to see: Lake Boren; horses, llamas, and Highland cattle in pastures on May Valley Road; Issaquah fish hatchery and historic depot museum; Anti-Aircraft Peak at Cougar Mountain Park; coal-mining artifacts

Maps: *DeLorme Atlas & Gazetteer—Washington,* page 46; King County Bicycle Map, kingcounty.gov/transportation/kcdot/Roads/Bicycling.aspx

Getting there: By car: Take I-90 east to I-405 south. Instead of taking the ramp onto I-405, remain in the right merge lane and take the exit to Coal Creek Parkway Southeast, turning left at the stoplight. Continue about 3 miles on Coal Creek Parkway, turn right onto Southeast 84th Way, and then another right into the Lake Boren Park parking lot. **By bus:** The park is on the 114 and 240 Metro bus routes. GPS: N47 31.659' / W122 09.962'

THE RIDE

This route sets off on a winding valley road for several miles until it challenges you on a climb that may have you crying "Uncle!"—if you can catch your breath to speak. It's a good test of stamina that rewards riders with an amazing view from the summit of Cougar Mountain.

The ride starts at Lake Boren Park in the town of Newcastle. Founded as a remote coal-mining town on the slopes of Cougar Mountain in the 1870s, the town relocated to its present site and has become a tony residential area. Heading out on Coal Creek Parkway, you might be surprised how quickly the suburbs surrender to farms and rich pastureland after you turn onto Southeast May Valley Road.

The two-lane road hugs the edge of a valley at the base of Cougar and Squak mountains. You'll pass pastures and corrals with spirited thoroughbreds and quarter horses, as well as fenced fields with what I'd call living lawn ornaments—Highland cattle, llamas, and alpacas.

After crossing SR 900, which serves as a pass between Cougar and Squak mountains, you come to Squak Mountain State Park. Trails on old logging roads and coal-mine railroads crisscross the park, but bicycles aren't allowed beyond the parking lot. Taking the shoulder after turning left onto busy Issaquah-Hobart Road, you may soon get the impression there are huge birds soaring over you. These are the hang-gliders and paragliders who launch near the summit of Tiger Mountain State Park from Poo Poo Point. Although a lot of scatological references have been made about that name, it refers to the steam whistles that used to echo up and down the valley during the heyday of the logging industry. You pass the field where the gliders land on your right.

Bike Shops

Bicycle Center of Issaquah: 121 Front St. North, Issaquah; (425) 392-4588; bicyclecenter.biz
REI Issaquah: 735 NW Gilman Blvd., Issaquah; (425) 313-1660; rei.com/stores/issaquah.html

You arrive in old town Issaquah about halfway through the bike loop. Owing its existence to the coal-mining and logging industries, the town has preserved many of its late nineteenth-century downtown buildings. You'll find cafes and coffee shops on Front Street, or you might want to visit the Issaquah Depot Museum. After turning left onto Newport Way in the late summer or fall, you can watch Chinook and coho salmon trying to clear the dam at the Issaquah State Salmon Hatchery.

Heading out of town on Newport Way, turn left, pass Tibbets Valley Park (if you're running low on water, this is a good place to replenish) and then

Cougar Mountain: The Cold War Era

The Cold War came to roost at the summit of Cougar Mountain in a big way beginning in the 1950s. As the name suggests, Anti-Aircraft Peak housed 90mm Skymaster anti-aircraft guns beginning in 1953 to ward off any aerial attack on Seattle from the Soviet Union. About the time the schoolchildren in the towns below were practicing ducking under desks for civil defense alerts, a Nike missile defense system replaced the guns from 1957 until 1967. The site consisted of three radars, barracks, mess halls, electricity generators, and control rooms.

Farther downhill (check a park map for directions) was the actual missile site, today marked by a large meadow with a low sand "blast berm" at one end. The Nikes were stored beneath the meadow in two-story-deep reinforced vaults, but six could be hoisted onto above-ground launchers during active Cold War alerts.

About 125 men were billeted at the two sites, and the missile crews worked in underground bunkers. Explore the fringes of the open area, and you'll find old cement sidewalks and stairways and cement pads for the barracks and operation buildings.

King County acquired the 17-acre site from the feds and made it the cornerstone of the 300-acre Cougar Mountain Regional Wildland Park, which opened in 1983 as an urban wilderness overlooking Bellevue, Issaquah, and Newcastle.

new residential condo developments until you see a left turn for the Cougar Mountain Zoological Park on Southeast 54th Street.

Soon you're heading up a climb that might make you think you're in a stage of the Tour de France. An essentially flat ride until this point, the route heads up switchbacks through woods that provide welcome shade on a sunny day. Not far from the base is the Cougar Mountain Zoo, which opened as a mom-and-pop operation in 1972 with fifty-three animals. Today the zoo is home to alpacas, emus, lemurs, cranes, macaws, and reindeer, as well as its namesake, cougars.

Thinking about the zoo animals might take your mind off the five switchbacks you swerve around on the way up. When you turn right onto Southeast 60th Street, you might wonder why the road engineers ended the wooded switchbacks and forced riders straight up a bare hillside for the next mile. Turning left onto Southwest Cougar Mountain Drive, the uphill pedaling is nearly complete and you can enjoy the views toward Lake Sammamish over the rooftops of hillside mansions. Eventually the blacktop ends and the road surface is crushed rock in Cougar Mountain Regional Wildland Park. Cougars don't live here anymore, although black bears and bobcats do. There's a

This picnic table has a "million dollar view" from the summit of Cougar Mountain Park.

thick second-growth forest along the road and occasional trails (no bicycling allowed) cut across the road.

There are a couple of places to check out from the parking lot at the end of the road. To the left is a short trail to the so-called "Million Dollar View," which has been devalued to about $500,000 as trees gone wild obscure the panorama from the summit. To the right is Anti-Aircraft Peak, the summit of Cougar Mountain and part of Seattle's defense shield during the Cold War era.

King County acquired the 17-acre site from the feds and made it the cornerstone of the 300-acre Cougar Mountain Regional Wildland Park, which opened in 1983 as an urban wilderness overlooking Bellevue, Issaquah, and Newcastle.

Needless to say, the ride from here is all downhill. Check your brakes. Retrace your route to Southeast 60th Street, turn left, and left again onto 168th Place Southeast. Stay on this arterial as it twists and turns downhill past upscale hillside homes. A left turn onto Lakemont Boulevard Southeast begins another downhill run. A right curve in the road here marks the original Newcastle town site and another parking lot for trails (no bicycling) into Cougar Mountain Park.

A concrete wall standing in a field on your right is the sole remains of the Coal Creek Hotel, which was going strong one hundred years ago. Coal mining flourished here in the late nineteenth and early twentieth centuries, with more than 250 miners employed. The park has preserved several artifacts from the mining days, including a coal-mine entrance, with interpretive signs. Hikers are warned to stay on the paths in the park to avoid the occasional sinkhole into a mineshaft.

Cougar Mountain–May Valley Loop

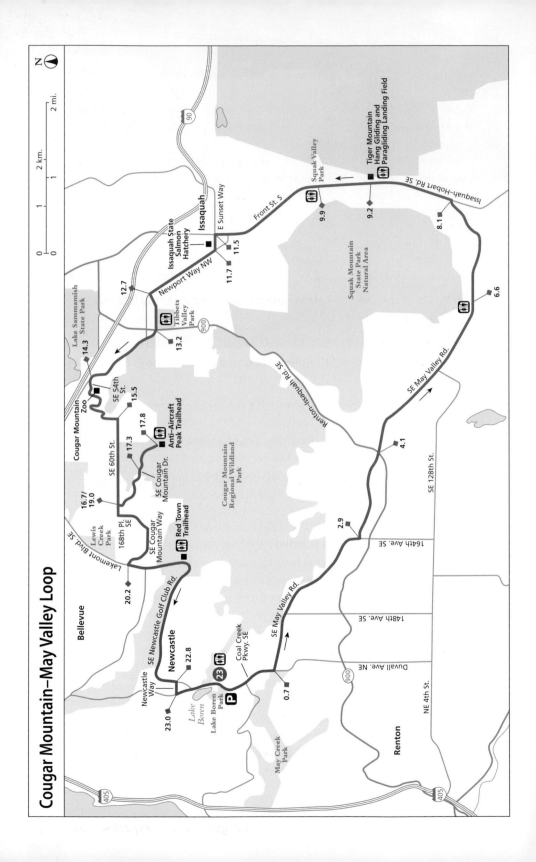

N

0   1   2 mi.

0   1   2 km.

Bellevue

Lake Sammamish State Park

Issaquah State Salmon Hatchery

Issaquah

E Sunset Way

Newport Way NW

11.5

11.7

12.7

Tibbets Valley Park

13.2

14.3

Cougar Mountain Zoo

SE 54th St.

15.5

SE 60th St.

17.3

17.8

Anti-Aircraft Peak Trailhead

Lewis Creek Park

16.7

19.0

168th Pl. SE

Lakemont Blvd. SE

SE Cougar Mountain Way

SE Cougar Mountain Dr.

Red Town Trailhead

20.2

SE Newcastle Golf Club Rd.

Newcastle

22.8

23

Newcastle Way

23.0

Lake Boren

Lake Boren Park

P

Coal Creek Pkwy. SE

405

405

Renton

NE 4th St.

Duvall Ave. NE

148th Ave. SE

164th Ave. SE

SE 128th St.

900

0.7

SE May Valley Rd.

2.9

4.1

SE May Valley Rd.

Renton–Issaquah Rd. SE

Cougar Mountain Regional Wildland Park

6.6

8.1

Squak Mountain State Park Natural Area

9.2

Tiger Mountain Hang Gliding and Paragliding Landing Field

9.9

Squak Valley Park

Front St. S

Issaquah–Hobart Rd. SE

900

May Creek Park

The route changes name to Southeast Coal Creek Newcastle Road at the right curve. Keep going to a stop sign and turn right downhill to Coal Creek Parkway. A vegetable stand at the corner provides juicy fruit and drinks during the season, and two nearby shopping centers offer groceries and coffee shops.

Turning left onto the Coal Creek Parkway bike lane, you'll return to Southeast 84th Way and the Lake Boren parking lot in less than a mile.

MILES & DIRECTIONS

0.0 Leaving the Lake Boren Park parking lot, turn left onto Southeast 84th Way. Begin the ride with a right turn onto the bike lane for Coal Creek Parkway Southeast.

0.7 Check for traffic and merge into the left-turn lane at the traffic signal for Southeast May Valley Road.

2.9 Road turns left, remaining Southeast May Valley Road.

4.1 Cross SR 900 at traffic signal. (This can be a long wait; there is a crosswalk button to activate the traffic light.)

6.6 Pass entrance to Squak Mountain State Park on left.

8.1 Turn left onto shoulder of Issaquah-Hobart Road Southeast.

9.2 Pass Tiger Mountain Hang Gliding and Paragliding Landing Field is on the right.

9.9 An unnamed park with pit toilets is located on left side of Issaquah Hobart Road Southeast; road becomes Front Street South.

11.5 Turn left onto West Sunset Way at the traffic signal.

11.6 Pass the Issaquah State Salmon Hatchery on your left.

11.7 Turn right onto Newport Way Northwest at the traffic light.

12.7 Turn left at traffic light; road remains Newport Way Northwest.

13.2 Pass through intersection of SR 900.

14.3 Turn left onto Southeast 54th Street; begin climb.

14.6 Ride past Cougar Mountain Zoo on the left.

15.5 Turn right onto Southeast 60th Street.

16.7 Turn left onto Southeast Cougar Mountain Drive.

17.3 Southeast Cougar Mountain Drive turns to packed gravel.

17.8 Park your bike at Cougar Mountain Park. When you're done exploring, retrace your route to Southeast 60th Street.

19.0 Turn left onto Southeast 60th Street, which curves to the left and becomes 168th Place Southeast.

20.2 Turn left onto Lakemont Boulevard Southeast.

20.9 Cougar Mountain Park hiking trails and exhibits on the left and right of road. Bicycles are not allowed on the trails.

22.8 Turn right onto Newcastle Way bike lane.

23.0 Turn left onto Coal Creek Parkway bike lane.

23.7 End of ride. Turn right onto Southeast 84th Way and take first right into Lake Boren parking lot.

RIDE INFORMATION

Local Events and Attractions:

Newcastle Days: September, Lake Boren Park, 13058 SE 84th Way, Newcastle

Salmon Days Festival: October; streets are closed throughout downtown Issaquah; salmondays.org

Issaquah Depot Museum: 150 1st Ave. Northeast, Issaquah; (425) 392-3500; issaquahhistory.org/issaquah-depot

Gilman Town Hall Museum: 165 SE Andrews St.; (425) 392-3500; issaquah history.org/gilman-town-hall-museum

Cougar Mountain Zoo: 19525 SE 54th St., Issaquah; (425) 392-6278; cougar mountainzoo.org

Squak Mountain State Park: parks.wa.gov/

Cougar Mountain Regional Wildland Park: kingcounty.gov/recreation/ parks/inventory/cougar.aspx

Restaurants

Issaquah Brewhouse: 35 W. Sunset Way, Issaquah; (425) 557-1911

XXX Root Beer Drive-in: Vintage drive-in with antique cars cruising the parking lot, 98 NE Gilman Blvd., Issaquah; (425) 392-1266; triplexrootbeer.com

Restrooms

Mile 0.0: Lake Boren Park (restrooms and water)

Mile 6.6: Squak Mountain Park (pit toilets)

Mile 9.2: Tiger Mountain Hang Gliding and Paragliding Landing Field (portable toilet)

Mile 11.6: Issaquah Fish Hatchery (restrooms and water)

Mile 12.9: Tibbets Valley Park (restrooms and water)

Mile 17.8: Cougar Mountain Regional Wildland Park (pit toilets)

Mile 20.9: Cougar Mountain Regional Wildland Park (portable toilets)

24

Sammamish River Trail

This route combines two flat, paved trails that are popular among bike commuters and recreational cyclists alike. The route follows the Sammamish River Trail from Redmond to Bothell and then picks up the Burke-Gilman Trail for 2 miles to the turnaround at Log Boom Park. Plentiful parks and restrooms mark the route.

Start: Marymoor Parking Lot K, Redmond

Length: 26.2 miles

Approximate riding time: 2 to 3 hours

Best bike: Road or hybrid bike

Terrain: Flat route on paved multi-use path

Traffic and hazards: Lots of different users—walkers, skaters, families on bikes, fast roadies—on this multiuse path. Watch for cross traffic in Bothell and Kenmore.

Things to see: Marymoor Park Velodrome, trailside sculpture in Redmond and Woodinville, waterfowl and raptors around the Sammamish River, Woodinville Wine Country, historic Bothell Landing Park, Lake Washington views at Tracy Owen Station at Log Boom Park

Maps: *DeLorme Atlas & Gazetteer—Washington,* page 46; King County Regional Trails Map, kingcounty.gov/recreation/parks/trails/regionaltrailssystem.aspx

Getting there: Heading east on SR 520 toward Redmond, take the West Lake Sammamish NE exit. Turn right at the bottom of the ramp, go 1 block, and turn left at the light into Marymoor Park at Northeast Marymoor Way. Entering the park, take the first or second left into parking lot K. (**Note:** $1 parking fee at Marymoor Park.) GPS: N47 39.890' / W122 07.283'

THE RIDE

It's no surprise that you'll find more bicyclists on the Sammamish River Trail than any other Seattle area trail except the Burke-Gilman. The King County Regional Trail is paved and represents 10.9 miles of flatness. It rolls through bicycle-friendly communities such as Redmond, and it connects to Seattle via the Burke-Gilman Trail to the west and to Issaquah via the East Lake Sammamish Trail to the south.

Even before daylight and after sunset during the winter months, you'll find Gortex-wearing commuters on lit-up bicycles heading to or from work in job centers at each end of the trail. During the day, recreational cyclists show up to ride this trail where all but one road crossing is an underpass, so they don't even have to slow down for crosswalks. Trail use reaches a peak on dry, sunny summer and fall weekends, when everyone from speedy cyclists in training to families with kids in training wheels share the trail with skaters, hikers, and dog walkers.

The Sammamish River Trail is the center link of the so-called "lakes to locks" trail system that today stretches for more than 40 miles from Issaquah through Redmond and onward to the canal locks in Seattle and beyond to the Puget Sound shoreline. That ride is essentially flat and passes regularly spaced public restrooms and water stops, as well as coffee shops and even a taproom that caters to cyclists.

This round-trip ride starts near the trail's end at Redmond's Marymoor Park. It continues through Woodinville, Bothell, and Kenmore to the turnaround at scenic Log Boom Park after the trail becomes the Burke-Gilman. If you forgot to pick up picnic supplies, there's a Subway concession next to the restrooms in the Marymoor parking lot. If you forgot to bring your bike, or don't have one, a Dasani Blue Bike rental stand near the Marymoor Velodrome lends out free Trek cruisers for the day.

Bike Shops

Bothell Ski & Bike: 8020 Bothell Way Northeast, Kenmore; (425) 486-3747; bikesale.com

Redmond Cycle: 7495 159th Place NE, Redmond; (425) 885-6363; redmondcycle.com

REI–Redmond: 7500 166th Ave. Northeast, Redmond; (425) 882-1158; rei.com/stores/redmond.html

Woodinville Bicycle: 13210 NE 175th St., Woodinville; (425) 483-6626; woodinvillebicycle.com

An artist painted these tree trunks aquamarine to highlight the problem of worldwide deforestation.

As you leave the parking lot and pick up the Sammamish River Trail, you'll soon realize that this river has been tamed. Originally more than 17 miles long, it meandered through a swampy valley between steep ridges on the east and west. In the past one hundred years, the river has been dredged and channeled several times, mostly recently in the 1960s. That Army Corps of Engineers project left a sterile, 12-mile ditch. Since then, this trail appeared on the levee, and the county improved fish habitat in the water and planted native trees and bushes on the riverbanks to attract birds and wildlife.

Heading north from Marymoor Park, you'll cross the Leary Way bridge (this is narrow and the approaches have sharp turns) and pass a couple of parks. You'll see carved totems and other "art in the park" sculptures as you ride past the Redmond city hall offices and commercial buildings. Keep your eyes on the trail, though, as this area can be crowded with lunchtime strollers.

About a mile ahead, you'll pass a pedestrian bridge that crosses the river. This heads over to the "soft-surface" trail for equestrians, mountain bikers, or anyone else. It runs between Leary Way and 116th Street, but may be extended in the future. Heading north, you might want to note the Northeast 145 Street crossing for your return trip. A ramp leads to a trail that crosses the river to Woodinville's "Wine Country," a collection of very bike-accessible wineries, as well as the Red Hook Brewery.

A popular midway stop is Woodinville's Wilmot Gateway Park, which features a welcoming pergola decorated with flowers, an expansive view to the river, and frequently used bike racks in front of the restrooms. From here the trail follows the river westward as it passes beneath a half-dozen highways and ramps that make up the complex I-405–SR 522 interchange. Shortly afterward, you'll pass the North Creek Trail on your right, which will one day become a major north-south trail connection to the Snohomish County Regional Interurban Trail in Everett.

The trail is interrupted by Woodinville Drive at mile 8.9. Follow the bike lane for a couple of blocks, then follow the signs for the trail across the street. Soon you'll cross a bridge and pass some houses with rickety docks where boats are moored. If you want to take a historic detour, turn right onto the bridge that crosses the river to Bothell Landing Park. Here you'll find some old structures from the town founded in the mid-1870s after the early Native American tribes were displaced. The park has an old one-room schoolhouse and an 1884 cabin in which the Beckstroms are said to have raised sixteen children.

Returning to the Sammamish River Trail, you'll pass over another bridge downstream, then ride through a short tunnel where the trail becomes the Burke-Gilman. This rail trail soon changes character, as it parallels commercial strip development along Bothell Way. Even more jarring is a grove of trees whose trunks have been painted a bright, aquamarine blue. An Australian artist included these trees in his Blue Tree project to draw attention to global deforestation.

The trail ducks below two busy intersections on underpasses as it enters Kenmore and the north shore of Lake Washington. This is a light industrial area, and home of a busy seaplane port. Use caution as you cross two streets on the Burke-Gilman before it reaches Tracy Owen Station at Log Boom Park, our halfway turnaround location. There's a newly built restroom here, drinking water, and views of Lake Washington and the seaplanes coming and going. It's another gathering point for cyclists to swap stories. For fast food, there are plenty of opportunities across Bothell Way. Enjoy the ride back to Marymoor Park.

MILES & DIRECTIONS

0.0 Turn left at the restrooms and Subway concession stand at the parking lot.

0.3 Stay right at junction, cross bridge, and turn right.

0.9 Go under the bridge, take the left fork and pedal up the ramp to cross Sammamish River on Leary Way bridge. Caution: Trail takes a sharp left turn coming off the bridge; watch for oncoming bikes.

1.0 Pass Dudley Carter and Luke McRedmond Parks on the right.

1.7 Ride carefully through a congested area adjacent to City Hall. There are lots of walkers here, especially at lunch hour.

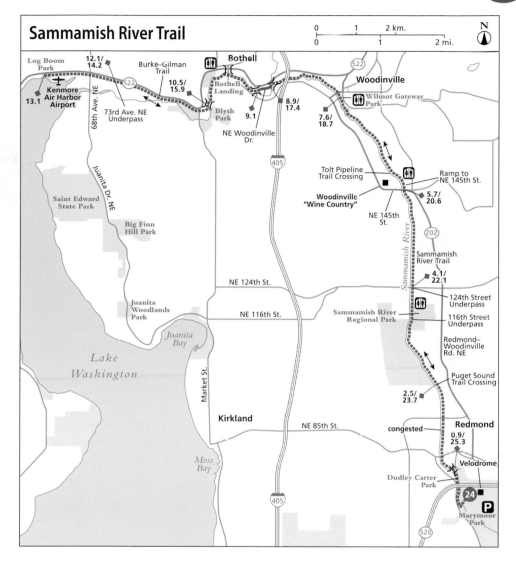

Sammamish River Trail

0 1 2 km.
0 1 2 mi.

N

2.5 Cross Puget Power Line Trail on right and pedestrian bridge on left that crosses the river to West of Sammamish River Trail and short continuation of the Puget Power Trail.

3.6 Pass exit and go beneath Northeast 116th Street overpass. Sixty Acres North and South soccer fields are here with lots of pedestrian traffic.

4.1 Pass exit and ride under Northeast 124th Street.

5.7 Ride under Northeast 145th Street. (Side trip: If you want to visit Red Hook Brewery and Woodinville Wine Country, turn right on the ramp after underpass and right again onto trail alongside Northeast 145th Street. Red Hook Brewery is on the right after crossing the bridge. A left turn before intersection leads to Chateau St. Michelle Winery and entertainment venue on Stimson Lane.)

5.9 Pass Northshore Athletic Fields.

6.0 Pass the Tolt Pipeline Trail junction on right.

7.6 Ride through Wilmot Gateway Park.

8.6 Pass underneath a busy interchange for I-405 and SR 522.

8.8 Cross a bridge and pass a trail junction with North Creek Trail on right; continue straight ahead.

8.9 Turn right onto bike lane along Woodinville Drive.

9.1 Look for continuation of trail on left side of road; carefully cross street.

9.2 Cross another bridge and take sharp right turn.

9.7 Cross 102nd Avenue Northeast; parking lot for trail.

9.9 Pass bridge on right over Sammamish River to Bothell Landing Park.

10.3 Take right fork across bridge; caution with sharp left immediately after bridge.

10.5 Sammamish Trail ends and Burke-Gilman Trail begins; enter a short tunnel.

12.1 Enter underpass for 73rd Avenue Northeast (192 Brewing Co.'s Lake Trail Taproom on left).

12.4 Enter underpass for 68th Avenue Northeast.

13.1 Arrive at Log Boom Park. Turn around and return to Marymoor Park.

15.9 After going through tunnel, follow the Sammamish River Trail to the left, instead of following trail straight ahead over bridge.

16.5 Pass bridge to Bothell Landing Park on left.

17.1 Turn left at trail junction and cross bridge.

17.5 Turn right at trail junction and cross bridge; North Creek Trail on the left.

20.6 Go beneath Northeast 145th Street (last chance for wineries).

25.3 Take the left lane and go over the bridge on Leary Way (do not pass under the bridge toward Redmond Town Center). Watch out for hairpin turn on other side.

Wine Country

A visit to the Woodinville Wine Country is a tasteful side trip for cyclists on the Sammamish River Trail whose refined taste buds require something besides an energy drink at mealtime. More than ninety wineries call Woodinville their home, and a side trail off the Sammamish River Trail leads cyclists to the front door of a few of them, as well as a regional brewer, Red Hook.

From the Sammamish River Trail, take the ramp on the north side of the Northeast 145th Street underpass up to the road, turn right onto a path adjacent to the road, and follow it across the river. Don't expect to see acres of vineyards here. The grapes for these wine makers are grown on the dry eastern side of the Cascade Mountains. These vintners take the juice, ferment it, blend it, and bottle it. Most have tasting rooms.

After crossing the river, look for Red Hook Brewery at the second driveway on the right. You can stop in the restaurant to taste the varieties of beer, or take one of the twice-daily tours.

Across Northeast 145th Street is a destination for any wine lover, the sumptuous grounds of the Chateau St. Michelle Winery. Housed in a French-style chateau, this was the first winery in the state. It offers free tours of its cellars and barrel-aging rooms, as well as free tastings.

The other trailside wineries are located either on Northeast 145th Street or around the corner on Redmond Woodinville Road Northeast.

- Chateau Ste. Michelle: 14111 NE 145th St., Woodinville; (425) 488-1133; ste-michelle.com
- Columbia Winery: 14030 NE 145th St., Woodinville; (425) 488-2776; columbiawinery.com//index.cfm
- Novelty Hill–Januik Winery: 14710 Woodinville Redmond Rd. Northeast, Woodinville; (425) 481-5502; noveltyhilljanuik.com
- Celaeno Winery: 15007 Woodinville Redmond Rd. Northeast, Woodinville; (425) 417-9725; celaenowinery.com
- Silver Lake Winery: 15029 Woodinville Redmond Rd. Northeast, Woodinville; (425) 485-2437; silverlakewinery.com

Other wineries are located farther north on Woodinville Redmond Road, or just east of the trail at the intersection of Northeast 145th Street and 148th Avenue Northeast. Check the map under "Visitor Info" at the Woodinville Wine Country website: woodinvillewinecountry.com.

25.9 Turn left at trail junction (right goes to West Lake Sammamish Parkway) and cross the bridge.

26.2 Trail ends at green restroom building and sandwich concession.

RIDE INFORMATION

Local Events and Attractions

Redmond Derby Days: Annual community festival surrounds the longest-running bicycle race in the nation. Held on a weekend in mid-July; redmond derbydays.com.

Concerts in the Park: Wednesday evenings throughout July at Wilmot Gateway Park, Woodinville

Flying Wheels Century: Largest century bike ride in Washington state begins and ends at Marymoor Park, early June; cascade.org/flying-wheels-summer-century

Sammamish River Trail: kingcounty.gov/recreation/parks/trails/regional trailssystem/sammamishriver.aspx

Burke-Gilman Trail: burkegilmantrail.org

Marymoor Park Velodrome: More than sixty race dates a year and seventy class days per year; Marymoor Park, Redmond, at Parking Lot I; velodrome.org/mva/

Dasani Blue Bikes: Free use of Trek cruiser-style bikes on Sammamish River Trail to registered riders; Marymoor Park, Redmond, at Parking Lot I; king county.gov/recreation/parks/inventory/marymoor/dasanibluebikes.aspx

Woodinville Wine Country: Seven wineries and one brewery are located along a trail extension across the river; Northeast 145th Street and Woodinville Redmond Road Northeast, map available under Tourist Info at woodinvillewinecountry.com.

The Blue Trees project: kondimopoulos.com/2011/11/blue-trees

Restaurants

192 Brewing Company, The Lake Trail Taproom: 7324 NE 175th St. (at North 73rd Avenue), Kenmore; (425) 424-2337; 192brewing.com

Red Hook Brewery, Woodinville Brewery & Forecasters Public House: 14300 NE 145th St., Woodinville; (425) 485-0761; redhook.com

Restrooms

Mile 0.0: Parking lot
Mile 3.9/22.3: Trailside (past soccer fields)
Mile 5.9/20.3: Trailside
Mile 7.6/18.7: Wilmot Gateway Park
Mile 9.9/16.4: Bothell Landing Park
Mile 13.1: Log Boom Park

Lake Sammamish Loop

This bike ride around Lake Sammamish offers more than a clockwise spin around a picturesque lake. It starts out as a flat jaunt on a rail trail that passes among expensive lakefront homes, climbs to lake overlooks from the hills above, and ends with a screaming downhill run to the start.

Start: Marymoor Parking Lot K, Redmond

Length: 23.5 miles

Approximate riding time: 2 to 3 hours

Best bike: Road or hybrid

Terrain: First half is on level rail trail; second half climbs into hills overlooking the lake.

Traffic and hazards: Watch for pedestrians on trails; bike lanes, wide shoulders, or sidewalks available on busy roads; others are low-traffic residential streets.

Things to see: Wildlife along Lake Sammamish shoreline; Marymoor Velodrome; a host of city, county, and state parks

Maps: King County Regional Bicycle Map, available in bike stores and online, kingcounty.gov/transportation/kcdot/Roads/Bicycling.aspx; Bicycling in Bellevue Map, available in bike stores, trail kiosks, and online, bellevuewa.gov/pdf/Transportation/bike_map_2009.pdf; *DeLorme Atlas & Gazetteer—Washington,* page 46

Getting there: Heading east on SR 520 toward Redmond, take the West Lake Sammamish Northeast exit. Turn right at the bottom of the ramp, go 1 block, and turn left at the light into Marymoor Park at Northeast Marymoor Way. Entering the park, take the first left into parking lot K. (**Note:** Parking costs $1 at Marymoor Park.) GPS: N47 39.890' / W122 07.283'

THE RIDE

Bicyclists love to ride around lakes. Large or small, at sea level or high in the mountains, there's something about large bodies of water surrounded by land that draws pedalers. Maybe it's the scenery. Or maybe it's the fact that you can't get lost as long as you travel in either a clockwise or counter-clockwise direction. Keep the lake either to your left or your right and you should return to your starting point.

Lake Sammamish is no different. A smaller twin to Lake Washington, the 7-mile glacially formed lake has been a longtime destination for bicyclists who used East and West Lake Sammamish Boulevards to encircle the lake. The loop became more popular with the opening of a gravel rail trail on the eastern shoreline in 2006.

Expect more bike commuters and recreational cyclists in the future. Development spurred by Microsoft and other tech companies has brought more potential cyclists to the eastern suburbs, and King County is replacing that gravel path with a preferable hard, blacktop surface. Meanwhile, the city of Bellevue has long-range plans to build a multipurpose trail along West Lake Sammamish Boulevard. Because of dangerous conditions on that road now, and the uncertain timing of construction in the future, this loop ride follows a route through hills west of the lake.

Starting at the parking lot on the west side of Redmond's Marymoor Park, the route follows the Marymoor Connector Trail that rolls for 1.5 miles through the park. Opened in 2009, the trail completed an off-road bicycling link from Seattle to Issaquah. Less than a mile from the trailhead is the entrance to the Marymoor Velodrome. Opened in 1975, the state's only bicycle track is home to several former Olympic medal winners. Track cyclists compete here four nights a week during the season, and you'll likely see someone training there whenever you visit.

The park trail crosses a finger of lake wetlands on a causeway, and then joins the East Lake Sammamish Trail. The trail connects Redmond and Issaquah along the old rail bed of the Burlington Northern Santa Fe Railway. The railroad abandoned the lakeside route in 1996, and the county

Bike Shops

Bicycle Center of Issaquah: 121 Front St. North, Issaquah; (425) 392-4588; bicyclecenter.biz
Redmond Cycle: 7495 159th Place NE, Redmond; (425) 885-6363; redmondcycle.com
REI–Issaquah: 735 NW Gilman Blvd., Issaquah; (425) 313-1660; rei.com/stores/issaquah.html
REI–Redmond: 7500 166th Ave. Northeast, Redmond; (425) 882-1158; rei.com/stores/redmond.html

announced its plans to build a rail trail. The idea didn't sit well with many adjoining property owners, who filed a lawsuit. Eventually a federal judge ruled that a trail was an appropriate use, and a crushed-rock trail opened in 2006.

This northern section of trail was the first to be widened and paved, followed by a section in Issaquah in 2013. Plans call for the seven or eight miles in between to be paved as well. If trail crews are paving during your ride, expect to detour onto the wide shoulder of East Lake Sammamish Boulevard as you continue south.

Your first unobstructed views of the lake emerge after passing the lakeside woods at the north end. Scan the snags for bald eagles or other large

Cascade Bicycle Club

Whenever talk rolls around to bicycling in the Seattle area, more than likely the Cascade Bicycle Club will be mentioned. At 15,000 members, the nonprofit is the largest bicycling club in the United States. Its paid staff and thousands of volunteers are involved in all facets of bicycling recreation, advocacy, and education. Volunteers lead some 1,300 free rides per year for anyone wearing a bicycle helmet, regardless of membership status.

The club offers seven major bicycling events annually. The aptly named Chilly Hilly bike ride around Bainbridge Island in February traditionally kicks off the recreational bicycle season in Seattle. The club's Seattle-to-Portland Bicycle Classic established in 1979 is the largest ride of the year and a rite of passage for Pacific Northwest bicyclists. The event draws 10,000 folks who ride 200 miles in one or two days to Portland, Oregon. This loop ride around Lake Sammamish is based on an option in its Flying Wheels event held every summer.

The club continuously advocates at city hall and the state capitol for better bicycling conditions on the streets and better laws to protect bicyclists. Elected officials who don't pay heed can find themselves left off the Cascade's list of endorsements come election day.

A sister organization, Cascade Bicycle Club Education Foundation, educates and consults with area agencies on how to create bicycle-friendly businesses and communities. It also hosts safe-cycling classes for children and adults, promotes bicycle commuting to businesses, and works on Safe Routes to Schools programs.

One of the foundation's most high-profile programs is the Major Taylor Project, a youth cycling program that incorporates fitness, bicycle maintenance, healthy living, and personal development.

The Cascade Bicycle Club's website is cascade.org.

Painted portraits decorate a trailside fence on East Lake Sammamish Trail.

birds of prey that snack on fish or critters in the marshes. Herons are often feeding near shore, and beavers seem to make a nuisance of themselves in locations around the lake.

After early settlement in the 1800s, Lake Sammamish provided a transportation route to Seattle and the Puget Sound. Coal, lumber, or other local resources were loaded on flat-bottomed boats that slowly made their way north into the twisting Sammamish River channel, which led to Lake Washington.

The lake commerce gave rise to a number of small towns along the shore. The current location of Sammamish Landing Park, for instance, is in the vicinity of Adelaide. Weber Point and Inglewood are other towns whose names survive on maps today. By far the largest community on this side of the lake was Monohon, located at the crossing of Southeast 33rd Street. The population had grown to 300 by 1925 when a lumber-mill fire wiped out the entire town.

Today, the trail passes a nearly uninterrupted series of lakefront homes with expansive views of the lake as far south as the entrance to Lake Sammamish State Park. If you want to avoid traffic and hills, this is a good place to return to Marymoor Park for a nearly 20-mile round-trip ride. A mile later, the loop turns right onto a bike lane at Southeast 56th Street (it becomes Northwest Sammamish Road) in a busy retail-commercial district.

If you're hungry, restaurants and coffee shops are located in the shopping center across Northwest Sammamish Road at the 10th Avenue Northwest intersection. The Pickering Farm Barn, an 1878 vintage dairy barn listed on the National Register of Historic Places, is next to the shopping center and hosts a farmers' market in season.

The route follows the base of the lake on West Lake Sammamish Parkway Southeast as it heads west toward Bellevue. As it pulls away from the lake, a slow but steady climb continues for about eight miles. You'll get a good view of Lake Sammamish, with Mount Baker in the distance, as you climb Southeast Newport Way. Look for a break in the trees that marks the entrance to an arched pedestrian bridge over I-90. Go easy on the other side, as it spirals steeply down to a 180-degree turn to continue west toward Bellevue.

As the I-90 Trail ends at Southeast Eastgate Way, you're deposited onto low-traffic residential side streets most of the way back to Marymoor Park. There are several parks located along this route. One of the most striking is the 80-acre Weowna Park on 168th Avenue Southeast. Its old-growth forest somehow escaped the logging in the early 1900s.

A fun stop on a hot day is Crossroads Park, at the corner of 164th Avenue Northeast and 8th Street Northeast, which features a water spray playground. A block away at 156th Avenue Northeast and 8th Street is Crossroads Mall, whose food court features many ethnic foods that reflect the diversity of this community.

Crossroads Park also marks the high point of this ride through the bluffs west of Lake Sammamish. Once the descent starts on Northeast 30th Street, it's a screaming 4-mile downhill to Marymoor. Just make sure your brakes have plenty of stopping power to negotiate stop signs at the bottoms of hills.

MILES & DIRECTIONS

0.0 Exit parking lot and turn left onto a paved trail—Marymoor Connector.

0.3 Pass entrance to Marymoor Velodrome on the left.

0.8 Cross Marymoor Park Road on trail.

1.3 Turn right at junction of Marymoor Connector Trail with East Lake Sammamish Trail.

1.9 Pass access to East Lake Sammamish Boulevard on the left. Pavement ends and crushed-rock surface begins.

2.3 Pass by Sammamish Landing Park on the right.

4.4 Access to East Lake Sammamish Boulevard intersection with Northeast Inglewood Hill Road.

9.0 Access to East Lake Sammamish Boulevard via 212th Way Southeast.

9.4 Paved portion of East Lake Sammamish Trail begins at Southeast 43rd Way.

9.7 Pass entrance to Lake Sammamish State Park boat launch area.

10.3 Cross Southeast 51st Street with the crossing signal.

10.7 Turn right onto Southeast 56th Street bike lane (trail continues straight to Northwest Gilman Boulevard).

11.0 Veer off street onto a wide sidewalk as bike lane ends; keep to the left as sidewalk splits ahead.

11.4 Bear to the right as sidewalk forks and pick up bike lane on Northwest Sammamish Road.

11.8 Entrance to Lake Sammamish State Park. Northwest Sammamish Road bears right and becomes West Lake Sammamish Parkway Southeast.

13.4 Pass entrance to Timberlake Park.

13.7 Enter roundabout in left lane, go three-fourths of the way (third right), and take 180th Avenue Southeast. Pass underneath I-90 overpass.

14.1 Turn right onto Southeast Newport Way.

14.9 Turn right onto short path that leads to pedestrian bridge over I-90. Use caution on the curving descent. At the base of the ramp make a 180-degree turn in the other direction and proceed on the I-90 Bike Path.

15.9 The trail ends; turn left onto Southeast Eastgate Way.

16.0 Turn right onto 161st Avenue Southeast.

16.1 Pass entrance to Spiritridge Park.

16.8 Turn right onto Southeast 24th Street. Bear left as it becomes 168th Avenue Southeast.

17.4 Pass by entrance to Weowna Park. Follow road to the left as it becomes Southeast 14th Street.

17.9 Turn right onto 164th Avenue Southeast. Pass Lake Hills Park.

19.2 Cross Northeast 8th Street and pass the Crossroads Park and water-spray playground on the left.

20.6 Turn right onto Northeast 30th Street. Pass by Ardmore Park on the right.

21.1 Turn left onto bike lanes on 172nd Avenue Northeast.

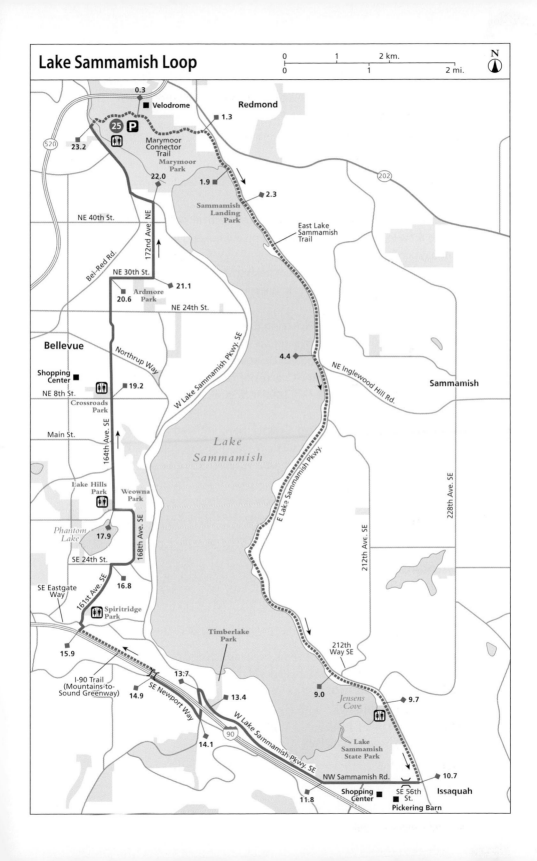

Lake Sammamish Loop

0   1   2 km.

0   1   2 mi.

N

Redmond

0.3

■ Velodrome

1.3

520

25 P

23.2

Marymoor Connector Trail

Marymoor Park

22.0

1.9 ■

2.3

Sammamish Landing Park

East Lake Sammamish Trail

NE 40th St.

Bel-Red Rd.

172nd Ave. NE

NE 30th St.

21.1

20.6   Ardmore Park

NE 24th St.

4.4

NE Inglewood Hill Rd.

Sammamish

Bellevue

Northrup Way

Shopping Center

NE 8th St.

19.2

Crossroads Park

164th Ave. SE

Main St.

W Lake Sammamish Pkwy SE

Lake Sammamish

228th Ave. SE

Lake Hills Park

Weowna Park

Phantom Lake

17.9

168th Ave. SE

SE 24th St.

E Lake Sammamish Pkwy.

212th Ave. SE

SE Eastgate Way

161st Ave. SE

16.8

Spiritridge Park

15.9

I-90 Trail (Mountains-to-Sound Greenway)

14.9

13.7

SE Newport Way

13.4

9.0   *Jensens Cove*   9.7

212th Way SE

Timberlake Park

90

W Lake Sammamish Pkwy. SE

14.1

Lake Sammamish State Park

10.7

NW Sammamish Rd.

11.8   Shopping Center

SE 56th St.

Pickering Barn

Issaquah

202

22.0 Turn left onto West Lake Sammamish Parkway bike lane.

23.2 Turn right into Marymoor Park at Northeast Marymoor Way.

23.4 Turn left at first parking lot, Parking Lot K.

23.5 End of ride.

RIDE INFORMATION

Local Events and Attractions

Redmond Derby Days: Annual community festival surrounds the longest-running bicycle race in the nation. Held on a weekend in mid-July; redmond derbydays.com.

Bellevue Strawberry Festival: Lots of fresh strawberries, other food, entertainment; late June in Crossroads Park, Bellevue; bellevuestrawberryfestival.org/Home.asp

Issaquah Farmers' Market at Pickering Barn: Farm-fresh foods, food vendors, entertainment, activities for kids; Saturday in Apr through Sept, Pickering Barn, 1730 10th Ave. Northwest, Issaquah; ci.issaquah.wa.us/index.aspx?NID=778

Lake Sammamish State Park: 512 acres of parkland with more than 1 mile of waterfront on Lake Sammamish; 2000 NW Sammamish State Park, Issaquah; parks.wa.gov/

Marymoor Park: 640-acre King County park with athletic fields, concert venue, climbing wall, canoeing; 6046 W. Lake Sammamish Park Northeast, Redmond; kingcounty.gov/recreation/parks/inventory/marymoor.aspx

Restaurants

Crossroads Mall food court: Ethnic foods, 15600 NE 8th St., Bellevue; cross roadsbellevue.com

Restrooms

Mile 0.0: Marymoor Park

Mile 1.9: Portable toilet on trail

Mile 2.3: Portable toilet on trail

Mile 9.4: Portable toilet on trail

Mile 9.7: Lake Sammamish State Park boat launch

Mile 11.8: Lake Sammamish State Park via main entrance

Mile 13.4: Timberlake Park

Mile 16.1: Spiritridge Park

Mile 17.9: Lake Hills Park

Mile 19.2: Crossroads State Park

Saint Edward State Park and Big Finn Hill Park

These two adjoining state and county parks provide a woodsy suburban setting for mountain bikers to improve their riding abilities. Novice mountain-bike riders can test their skills on some forgiving trails at Saint Edward State Park, home to an abandoned 1920s-era seminary. As confidence grows, they can venture onto more technical single track that meanders through the forests at Big Finn Hill Park.

Start: Saint Edward State Park in Kenmore or Big Finn Hill Park in Kirkland

Length: 9.0 miles of bike routes on a total 16 miles of single track in both parks

Approximate riding time: 1 to 3 hours

Best bike: Mountain bike

Terrain: Rolling terrain with a few notable climbs. The trail is hard-packed dirt, maintained so that most areas can handle a few days of rain without becoming muddy. Bikers might want to consider long pants to prevent getting raked by blackberry bush thorns in areas away from dense forest canopy.

Traffic and hazards: Watch for traffic when crossing Juanita Drive Northeast. The park trails are a popular destination for people hiking and walking dogs.

Things to see: Saint Edward Seminary, Lake Washington shoreline, Bastyr University campus, beaver pond

Maps: Saint Edward State Park and Big Finn Hill Park trail maps at your .kingcounty.gov/ftp/gis/Web/VMC/recreation/BCT_BigFinnHill_brochure.pdf; *DeLorme Atlas & Gazetteer—Washington,* page 46

Getting there: **By car:** From northbound or southbound I-405, take exit 20A and turn west onto Northeast 116th Street. Go 1.5 miles to intersection, where the road becomes Juanita Drive Northeast. Continue 3 miles to reach Big Finn Hill Park on the right; go another 1 mile to Saint Edward State Park on the left (follow signs for parking). From Seattle, travel north on Lake City Way Northeast, which becomes Bothell Way Northeast. Turn right on 68th Avenue Northeast, which becomes Juanita Drive Northeast, and arrive at Saint Edward State Park on the right at about 1.7 miles; Big Finn Hill Park is another mile down Juanita Drive Northeast on the left. (**Note:** A Discover Pass is required for Saint Edward State Park; parking at Big Finn Hill Park is free.) **By bus:** Metro routes 234, 244, and 935 serve Saint Edward State Park; 230 and 935 serve the vicinity of Big Finn Hill Park. GPS: St. Edward State Park, N47 43.978' / W122 15.350'; Big Finn Hill Park, N47 43.457' / W122 14.283'

THE RIDE

Saint Edward State Park and Big Finn Hill Park are popular close-by destinations for mountain bikers who want to improve their cross-country skills by finding increasingly challenging single-track routes through the woods.

The trails and locations of the two parks are so intertwined that the two park names are interchangeable among mountain bikers in the Seattle area. You can start in one and ride to the other by merely crossing a couple of streets. That's why they've been included here together. Let's try to unravel the two.

Saint Edward State Park, 316 acres overlooking Lake Washington, was owned by the Roman Catholic Archdiocese of Seattle from the 1920s to 1977, when the state acquired it. The imposing, four-story Catholic seminary built in the 1920s still stands on a hilltop and is listed on the National Register of Historic Places. The Washington State Ghost Society is greatly interested in the abandoned building.

Bastyr University, a college devoted to natural health arts and sciences, owns a small portion of the former archdiocese property and shares the entrance with the park. A Discover Pass is required at the park, and parking can get congested on sunny weekends with picnic grounds, baseball and soccer fields, and a big playground.

A forest, last logged in the 1920s, surrounds the developed areas of the park. The trails that wind between those Douglas fir, western red cedar, hemlock, and big-leaf maples draw mountain bikers and hikers alike. A map available at a kiosk in front of the administration building, the old gymnasium, shows which trails mountain bikers can use. Be kind and stay off trails where biking is prohibited.

The mountain-bike trails north of the entrance road—Entrance, Volunteer, Juanita, and Arrowhead Trails—are generally smooth and a good place to warm up. Green mountain bikers will be comfortable testing themselves here to practice crossing bridges, making tight turns while pedaling up or down short hills, and feeling the rhythm of slightly banked turns. The 1.2-mile loop can be ridden in either direction; just watch out for hikers.

Bike Shops

Bothell Ski and Bike: 8020 Bothell Way Northeast, Kenmore; (425) 486-3747; bikesale.com
Kirkland Bicycle: 208 Kirkland Ave., Kirkland; (425) 828-3800; kirklandbikes.com
Kirkland Cycle: 201 S. 6th St., Kirkland; (425) 241-2026; kirklandcycle.com

You can continue the loop ride by following a trail marked Storage Sheds that follows the Perimeter Trail to Seminary Trail and ends at the scenic undeveloped beach on Lake Washington. Remember, other trails in this area are closed to bikes so you'll have to slog your way back up this steep hill.

If you're ready for more challenges, then it's time to head to Big Finn Hill Park, 220 acres operated by King County about a mile to the south. The county park is split by Juanita Drive Northeast. On the east are parking lots for more than 200 cars, seasonal restrooms (portable toilets in the winter), athletic fields, and some trails. The west side is strictly forests and trails.

Mountain bikers have been sharing these trails with hikers and dog walkers since the 1990s. Rogue trails and technical structures have popped up over the years, prompting the parks department, a neighborhood association, and the Evergreen Mountain Bike Alliance to work on restoring some order in the forest. The group seeks to improve trail maintenance, map out perimeter routes, and preserve the forest by limiting the spread of rogue trails. Although the trails will be open to everyone, some will be recommended for walkers and joggers, while others will be geared to mountain bikers. The partners already have built a wooden trail bridge over Denny Creek to improve a muddy trail crossing that filled the creek with sediment downstream.

Mountain bikers can park their vehicles at Big Finn Hill Park and ride several loops described below, or use the paths to ride up to Saint Edward State Park.

The Beaver Pond Loop (1.2 miles) is one of the easiest on the eastside. It starts at the seasonal restroom facility located between the baseball and soccer field. This loop goes over a short bridge then skirts an ever-growing beaver pond. You can see where the pond has obliterated an old trail. This route

Mountain bikers can coast downhill to Lake Washington, but face a steep return climb.

actually leaves the park and takes a right turn onto a sidewalk on 84th Avenue Northeast for a short distance before re-entering the park and taking the high ground around the south side of the pond. After passing a rear entrance to the athletic fields at Finn Hill Middle School, the trail comes to a dirt hillside with man-made embankments, then heads left to the wooden bridge over Denny Creek. An uphill climb returns to the start.

A shorter loop (0.7 miles), dubbed the Northside Loop, starts on a path across the entrance road from the soccer field. It climbs through the woods to the back of some houses on Northeast 140th Street. Continuing left, mountain bikers ride a bluff overlooking Juanita Drive, then return via an exciting downhill cruise around some sharp bends.

The Westside Loop is a challenging and fun 2-mile tour of the 135 acres of woodland across the road. It starts at the restrooms and ducks into the woods at the far end of the soccer field. This route crosses Juanita Drive and turns left along the shoulder to a path on the right just before a guardrail. A short climb leads to a left turn that begins a clockwise route around the perimeter of this forest. Keep turning left at trail junctions to stay on the main loop, as the right turns mostly head into the labyrinth of trails that crisscross the woods. These are worth exploring later to improve such skills as jumping, turning, and balance. Narrow paths that branch left connect to some adjoining neighborhoods.

Connector trails link Big Finn Hill with Saint Edward State Park so you can visit both without getting into your car. From Big Finn Hill Park, the connector route starts at a kiosk at the north end of the Westside Loop and crosses Northeast 138th Place and Holmes Point Drive Northeast on its way to the entrance at Saint Edward Park. The right fork is more direct, but still features some interesting turns and a narrow bridge—actually a wide plank—over a muddy depression. The left fork dips to the edge of some wetlands and crosses a crazy steep ravine named Gravity Shoot where you can see if your downhill speed gives you enough momentum to make it up the other side.

This last is one of the many challenges you'll encounter in the two parks and demonstrates why mountain bikers keep coming back as their skills improve.

MILES & DIRECTIONS

Saint Edward Loop (3.1 miles)

0.0 Start at Arrowhead Trail, located on Saint Edward State Park Access Road where the entrance road splits into driveways for various parking lots. Head back toward the entrance with the access road on your right.

0.2 At trail junction, take right path onto Volunteer Trail, then go left where it splits.

0.7 Arriving at park entrance, veer left onto Juanita Trail, a curvy route along Juanita Drive.

1.1 Make a sharp left at hairpin turn onto Arrowhead Trail. Stay on this wide trail.

1.4 Turn right onto a trail marked Storage Sheds about 50 feet after passing the junction with Volunteer Trail. There are a couple of hills.

1.6   Cross the parking lot to Perimeter Trail on the other side; it follows the right edge of the field.

1.8   Follow the Perimeter Trail by taking a hard right.

1.9   Turn right onto Seminary Trail for 0.5 mile downhill to the Lake Washington beach. (A left turn avoids a steep uphill return climb.)

2.4   Arrive at pit toilets and then the beach. The Beach and South Ridge Trails are not open to bicycles. Retrace your route back uphill.

2.9   Arrive at Perimeter Trail; turn left to follow trail along edge of field.

3.0   Turn right at parking lot and continue to exit to return to trailhead.

3.1   Arrive at trailhead. End of loop.

Beaver Pond Loop (1.2 miles, Big Finn Hill Park)

0.0   Start at seasonal restrooms between baseball field and soccer field near Juanita Drive park entrance. Pass through gate that blocks entrance road.

0.1   Turn right onto gravel trail, take the first left over a low hill, and then left at T intersection.

0.2   Cross a wooden bridge and take immediate left. The trail follows creek on the left and beaver pond on the right.

0.5   After short climb, take side trail left and exit park and turn right onto sidewalk along 84th Avenue Northeast.

0.6   Turn right onto path that returns to park through opening in the fence. This route has climbs but stays out of beaver pond.

0.8   Arrive at rear entrance to Finn Hill Middle School athletic fields. Follow trail right to steep dirt hillside; pick your line and turn left at the bottom.

1.0   Cross wooden bridge over Denny Creek, then take right fork uphill to the start at parking lot.

1.2   End of loop.

Northside Loop (0.7 miles, Big Finn Hill Park)

0.0   Start at trailhead at edge of woods across the park entrance road from the soccer field. Turn left onto main trail, then turn right at first junction to head uphill, bearing left after cresting the hill.

0.1   Take the right junction, which goes uphill.

0.2   Follow trail left before it arrives at entrance to Northeast 140th Street.

0.4   Follow main track and turn left at apartment complex on your right. Keep Juanita Drive to your right.

Saint Edward State Park and Big Finn Hill Park

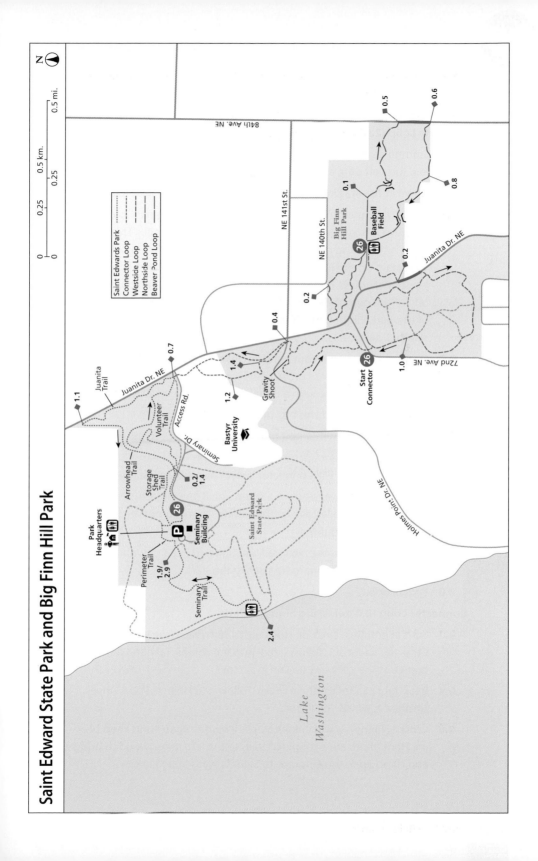

0.5 Take the left fork (right goes to Juanita Drive) and then a right fork that makes a twisting downhill run back to the trailhead.

0.7 End of loop.

Westside Loop (2.0 miles, Big Finn Hill Park)

0.0 Starting at seasonal restrooms, ride along right side of soccer field and turn left onto a trail at the far end.

0.2 Arrive at Juanita Drive, cross road, and turn left onto far shoulder.

0.3 Turn right onto dirt path just before guardrail begins. Go uphill and turn left at a well-worn trail at the top of the hill. (This loop takes a clockwise route around the west side of Big Finn Hill Park. To remain on the loop, continue taking the left branches at trail junctions, unless it looks like the left is a spur trail heading into one of the neighborhoods that border the south and west sides of the park. Right turns head into a multitude of single-track and skill-building trails.)

0.7 Turn right to stay on main trail and bear left at the next fork. (The left branch ends in a dense grove of evergreens along Northeast 132nd Street and passes through a bog before returning to Westside Loop.)

0.8 Take the right fork at this trail junction.

1.0 Pass a fallen log on the right that's used for balance training.

1.2 Take right fork at entrance kiosk. (Left crosses Northeast 138th Place and joins Big Finn Hill Connector Loop.) Then take a left fork.

1.4 Take the right fork and attack a steep uphill (the left returns to Juanita Drive). Take the left fork at the summit (some jumps are located in a clearing on the right).

1.6 Take a sharp left at the next trail junction and head downhill to Juanita Drive, retracing your route back to the start.

2.0 End of loop.

Connector Loop (2.0 miles, Big Finn Hill Park)

0.0 Start at entrance kiosk on Northeast 138th Place (see Westside Loop). Cross the street and follow a trail into the woods. Take the right branch at the split and stay on main trail.

0.4 Bear right at a fork in the trail and follow it to Holmes Point Drive Northeast, which you'll cross.

0.6 Cross a skinny—a wide plank across a muddy spot—and keep bearing right (there are a couple of trails to the left), cross wooden bridge, and climb up to the entrance to Saint Edward State Park.

0.8 Cross the access road to the trail junction of Entrance and Volunteer Trails at the state park. Retrace your route.

0.9 Make a sharp right turn downhill immediately after crossing the wooden bridge. A wooden walkway on the right returns to Bastyr University, so bear left and use caution among the tree roots at the edge of a wetlands.

1.2 Turn left, pedal up a steep hill

1.4 Join the main trail and veer right, cross Holmes Point Drive Northeast, then take a right fork.

1.5 Arrive at steep ravine. You can either take the steepest route on a wide trail directly in front of you, a slightly less steep trail to the right, or a trail on the left that completely skips the ravine and meets the main trail farther south. If you cross the ravine, continue straight along a bluff that's high above Holmes Point Drive.

1.8 Bear right at trail junction and ignore trail spurs to the left and right.

2.0 Arrive at kiosk. End of ride.

RIDE INFORMATION

Local Events and Attractions

Saint Edward State Park–Kenmore Summer Concert Series: Thursday nights in July and August; kenmorewa.gov/events

Bastyr University: Free tours of medicinal herb garden; annual Herb and Food Fair in late May or early June; bastyr.edu

Restaurants

Sandwich shops and grocery-store deli in shopping center at Northeast 141st Street and Juanita Drive.

Restrooms

Mile 1.6: Saint Edward State Park, administration offices (old gymnasium)

Mile 2.4: Saint Edward Loop, at Lake Washington beach (pit toilets)

Big Finn Hill Park: Seasonal restrooms between soccer and baseball fields (portable toilets in winter near gate)

Thrilla in Woodinvilla Loop

The Thrilla is a strenuous, all-season bike route to help mountain bikers stay in shape in the rainy season when local trails are muddy or closed. There's no single-track technical riding like you'd find throughout the forest of the Pacific Northwest. What you do find are some gut-busting hills, some white-knuckle descents, and plenty of soft surface trails in a few parklike settings.

Start: Parking lot on 145th Street Northeast adjacent to Sammamish River Trail

Length: 18.6 miles

Approximate riding time: 2 to 3 hours

Best bike: Mountain bike

Terrain: Hilly. The route is mostly dirt, wood chips, and gravel, although some rural roads.

Traffic and hazards: Most of the bike route is off-road; the short on-road stretch has very little traffic. Use care at road crossings and make sure your brakes are in good working order for steep descents.

Things to see: Sammamish River Trail, Redmond Watershed Preserve, views from open landscapes around hilltops in utility corridors

Maps: Other options for Thrilla ride, trails.evergreenmtb.org/wiki/Trail:Thrilla_Route; *DeLorme Atlas & Gazetteer—Washington,* page 46

Getting there: By car: From I-405, take exit 20 (Totem Lake Mall) to Northeast 124th Street. Go east less than a mile and make a slight left onto 132nd Place Northeast. Continue north for 1.3 miles and turn right onto Northeast 143rd Place. Follow the arterial to the east as it becomes Northeast 145th Street (SR 202) and follow it across the Sammamish River to a traffic circle. Go three-quarters of the way around the circle and exit at Village Road, which leads to the gravel parking lot. GPS: N47 43.991' / W122 08.662'

THE RIDE

You'll need your "stump-puller" gear to get up some of the steeps on the Thrilla in Woodinvilla ride, as well as a good set of brakes for a dizzying descent heading home.

This route gravitates toward utility rights of way and wooded park trails that remain hidden from dense residential development in the Union Hill–Novelty Hill area east of the Sammamish River.

The Evergreen Mountain Bike Alliance holds weekly evening Thrilla training rides on various routes throughout the ridges east and west of the Sammamish River in this area. Many start at the Red Hook Brewery just west of the Sammamish River Trail on 145th Street Northeast. At 18.6 miles, this would be one of the shortest, putting it in the "French Vanilla Thrilla" category. Longer ones are nearly 40 miles. The route also uses much of mid-January's Stinky Spoke mountain-bike ride.

After opening with a level 3.3-mile ride along the Sammamish River Trail, the route turns left onto the soft-surface Power Line Trail. It's marked with a sign and a kiosk, as well as an array of high-voltage transmission lines that the Puget Sound Power and Light Company stretched above your head to help you find your way. Those power lines, installed in the mid-1960s, will be your waymark for the next eight or nine miles. Also look for a small badge with a "T" inside of it on posts or poles. This clarifies the direction of the Thrilla trail at some confusing intersections.

About halfway up the hill, cross a busy street (SR 202, Redmond Woodinville Road Northeast) at the crosswalk, then turn left and then right to follow the trail right up the hill. There are a couple of options to get up this hill: A utility road takes a steep shot uphill, while a trail winds through the undergrowth to smooth out the slope a bit.

For the next 3 miles, you'll follow this power line corridor across a few minor and major road crossings. You'll see signs for trails to Juel Community

Bike Shops

Bothell Ski & Bike: 8020 Bothell Way Northeast, Kenmore; (425) 486-3747; bikesale.com

Redmond Cycle: 7495 159th Place NE, Redmond; (425) 885-6363; redmondcycle.com

REI–Redmond: 7500 166th Ave. Northeast, Redmond; (425) 882-1158; rei.com/stores/redmond.html

Woodinville Bicycle: 13210 NE 175th St.; Woodinville; (425) 483-6626; woodinvillebicycle.com

The last leg of the Thrilla ride uses the hilly Tolt Pipeline trail.

Park on the left and then Farrel McWirther Park on your right. At the latter, take the left fork to bypass the park and keep going until the trail ends at 196th Avenue Northeast, where you turn left.

The Thrilla route follows not-too-thrilling rural roads for the next couple of miles until you ride past a gate onto a path and attack Horse Pasture Hill, which climbs to the top of the ridge under the power lines.

Soon you'll enter the 800-acre Redmond Watershed Preserve property. The city started buying parcels on the ridge in 1926 to create a source of protected drinking water. Although the water never met state standards, the property became a refuge with large stands of forest and wildlife. Watch the trail for garter snakes and listen for Steller's jays in the trees. More serious animals such as bears, bobcats, and even cougar have been spotted in this preserve as well.

A right turn on the Trillium Connector goes to the restrooms in the 218th Avenue Northeast parking lot—the only legit bathroom break until you return to the Sammamish River Trail. The thick stands of second-growth Douglas fir and western hemlock here are more reminiscent of a national—not municipal—park.

Returning to the Trillium Trail junction, turn right on the Power Line Trail and follow it into the dense woods. Remain under forest canopy as you turn left at the Pipeline Regional Trail and pedal along the curvy, dirt (or muddy in the winter) trail for a couple of miles. Turn right when the Collin Creek Trail suddenly appears.

Leaving the watershed preserve, you cross several streets—Sun Break Way is the first. The trail name becomes Bear Creek Ridge Trail and then Trilogy Watershed Trail, named for the 1,000-acre residential commercial community through which it passes.

The gravel trail through the Trilogy development is about a mile long and ends at another utility corridor—the roller-coaster Tolt Pipeline Trail. Turn left and follow this 100-foot-wide passage for nearly six miles to the Sammamish River Trail.

Although bicyclists can ride the dirt trail, it's painfully obvious that the pipeline route was chosen in 1963 to ship water by the shortest distance—a 12-mile straight line—from the Tolt River Watershed above Duvall in the Cascade foothills to Blyth Park on the Sammamish River in Bothell. There are no switchbacks and no grading.

The trail is bounded by horse farms and upscale homes. From where you join it, the trail heads downhill to a bridge over Bear Creek, and then begins a 2-mile climb to the next ridge. Once there, you'll toodle along more or less on level ground until making a harrowing descent to a road crossing (148th Avenue Northeast) at the bottom of the hill. Considering the road at the bottom and some other obstacles, you will not want to go down this hill at top speed.

After crossing the road you head across a field and once again pick up the Sammamish River Trail. Turn left for the short trip back to the parking lot.

MILES & DIRECTIONS

0.0 Exit parking lot on path and turn right onto trail ramp and a sharp left onto Sammamish River Trail, heading south. Cross under Northeast 145th Street.

1.6 Cross under Northeast 124th Street.

2.1 Cross under Northeast 116th Street.

3.3 Left turn onto Power Line Trail, which is not paved. Start climbing uphill, bearing left when the trail forks.

3.6 Cross SR 202 (Redmond Woodinville Road Northeast) and look for trail on left after crossing the street.

3.9 Cross Northeast 104th Street, a residential street.

4.3 Cross Northeast 110th Street and follow trail as it turns right.

5.0 Veer left of a white fence that marks a sediment pond and cross 172nd Place Northeast.

5.9 Cross Avondale Road at the crosswalk and follow the trail.

6.0 Cross a bridge after the trail bends right, followed by a left turn onto the power line trail.

6.3 Go straight through trail junction and then take two left forks, following a sign toward 196th Avenue Northeast.

6.6 Turn left onto 196th Avenue Northeast, a rural paved road.

6.9 Turn right onto Northeast 116th Street.

7.4 Ride through intersection with 204th Avenue Northeast.

7.5 Turn right onto 206th Avenue Northeast.

7.8 Turn left onto Northeast 112th Street. This road ends at a gate and fence; go to the right side of this and pick up the trail that continues in an easterly direction.

8.1 Power Line Trail veers to the right, away from utility road for a short distance. Look for Power Line Trail map posted at this location.

8.5 Right turn on Trillium Connector Trail.

8.7 Restrooms at Redmond Watershed Preserve. Retrace route to Power Line Trail.

8.8 Right turn on Power Line Trail after return to junction. Follow the trail as it bends to the right and then curves to the left.

8.9 Continue straight on Power Line Trail as it enters the forest. Follow the trail that meanders through the forest and cross a bridge.

9.3 Turn left onto Pipeline Regional Trail toward Siler's Mill (hiker only) and Collin Creek Trail. Remain on this arterial trail, passing one trail on the left and two on the right. Follow "T" markings on signposts.

10.6 Turn right onto Collin Creek Trail.

11.0 Turn left on Collin Creek Trail (right turn is hiker only).

11.5 Cross Sun Break Way. Remain on the trail, which becomes Bear Creek Ridge Trail.

11.7 Cross Northeast 133rd Street and remain on the trail, which becomes the Trilogy Watershed Trail.

12.1 Cross 232nd Avenue Northeast on crosswalk and turn right, following the trail. Pass pond on the right and three wooden bridges.

12.7 Turn left onto Tolt Pipeline Trail. Cross 227th Avenue Northeast.

13.1 Cross 221st Avenue Northeast.

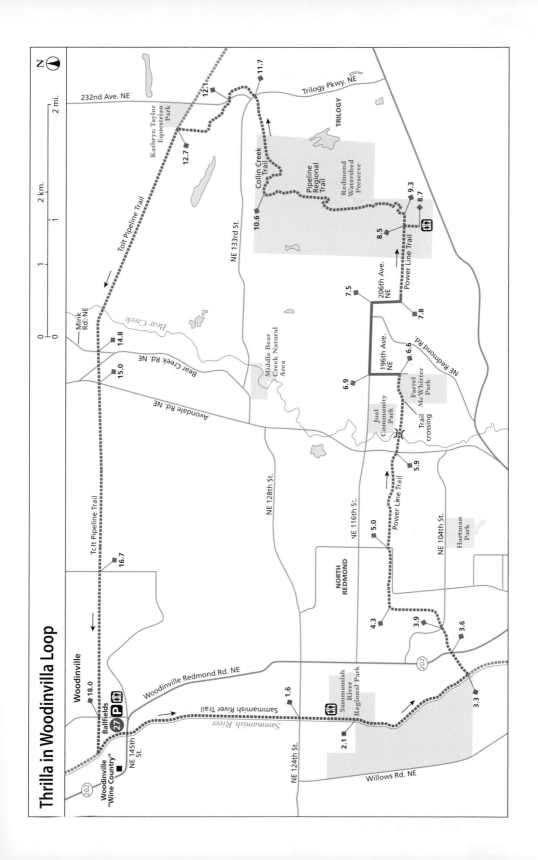

Thrilla in Woodinvilla Loop

13.5 Cross 216th Avenue Northeast.

13.7 Cross Northeast 143rd Street.

14.4 Continue through Bear Creek parkland.

14.8 Cross Mink Road Northeast.

14.9 Cross Bear Creek Road Northeast.

15.0 Cross Avondale Road Northeast.

15.6 Cross Northeast 146th Street.

16.2 Top of the climb; then it levels out.

16.7 Cross 168th Avenue Northeast. Starts downhill.

18.0 Cross 148th Avenue Northeast at the bottom of the hill.

18.3 Turn left onto Sammamish River Trail.

18.6 Take ramp on left side of Sammamish River Trail to parking lot. End of ride.

RIDE INFORMATION

Local Events and Attractions

Stinky Spoke Poker Ride: An 18-mile-ride fund-raiser for the Little Bit Therapeutic Riding Center; mid-January; stinkyspoke.org

Thursday evening Thrilla bike rides: Starts at 6 p.m. (wear headlamps and taillights in the winter). Check Evergreen Mountain Bike Alliance Calendar at evergreenmtb.org/recreation/calendar_view.php.

Restaurants

Red Hook Brewery, Woodinville Brewery & Forecasters Public House: 14300 NE 145th St.; Woodinville; (425) 485-0761; redhook.com

Restrooms

Mile 1.9: Sammamish River Trail

Mile 8.7: Redmond Watershed Preserve

Mile 18.4: Sammamish River Trail

Far Eastside

Single track bobs and weaves through the forest.

There's a lot of green open space farther east in King County as the so-called Issaquah Alps rise above the landscape and roll into the deep forests of the Cascade Mountains.

This is prime mountain-biking habitat. Mountain bikers can hone their single-track and freestyle skills at the Duthie Hill Mountain Bike Park and put them to use in the Tiger Mountain State Forest, Grand Ridge Park, and the remote Middle Fork of the Snoqualmie River.

Also, road cyclists should enjoy the rolling hills along the wide river valleys that pass little towns left over from the railroading and dairy farming days. Meanwhile, two routes take in stunning views of Snoqualmie Falls, and a rail trail passes through a 2.2-mile-long tunnel that crosses a pass in the Cascades.

Fall City–Carnation Loop

The flat Snoqualmie Valley and the ridges bordering it are a popular destination for cyclists looking for good country air and low traffic. So many clubs and charities sponsor rides on these farm roads that riders might have difficulty distinguishing the directional markings painted at the intersections.

Start: Totem pole in Fall City

Length: 30.3 miles

Approximate riding time: 2.5 to 3.5 hours

Best bike: Road or hybrid

Terrain: The route is mostly flat with one notable climb to Ames Lake. The entire route is paved.

Traffic and hazards: Redmond–Fall City Road (SR 202) is a busy highway, but it has a wide shoulder. The route also uses Duval-Carnation Road (SR 203) for a short distance; it's also busy but has a separated bike path or wide shoulder. The other roads have no shoulders but little traffic. The only hazards are crossing SR 202 in two places.

Things to see: Fall City totem pole, historic displays in Olive Taylor Quigley riverfront park in Fall City, antique shops in Carnation, Tolt-MacDonald Park, Remlinger Farms, Jubilee Farms, flower farms, dairy farms, and former Carnation Dairy Farm

Maps: *DeLorme Atlas & Gazetteer—Washington,* page 46; King County Bicycle Map, kingcounty.gov/transportation/kcdot/Roads/Bicycling.aspx

Getting there: By car: Take Eastbound I-90 to exit 22. Turn left on Southeast 82nd Street and right on Southeast High Point Way. The road becomes Preston–Fall City Road Southeast. Continue for nearly 4 miles to Southeast Redmond Fall City Road (SR 202) and turn left. You can park on the right side of road next to the riverfront park. The bike ride starts at the totem pole at Southeast 42nd Place and SR 202. GPS: N47 34.136' / W121 53.572'

THE RIDE

The farmer who erected the hand-carved sign, HOLY LAND, overlooking the Snoqualmie Valley chose an apt name for this picturesque area. Trapped between two ridges, the Snoqualmie River meanders back and forth through rich bottomland that was a center for dairy industry research and is now becoming home to immigrant farmers who grow colorful and fragrant crops for the cutflower trade.

The smooth, low-traffic farm-to-market roads draw cyclists who enjoy logging flat miles through a bucolic countryside with a well-placed stop for refreshments. For vertical challenges, there's Tolt Hill on the west and the low shoulder of the Cascade foothills to the east.

The ride starts at the totem pole in Fall City, a crossroads on the Snoqualmie River that got its start in the 1850s as a trading post with local tribes. It later grew as a port for flat-bottomed steamboats that plied the river. The town takes its name from Snoqualmie Falls, a 260-foot waterfall about four miles upstream. The 30-foot totem pole across the street from the Fall City Library depicts the story of a journey taken by Moon Child, at the base of the pole, who is protected by Quq the Raven, at the top. While their journey involved traveling by canoe on the Snoqualmie River, we start our journey by heading out of town on streets that bear both their current and historical names.

Bike Shops

Bicycle Center of Issaquah: 121 Front St. North, Issaquah; (425) 392-4588; bicyclecenter.biz

Redmond Cycle: 7495 159th Place Northeast, Redmond; (425) 885-6363; redmondcycle.com

REI–Issaquah: 735 NW Gilman Blvd., Issaquah; (425) 313-1660; rei.com/stores/issaquah.html

On the outskirts of town the route picks up Southeast Issaquah–Fall City Road, which follows the route of an 1887 wagon road from Fall City to Renton. Except for the subsequent paving, the road exists much as it did in the beginning. It starts climbing uphill through some woods as it leaves town, but the bike route turns away instead of making the arduous trip up and over the Sammamish Plateau.

A mile after leaving that historic corridor, the route picks up Southeast Redmond–Fall City Road (SR 202). Watch for traffic before crossing and picking up the wide road shoulder. (If you want to avoid SR 202, the upcoming climb, and about 11 miles of pedaling, you can continue north on 308th Avenue Southeast. It picks up the West Snoqualmie River Road and travels all the way to Carnation.)

The snow-capped Cascades create a backdrop for these cows in pasture.

The route rolls along at the base of a ridge for the next 5.5 miles. There isn't much to see through here except for an occasional farm and the Patterson Creek Natural Area. Although the climb up Northeast Ames Lake Road is strenuous, the shady, quiet road with a pleasant babbling brook alongside is a welcome relief from the noise of the state highway.

There are a number of large-lot subdivisions with grand entrances along the road; the one for Quail Creek about 1.5 miles up the hill also marks the start of a pleasant descent into the valley. As you pick up speed, look for the left turn onto West Snoqualmie Valley Road Northeast across from the Daniels Ranch subdivision. Coasting downhill, you suddenly pass from shady forest to the pastoral scenery of the Snoqualmie Valley. This road bordering the western side of the valley is another historic corridor. Built piecemeal as a wagon road, it served farms along the base of the ridge away from the river.

At the intersection of Northeast 80th Street, you'll see the distinctive blue hay barn and matching milk house of the Vandermeer-Sinnema dairy farm. Pausing to look back to the left, you'll see the old one-room schoolhouse for the community of Vincent. Minutes from the Microsoft campus in Redmond today, this area was very isolated when the schoolhouse was built in 1905. It served about twenty children at a time in all grades. It closed in 1947.

Best Bike Rides Seattle

The bike route heads into the rich bottomland of the Snoqualmie Valley after a right turn at a weathered red barn. Originally an area of subsistence farms and later crop farms supporting the local dairy industry, much of the land is now planted in dizzying displays of flowers that change from spring through fall.

The farmers responsible for this transformation are Hmong tribesman who settled here as refugees from embattled Laos in the 1970s through the '90s. Thousands came to Washington state. As they were farmers in their homeland, many leased land in Carnation, Duvall, and Fall City to grow flowers and some vegetable crops. They sell their harvest at the flower stalls at Pike Place Market in Seattle, farmers' markets, and even from the backs of cars parked along the roadside throughout the Puget Sound area. If you want to buy a bouquet, there are usually a few for sale at a flower stand at the turn from 284th Avenue Northeast onto Northeast Carnation Farm Road. As you approach and make this turn, you'll see the bright red roofs of a large farm compound perched on a hillside on Northeast Carnation Farm Road. This is the old Carnation Stock Farm, parts of which date back to 1912, and is the birthplace of "contented cows." (See sidebar.)

Carnation Stock Farm

Eldridge A. Stuart and his partner developed a method to create evaporated milk in the late 1800s, before home refrigerators became commonplace. A few years later, after creating the Carnation brand name, he came up with the slogan "Carnation Condensed Milk, the milk from contented cows."

In 1908, he bought an undeveloped farm on what is now Carnation Farm Road and started building a dairy-cow breeding and research facility. Soon, the entire valley was devoted to the dairy industry and the local town of Tolt had changed its name to Carnation. Many of the hay barns that dot the valley date back to that era.

The dairy farm itself was such a success that Carnation cows held world milk-production records for thirty-two years in a row. One record-setter from 1920—Segis Pietertje Prospect—is memorialized at the entrance of the old research facility on Carnation Farm Road in a bigger-than-life statue.

Carnation eventually diversified into other food lines, and Swiss multinational Nestlé bought it in 1985. The 818-acre Carnation Farm is now home to Camp Korey, a no-cost camp for children with life-threatening diseases and their families. In recent years, it has been a rest stop on the Flying Wheels Summer Century bike ride.

Passing the Carnation Farm and Chinook Bend Natural Area, the route crosses the Snoqualmie River and arrives via back roads to the town of Carnation. Originally incorporated as Tolt in 1912, town fathers renamed it after the huge dairy farm in 1917. SR 203, also known as Tolt Avenue, is lined with coffee stands, small cafes, and taverns where cyclists can find refreshment. There's also a market to buy supplies for a picnic at the nearby Tolt-MacDonald Park at the confluence of the Snoqualmie and Tolt Rivers or the Nick Loutsis Park on the Snoqualmie Valley Trail.

Leaving town, the route crosses two more bridges before it turns onto West Snoqualmie River Road. This is another historic road that has changed little, except for paving, since the early 1900s. Bicyclists enjoy these 6 miles of flat, winding river road with little traffic as it passes old dairy farmsteads. The nearby Cascade foothills provide a scenic backdrop to the pastures and fields of flowers.

Of note along this road is the Jubilee Farm, where local families become members and can pick their own organically grown produce from the fields or buy food in the store. Use caution crossing SR 202 and return to the outskirts of Fall City.

MILES & DIRECTIONS

0.0 Facing the totem pole on Southeast 42nd Street with the Fall City Library at your back, head left and pass the Fall City Elementary School.

0.2 Turn left on 332nd Avenue Southeast.

0.7 Turn right on Southeast 46th Street, which becomes Southeast Issaquah–Fall City Road.

3.1 Turn right on Southeast 40th Street (left continues as Southeast Issaquah Fall City Road).

3.7 Turn left onto 308th Avenue Southeast.

4.0 Turn left onto SR 202, also known as Southeast Redmond–Fall City Road. Watch for traffic.

5.2 Continue straight through traffic light at 292nd Avenue Southeast on the left.

7.9 Ride past Northeast Tolt Hill Road on the right.

9.7 Turn right onto Northeast Ames Lake Road, which immediately starts ascent.

12.0 Pass Northeast Union Hill Road on the left.

Fall City–Carnation Loop

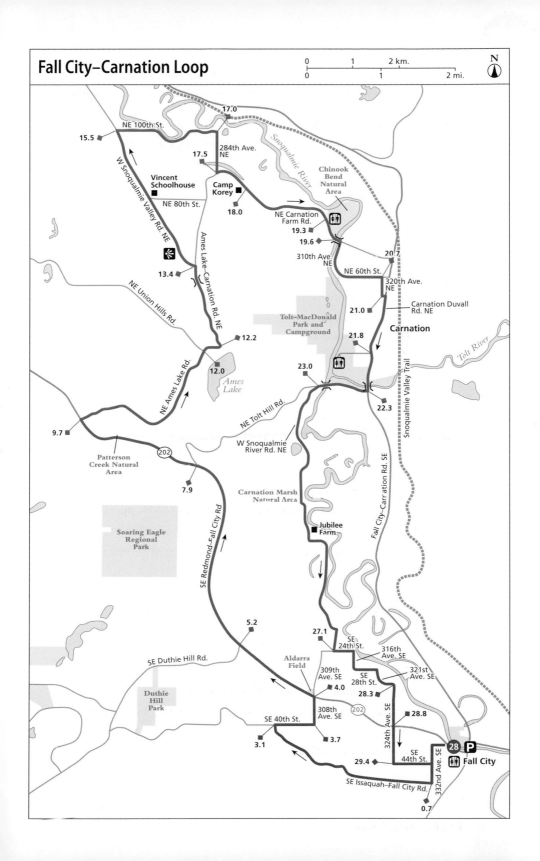

Scale:
0 — 1 — 2 km.
0 — 1 — 2 mi.

N

17.0

NE 100th St.

15.5

284th Ave. NE

17.5

Snoqualmie River

W Snoqualmie Valley Rd. NE

Vincent Schoolhouse

Camp Korey

NE 80th St.

18.0

NE Carnation Farm Rd.

19.3

19.6

Chinook Bend Natural Area

20.7

310th Ave. NE

NE 60th St.

320th Ave. NE

Carnation Duvall Rd. NE

13.4

NE Union Hills Rd.

Ames Lake–Carnation Rd. NE

21.0

Tolt–MacDonald Park and Campground

21.8

Carnation

12.2

NE Ames Lake Rd.

12.0

Ames Lake

23.0

22.3

Tolt River

Snoqualmie Valley Trail

9.7

NE Tolt Hill Rd.

W Snoqualmie River Rd. NE

Patterson Creek Natural Area

202

7.9

Carnation Marsh Natural Area

Fall City–Carnation Rd. SE

SE Redmond–Fall City Rd

Soaring Eagle Regional Park

Jubilee Farm

5.2

27.1

SE 24th St.

316th Ave. SE

SE Duthie Hill Rd.

Aldarra Field

309th Ave. SE

4.0

SE 28th St.

321st Ave. SE

28.3

Duthie Hill Park

308th Ave. SE

202

28.8

SE 40th St.

324th Ave. SE

3.1

3.7

29.4

28

Fall City

332nd Ave. SE

SE 44th St.

SE Issaquah–Fall City Rd.

0.7

12.2 Follow Northeast Ames Lake Road to the left as it becomes Ames Lake–Carnation Road.

13.4 Turn left onto West Snoqualmie Valley Road Northeast; this can be easy to miss if you're speeding downhill. Look for a sign for Daniels Ranch subdivision on the right.

14.5 Pass Northeast 80th Street on the right; this is the historic community of Vincent.

15.5 Turn right onto Northeast 100th Street.

17.0 Turn right at 284th Avenue Northeast.

17.5 Turn left onto Northeast Carnation Farm Road.

18.0 Pass Camp Korey, former site of huge Nestlé dairy operation.

19.3 Pass by the Chinook Bend Natural Area.

19.6 Cross bridge over Snoqualmie River and turn right onto 310th Avenue Northeast. Road turns and becomes Northeast 60th Street.

20.7 Turn right onto 320th Avenue Northeast.

21.0 Turn left onto Northeast 55th Street and an immediate right onto a protected bike lane adjacent to Carnation Duvall Road Northeast, SR 203. Enter the town of Carnation.

21.8 Pass entrance to Tolt-MacDonald Park on right at Northeast 40th Street. (Turn right for restrooms, drinking water, exhibits, and camping.)

22.3 Cross over the Tolt River Bridge and turn right onto Northeast Tolt Hill Road. Then cross the Snoqualmie River Bridge.

23.0 Turn left onto West Snoqualmie River Road Northeast. Road name changes repeatedly as it follows the Snoqualmie River; follow the main arterial.

27.1 Turn left onto Southeast 24th Street.

28.3 Road turns right and becomes 324th Avenue Southeast.

28.8 Cross Southeast Redmond–Fall City Road; busy crossing.

29.4 Turn left onto Southeast 44th Street.

29.9 Turn left onto 332nd Avenue Southeast.

30.1 Turn right onto Southeast 42nd Street.

30.3 Ride ends between totem pole and library building.

RIDE INFORMATION

Local Events and Attractions

Flying Wheels Summer Century: Various distances; presented by Cascade Bicycle Club in late May or early June; starts in Redmond with routes through Snoqualmie Valley; cascade.org/flying-wheels-summer-century

Tour de Peaks: Various distances; presented by Snoqualmie Valley Hospital District in July or August; starts in North Bend with routes throughout the valley; tourdepeaks.org

Remlinger Farm: A 200-acre working farm and tourist center with a restaurant, ice-cream parlor, and amusement park; 32610 NE 32nd St., Carnation; remlingerfarms.com

Tolt-MacDonald Park and Campground: A 574-acre park operated by King County. Tent sites as well as cabins and yurts for camping at the confluence of the Snoqualmie and Tolt rivers. Entrance at Northeast 40th Street, Carnation; kingcounty.gov/recreation/parks/inventory/toltmacdonald.aspx.

Restaurants

Fall City Roadhouse: American cuisine in historic location, 4200 Preston-Fall City Rd. Southeast, Fall City; fcroadhouse.com/

Small Frye's: Take-out and picnic-style burger joint, 4224 Preston–Fall City Rd. Southeast, Fall City

Restrooms

Mile 0.0: Fall City Library, 33415 SE 42nd Place, Fall City (ask for key at front desk)
Mile 19.3: Chinook Bend Natural Area (pit toilets)
Mile 21.8: Tolt-MacDonald Park (pit toilets)

This paved rail-trail ride through thick, Pacific Northwest forest offers a whole new view of the Snoqualmie Falls from about a half-mile distance. Most of the trail is an easy grade for just about everyone. The only hitch is a missing trestle that requires a dip into the Raging River Valley and a short series of switchbacks up the other side. As part of the Mountains to Sound Greenway, this King County Regional Trail links with other paved and unpaved trails.

Start: Preston-Snoqualmie Trailhead parking in Preston

Length: 11.3 miles round-trip

Approximate riding time: 1 to 2 hours

Best bike: Road, hybrid, or mountain bike

Terrain: Easy railroad grades, except for ravine at Raging River. Paved trail, 10 to 12 feet wide.

Traffic and hazards: There is one road crossing on a crosswalk at Preston–Fall City Road Southeast; hikers, runners, and dog walkers

Things to see: Old Preston mill and Preston community center (off trail), 1915 bridge from Sunset Highway, mature forests, and view of Snoqualmie Valley and Snoqualmie Falls

Maps: *DeLorme Atlas & Gazetteer—Washington,* page 46; King County Regional Trail Maps, kingcounty.gov/operations/GIS/Maps/VMC/ Recreation.aspx#6366BDAC031C4B179A0225581D55A339

Getting there: By car: Take eastbound I-90 to the Preston–Fall City exit 22. Turn left at the end of the ramp onto Southeast 82nd Street, cross I-90, then turn right onto Southeast High Point Way. Just past the Preston Athletic Fields and Park turn left onto Southeast 87th Place and park. **By bus:** Metro route 209 serves the vicinity. GPS: N47 31.347' / W121 56.028'

THE RIDE

A couple of missing railroad trestles are all that's lacking to make the Preston-Snoqualmie Trail a truly awesome connection in a cross-county off-road bicycle corridor.

The rail trail follows a mostly easy grade from Preston to within about a mile of the town of Snoqualmie. Unfortunately, the town—and a connection to the Snoqualmie Valley Regional Trail—is inaccessible from the end of the trail because of missing trestles and private-property trespassing issues. Another missing trestle about midway creates a notable road and river crossing.

Still, the Preston-Snoqualmie Trail is a great ride in any season. The trail is shaded by giant evergreens and big-leaf maples in the summer, and in the fall those maple leaves cover the ground in bright yellow. In the rainy winter and spring seasons, the pavement prevents bicyclists from getting bogged down in mud, and the bare trees yield dazzling views of the ridge across Snoqualmie Valley and Snoqualmie Falls.

The trail follows the grade of the Seattle, Lakeshore, and Eastern Railway that laid tracks through here for a rail line between Seattle and Fall City in the late 1880s. That railroad also is responsible for right-of-ways that now carry the Burke-Gilman Trail and the East Lake Sammamish Trail, as well as the tourist train operated by the Northwest Railway Museum in Snoqualmie.

This bike ride starts at the Preston-Snoqualmie Trailhead and parking lot located just past the Preston Athletic Fields and Park, where you'll find water and restrooms. It immediately enters a mature second-growth forest with wildlife corridors all the way from Issaquah into the Cascade Mountains. Don't be surprised to see warnings for bear sightings posted at the trailhead.

Bike Shops

Bicycle Center of Issaquah: 121 Front St. North, Issaquah; 425-392-4588; bicyclecenter.biz
Preston Bicycle Repair: 8428 SE Preston–Fall City Rd., Preston; (425) 222-3590; pbronline.us
REI–Issaquah: 735 NW Gilman Blvd., Issaquah; (425) 313-1660; rei.com/stores/issaquah.html
Singletrack Cycles: 119 W. North Bend Way, North Bend; (425) 888-0101; stcycles.com

The trail follows an effortless downhill grade for the first couple of miles. Some traffic noise drifting up from I-90 and Preston–Fall City Road Southeast is the only disturbance of the peace. At a fork in the trail, the route turns right to avoid the missing railroad trestle that has caused lots of consternation

Moss covers this old bridge that was part of the first automobile highway that crossed the state.

over the years. The original wooden trestle that spanned the Raging River collapsed while a freight train was crossing in 1900, killing the engineer. The Northern Pacific Railway, which had acquired the railroad, replaced it with a steel structure the following year. When the railway fell under the domain of Burlington Northern Railroad after 1970, the new owners abandoned the line and removed the trestle.

King County fashioned a scenic crossing that uses an historic highway bridge over the Raging River. Check your brakes before heading down that right fork that ends at a stop sign on Southeast Preston–Fall City Road. Use the crosswalk, then turn right behind the concrete barriers. It might seem like you're backtracking, but you'll make a left turn onto quiet Southeast 68th Street that puts you in the right direction.

The old narrow bridge over Raging River is a vestige of the Sunset Highway, the first automobile route over the Cascade Mountains completed in 1915. From the east, the original route followed the South Fork of the Snoqualmie to North Bend, Snoqualmie, and Fall City, then up this way on its way to Preston and west toward Seattle. A few years later, a shortcut took motorists directly between Preston and North Bend.

There are several tall stands of Douglas fir and western red cedar covered in moss along the river. Follow the detour back up to the barricade along

Southeast Preston–Fall City Road until you come to a hillside with seven switchbacks on a narrow gravel path. You'll need to dismount to negotiate these tight turns going uphill or downhill.

After you reach the top of the hill, the trail is fairly level as it follows the contours of a ridge south of the Snoqualmie River. There's an old second-growth forest up here, but looking across through breaks in the trees you can see the ridge north of the river and some snowy peaks in the Cascades.

There's another crossing and trailhead at Lake Alice Road Southeast (this area is called the Lake Alice Plateau); then it's a free ride to the end of the trail. Lean your bike against the fence and walk a few feet to the left for a view of Snoqualmie Falls, about a half-mile away. At 268 feet high, the falls are 100 feet higher than Niagara Falls. Although it appears the branches of the large evergreens are trimmed to frame the view, some other trees have been growing that could obscure this vantage point in the summer.

Although there's a big chain link fence with a No Trespassing sign blocking the trail, you are correct to assume that the railroad did not stop here. It continued past here to the town of Snoqualmie. Unfortunately, plans to extend the trail those final 2 miles to Snoqualmie back in the 1980s ran afoul of a

Mountains to Sound Greenway

The Preston-Snoqualmie Trail is just one of a network of biking and hiking trails in the Mountains to Sound Greenway, an area comprising 1.5 million acres along I-90 corridor between Ellensburg on the eastern slope of the Cascades to Seattle on the shores of Puget Sound.

The Greenway Trust is not a governmental institution. Members of the trust come from a wide range of business and environmental backgrounds and work together to conserve and enhance the landscape, avoiding the sprawl that marks so many interstate highways. One of their goals is to connect all the regional trail systems throughout the Greenway so hikers and bicyclists can travel safely off-road from one place to another. At last count, they're focusing their efforts on seven "missing links" in the regional trail system between Seattle and Ellensburg.

One of those is the gap between the end of the Preston-Snoqualmie Trail to the Snoqualmie Valley Regional Trail east of Snoqualmie Falls. Another is the 1-mile gap in the Snoqualmie Valley Regional Trail at the Snoqualmie Mill site. Gaps in Seattle, Bellevue, and Issaquah are also under review. Closing these "missing links" would create an off-road trail all the way from the Seattle waterfront to Ellensburg. Learn more at mtsgreenway.org.

number of entities who laid claim to the corridor. Lately, the county and city of Snoqualmie are seeking ways to connect the Preston-Snoqualmie Trail with the Snoqualmie Valley Regional Trail. One plan would involve a bridge over the river just east of Snoqualmie Falls.

From the dead end, retrace your ride to the trailhead. Remember to dismount when heading down those switchbacks, and watch for fast-moving traffic when you cross Preston–Fall City Road Southeast. Then shift down to your granny gear to get up the hill to return to the railroad grade.

MILES & DIRECTIONS

0.0 Follow an access road to the well-marked trailhead southeast from the parking lot.

1.9 Paved trail makes a hard right turn and goes down a steep grade.

2.1 Stop at crosswalk at bottom of the grade and cross Preston–Fall City Road Southeast; turn right after crossing and follow the trail behind the barriers that separate it from the road.

2.2 Turn left onto Southeast 68th Street, cross a bridge over Raging River, then follow the signs back to the trail.

2.4 Rejoin trail behind concrete barriers along Preston–Fall City Road Southeast.

2.6 Follow packed-gravel trail that veers to the right, and dismount for a series of seven short switchbacks that climb the hill.

2.7 Return to paved Preston-Snoqualmie Trail at the top of the grade.

3.7 Ride across Lake Alice Road Southeast trailhead.

4.2 Pass private driveway.

4.3 Dirt trail on right goes to Azalea Park on Douglas Avenue Southeast in Snoqualmie Ridge development.

4.6 Dirt trail on right goes to Deep Creek Trail and Whitaker Trail in Snoqualmie Ridge development.

5.6 Trail ends at private gate; scenic view of Snoqualmie Falls from benches on the left. Retrace your route back to trailhead.

7.4 Ride across Lake Alice Road Southeast.

8.4 Dismount and begin downhill switchbacks on gravel path as paved trail ends.

8.5 Take trail on left side of barriers along Preston–Fall City Road Southeast.

Preston-Snoqualmie Trail

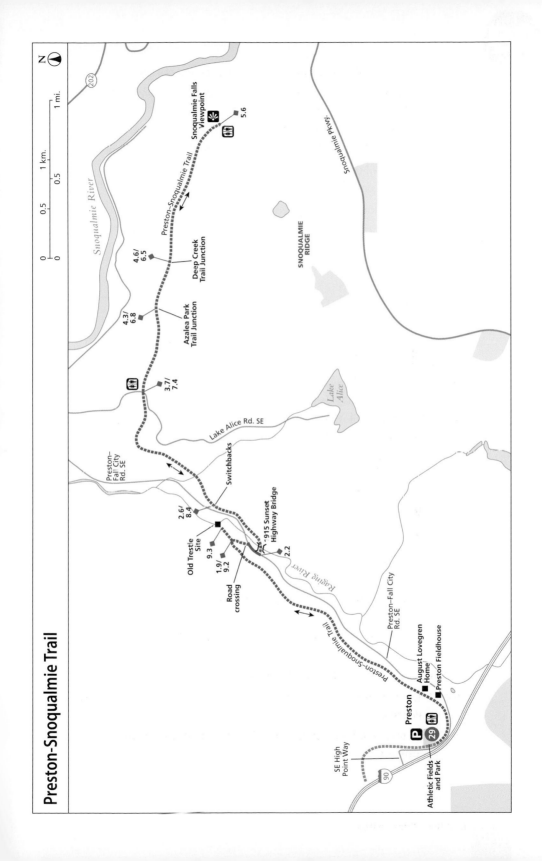

N

1 mi.

1 km.

0   0.5   1   0.5

Snoqualmie River

202

Preston-Snoqualmie Trail

Snoqualmie Falls Viewpoint

5.6

Deep Creek Trail Junction

4.6/ 6.5

Azalea Park Trail Junction

4.3/ 6.8

3.7/ 7.4

SNOQUALMIE RIDGE

Snoqualmie Pkwy.

Lake Alice

Lake Alice Rd. SE

Preston– Fall City Rd. SE

Switchbacks

2.6/ 8.4

Old Trestle Site

9.3

1.9/ 9.2

Road crossing

915 Sunset Highway Bridge

2.2

Raging River

Preston-Snoqualmie Trail

Preston–Fall City Rd. SE

August Lovegren Home

Preston Fieldhouse

Preston

P

29

SE High Point Way

90

Athletic Fields and Park

8.7 Take trail to left and join Southeast 68th Street; cross bridge.

8.9 Turn right onto trail behind barriers on Preston–Fall City Road Southeast.

9.1 Turn left at crosswalk on Preston–Fall City Road Southeast; carefully cross this busy road and throw it in your granny gear to go uphill.

9.2 At the top of the climb, turn right and take the short detour on the gravel to a bench overlooking a hillside.

9.3 This is the location of the missing railroad trestle across Raging River and Preston–Fall City Road. Turn around and head back to the trail.

11.3 End of trail.

RIDE INFORMATION

Local Events and Attractions

August Lovegren House: Historic two-story home built by owner of Preston Mill in 1904. Lovegren was a Swedish immigrant who invested in the mill just after the Great Fire of 1889, when lumber for the rebuilding of Seattle was needed. He was responsible for bringing many Swedes to the Preston–Fall City area; 8612 310th Ave. Southeast, Preston

Preston Mill Park: Not much remains of the old mill, most of which burned down in 1990. Now owned by King County Parks and Recreation Department; Preston–Fall City Road, Preston

Treehouse Point: Overnight lodging in treehouses and home base for Pete Nelson of Treehouse Masters on Animal Planet; 6922 Preston-Fall City Road Southeast, Preston; treehousepoint.com

Works Progress Administration Fieldhouse, Preston: Built in the late 1930s, the Preston community center features a river-rock exterior; 8625 310th Ave. Southeast, Preston

Restaurants

XXX Root Beer Drive-in: Vintage drive-in with antique cars cruising the parking lot; 98 NE Gilman Blvd., Issaquah; (425) 392-1266; triplexrootbeer.com

Restrooms

Mile 0.0: Portable toilet at trailhead
Mile 3.7/7.4: Portable toilet
Mile 5.6: Portable toilet

Rattlesnake Lake and Snoqualmie Falls Loop

Starting at the home of the Northwest Railway Museum, this ride passes through historic downtown Snoqualmie to a rail trail that ends at scenic Rattlesnake Lake. The downhill return to the valley visits North Bend and elk habitat near the base of Mount Si. After passing a placid old mill pond, the route swings by the thunderous Snoqualmie Falls before it concludes back in downtown.

Start: Parking lot at Railroad Avenue and Fir Street in downtown Snoqualmie

Length: 25.2 miles

Approximate riding time: 2.5 to 3.5 hours

Best bike: Hybrid or road bikes with wider tires

Terrain: Flat valley roads; one long climb on railroad grade (less than 3 percent)

Traffic and hazards: Mostly low-traffic country roads and rail trail; hazards include storm grates on Southeast Cedar Falls Road, a roundabout in North Bend, and traffic at Snoqualmie Falls

Things to see: Northwest Railway Museum, historic downtowns of North Bend and Snoqualmie, Rattlesnake Lake, Cedar River Watershed Education Center, Snoqualmie Falls, wildlife

Maps: *DeLorme Atlas & Gazetteer—Washington,* pages 46, 47, 61; King County Bicycle Map, kingcounty.gov/transportation/kcdot/Roads/Bicycling.aspx

Getting there: By car: Take I-90 east to exit 25. Turn left at the end of the ramp onto Snoqualmie Parkway and continue for 3.5 miles to a T intersection. Turn right onto Railroad Avenue, and then go another 0.5 mile to turn right onto Fir Street and enter a parking lot. **By bus:** Metro bus route 209 and 215 serve downtown Snoqualmie. GPS: N47 31.839' / W121 49.631'

THE RIDE

Downtown Snoqualmie is nothing like the modern master-planned community of Snoqualmie Ridge that you cross to get here. Downtown is the preserved old-timey commercial district for farmers and loggers who settled in the Upper Snoqualmie Valley in the second half of the nineteenth century, followed by the railroaders who worked here beginning in the 1890s.

Give yourself extra time to ride this route if you're a railroad buff, as you'll want to stop at the Northwest Railway Museum that you pass 1 block after leaving the parking lot on Fir Street. The museum is housed in Snoqualmie Depot, built in 1890. In addition to its collections and displays, the museum is also the ticket office for the Snoqualmie Valley Railroad tourist train that runs for 5.5 miles between Snoqualmie Falls and North Bend on weekends. On your return from Snoqualmie Falls, you'll pass more than seventy vintage locomotives and passenger and freight cars in the museum's collection stored on railroad tracks.

Heading down Railroad Avenue you'll pass old storefronts in the historic district that contain cafes, shops, a brewery, and a candy store. Turning left, the route rolls along the Snoqualmie River that flows behind downtown. The river left behind several oxbow lakes around the valley where it changed channels after floods.

Riding on Park Street, you'll cross Meadowbrook Way and pass athletic fields before you come upon Meadowbrook Farm Park on the right. Keep your eyes peeled for an elk herd that likes to browse in the field of this open-space park. Native inhabitants maintained this grassland as a hunting ground, and white settlers later created the nation's largest hop farm here before it became a dairy farm.

Turn left into the Mount Si Golf Course entrance, ride through the parking lot, and join the Snoqualmie Valley Trail on the right as it extends past a putting green and through the golf course.

This route uses the trail for 9.5 miles. It's crushed rock the entire way, which is why a hybrid bike or road bike with wider tires—28 mm and above—is recommended. The trail takes a flat, straight heading across the valley to North Bend, where a display marks the long-gone railroad station. Even though the trail looks flat, you might notice that your pace begins to slow after you leave town.

Bike Shop

Singletrack Cycles: 119 W. North Bend Way, North Bend; (425) 888-0101; stcycles.com

The trail crosses North Bend Way, passes beneath I-90, and spans the churning South Fork of the Snoqualmie River before it starts a slightly steeper

Mount Si dominates the landscape near the North Fork of the Snoqualmie River at Three Forks Natural Area.

grade. The trail cuts through the shade of large evergreens and emerges at Rattlesnake Lake, a 111-acre lake about 500 feet higher than North Bend. The crystal-clear lake contains the remains of Moncton, a town that stood on the shoreline of a smaller Rattlesnake Lake until the construction of a nearby dam by Seattle Public Utilities flooded it in 1915. The rocky outcrop of Rattlesnake Ledge is reflected in the lake from more than 1,000 feet above. Trails on the lake's south shore visit the Cedar River Watershed Education Center, which houses displays about the region's wildlife, forests, and water. It's also the only place for restrooms and drinkable water.

If you feel comfortable speeding downhill on a road, return to North Bend via Cedar Falls Road Southeast, which is the road next to the education center. Otherwise, take the Snoqualmie Valley Trail back downhill. Both meet Southeast North Bend Way as it heads toward North Bend. That road was part of the Sunset Highway that opened in 1915 as the first cross-state automobile road.

If some of the scenery around North Bend looks familiar, you might recognize that the opening scenes for David Lynch's cult-hit TV show *Twin Peaks* were shot around here. That craggy mountain to the right is Mount Si, seen in every episode opener. A popular hiking destination, the old volcano rises 3,500 feet from the surrounding landscape and is a prominent peak recognizable from Seattle.

Heading north on 428th Avenue Southeast, you'll cross the Middle Branch and North Branch of the Snoqualmie River in quick succession, entering the Three Forks Natural Area (the South Fork Snoqualmie River joins just downstream). Located at the foot of Mount Si State Park, the natural area protects a habitat for elk, deer, bear, cougar, bobcat, and river otters that visit or make their homes here. Such birds of prey as bald eagles, hawks, and peregrine falcons also hunt in the forests and along the river.

The route turns left along the Snoqualmie River on Southeast Reinig Road. It passes the old railroad trestle that dead-ends in midair after crossing the Snoqualmie River, thus requiring the 2-mile on-road detour. Take the right fork after the bridge to remain on the portion of Reinig Road that at one time served a neighborhood for workers at the Snoqualmie Falls Mill. That mill is gone now, as are the houses. What remains, however, is the peaceful Mill Pond that held logs on their way to the sawmill.

The route dumps onto busy SR 202 for a few feet before turning left into the parking lot for Snoqualmie Falls, a spectacular scenic attraction. The Snoqualmie River plunges 268 feet over a rocky precipice here, creating a cloud of spray that can douse visitors a half-mile away. By comparison, the tallest of the Niagara Falls is 167 feet. Snacks and restrooms are open for the 1.5 million people who visit annually, and the Salish Lodge offers rooms and dining. The falls provides electricity through two hydroelectric power plants, one more than one hundred years old. The heaviest flows are usually in the spring, when snowmelt combines with rainfall.

To finish up the ride, merge back onto SR 202 toward Snoqualmie. If traffic is heavy, you can take a sidewalk over the bridge that spans Snoqualmie River right above the falls. The road returns to the Fir Street parking lot, passing dozens of locomotives and passenger and freight cars on a railroad siding.

MILES & DIRECTIONS

0.0 Turn left out of parking lot onto Fir Street. Turn right onto shoulder of Railroad Avenue (SR 202).

0.1 Turn left onto South King Street, ride 1 block, and turn right onto Falls Avenue Southeast.

0.4 Turn left onto South Newton Street, ride 2 blocks, and turn right onto Park Avenue Southeast.

0.9 Cross Meadowbrook Way Southeast.

1.1 Pass entrance to Centennial Fields Park.

1.6 Turn left into entrance to Mount Si Golf Club. Continue into the parking lot and pick up the gravel pathway on the right that passes a practice putting green. This is the Snoqualmie Valley Regional Trail.

3.5 Cross over Main Street in North Bend.

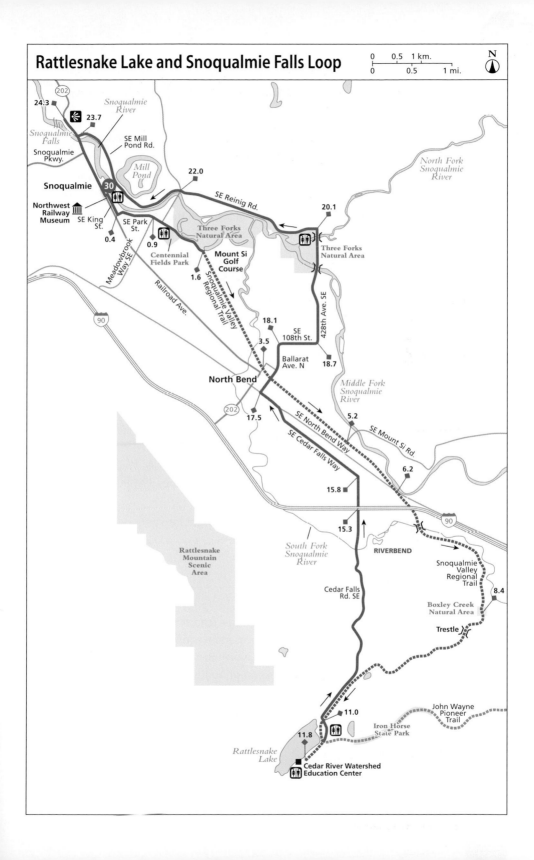

Rattlesnake Lake and Snoqualmie Falls Loop

0   0.5   1 km.
0   0.5   1 mi.

N

Snoqualmie River

24.3
23.7

Snoqualmie Falls
Snoqualmie Pkwy.

SE Mill Pond Rd.

Mill Pond

22.0

SE Reinig Rd.

North Fork Snoqualmie River

Snoqualmie

30

20.1

Northwest Railway Museum

SE King St.

SE Park St.

0.4

0.9

Three Forks Natural Area

Three Forks Natural Area

Centennial Fields Park

Mount Si Golf Course

1.6

Meadowbrook Way SE

Snoqualmie Valley Regional Trail

Railroad Ave.

90

18.1

SE 108th St.

3.5

428th Ave. SE

Ballarat Ave. N

18.7

Middle Fork Snoqualmie River

North Bend

202

17.5

SE North Bend Way

5.2

SE Mount Si Rd.

SE Cedar Falls Way

6.2

15.8

15.3

90

Rattlesnake Mountain Scenic Area

South Fork Snoqualmie River

RIVERBEND

Snoqualmie Valley Regional Trail

8.4

Cedar Falls Rd. SE

Boxley Creek Natural Area

Trestle

John Wayne Pioneer Trail

11.0

Iron Horse State Park

11.8

Rattlesnake Lake

Cedar River Watershed Education Center

5.2 Cross Southeast Mount Si Road.

6.2 Follow trail across Southeast North Bend Way and pass beneath I-90.

8.4 Pass trail to Boxley Creek Natural Area.

11.0 Turn right off of Snoqualmie Valley Trail, cross Cedar Falls Road Southeast, and follow trail to Rattlesnake Lake.

11.8 Arrive at Cedar River Watershed Education Center. Return on Southeast Cedar Falls Road. The road becomes 436th Avenue Southeast.

15.3 Pass the Riverbend Cafe and General Store on the left side of the road, then cross I-90 on an overpass.

15.8 Turn left onto Southeast Cedar Falls Way.

17.1 Take the third exit off the roundabout onto East North Bend Way.

17.5 Turn right onto Ballarat Avenue North.

18.1 Turn right onto Southeast 108th Street (Northeast 12th Street).

18.7 Turn left onto 428th Avenue Southeast.

20.1 Turn left onto Southeast Reinig Road.

22.0 Take the left fork to remain on Southeast Reinig Road.

22.3 Take right fork to go on Southeast Mill Pond Road.

23.7 Turn left to stay on Southeast Mill Pond Road, then turn right onto Railroad Avenue (SR 202).

24.3 Carefully turn left into parking lot for Snoqualmie Falls. Walk your bicycle to the overlook. Then turn right onto Railroad Avenue (SR 202) to finish the loop.

25.2 Turn right onto Fir Street, and then turn right into parking lot. End of ride.

RIDE INFORMATION

Local Events and Attractions
Railroad Days: Summer festival in Snoqualmie featuring vendors, train rides, and an outdoor car show; mid-August; railroaddays.com

Festival at Mount Si: Summer festival in North Bend featuring vendors, contests, and entertainment; second weekend of August; festivalatmtsi.org

Tour de Peaks: Bike tour in Snoqualmie Valley in July or August; tourdepeaks.org

Northwest Railway Museum: Housed in the restored 1890 Snoqualmie railroad depot; open seven days a week; train rides on weekends in summer; 38625 SE King St., Snoqualmie; trainmuseum.org

Cedar River Watershed Education Center: Displays, education programs, and guided tours presented by Seattle Public Utilities, which operates the source of Seattle's water; 19901 Cedar Falls Rd. Southeast, North Bend; seattle.gov/util/EnvironmentConservation/OurWatersheds/CedarRiver Watershed/CedarRiverEducationCenter/index.htm

Restaurants
Scotts Dairy Freeze: Ice cream and burgers since the 1950s; 234 E. North Bend Way, North Bend; (425) 888-2301
Snoqualmie Brewery and Taproom: Local brewery and cafe; 8032 Falls Ave. Southeast, Snoqualmie; (425) 831-2357; fallsbrew.com

Restrooms
Mile 0.1: Sandy Cove Park (portable toilets)
Mile 1.1: Centennial Fields Park
Mile 11.8: Cedar River Watershed Education Center
Mile 20.1: Three Forks Natural Area (pit toilets)
Mile 24.3: Snoqualmie Falls State Park

Historic Rail Lines

Two historic rail lines are preserved in the Snoqualmie Valley, one as a rail trail and the other as a tourist train.

The Snoqualmie Valley Regional Trail crosses the Lower and Upper Snoqualmie Valleys for 31.5 miles as a crushed-rock rail trail. Starting at the north end in Duvall, the former route of the Chicago-Milwaukee, St. Paul, and Pacific Railroad passes through Carnation and then climbs up an easy grade along a ridge to reach the elevation of the Upper Snoqualmie Valley at Snoqualmie Falls. The trail suffers a 1-mile missing link on private land near the falls, but begins again at the Reinig Road trestle over the river. It continues through the Three Forks Natural Area, Mount Si Golf Course, and North Bend before it crosses the South Fork of the Snoqualmie River and climbs a grade to Rattlesnake Lake.

The other abandoned railway in the valley still runs as a tourist train. The Northwest Railway Museum runs weekend excursions for 3.5 miles between Snoqualmie Falls and North Bend on the former Northern Pacific Railway North Bend branch. That route dates to 1889 when it was constructed by the Seattle, Lake Shore, and Eastern Railway.

Duthie Hill Mountain Bike Park Loop

Duthie Hill Park is nothing less than an outdoor amusement park for mountain bikers. The 130-acre county park in the Issaquah Highlands features single-track trails and freestyle runs that are suitable for all levels. Dedicated solely to the pursuit of mountain biking, the park was developed by the King County Parks and Recreation Department in conjunction with the Evergreen Mountain Bike Alliance.

Start: Duthie Hill Park parking lot at 27101 SE Duthie Hill Rd. in Issaquah

Length: 5.4 miles

Approximate riding time: 1.5 to 2 hours

Best bike: Mountain bike

Terrain: Short climbs and descents. Trail is packed-dirt single-track that's good for riding even in wettest weather; typical roots and rocks found in most Northwest forests.

Traffic and hazards: No cars and few, if any, hikers. One-way single tracks are graded for level of difficulty, and more challenging technical options can be avoided.

Things to see: Thick forest of second-growth Douglas fir and western hemlock, 600-foot-long boardwalk through marsh, all manner of dirt and wooden jumps, mountain biking classes and clinics

Maps: *DeLorme Atlas & Gazetteer—Washington,* page 46; King County Backcountry Trails, your.kingcounty.gov/ftp/gis/Web/VMC/recreation/BCT_DuthieHill_brochure.pdf

Getting there: By car: Heading east of I-90, take exit 18 for Highlands Drive. Stay left on ramp and follow Highlands Drive about 2 miles. Turn right on Southeast Issaquah–Fall City Road for 2 miles, then go straight on Southeast Duthie Hill Road as Issaquah–Fall City Road turns right. Look for the Duthie Hill Park entrance on the right in about another mile. Overflow parking: Cascade Ridge Elementary School, 2020 Trossachs Blvd.

Southeast, Sammamish. Continue 0.6 miles on Duthie Hill Road, then turn left onto Trossachs Boulevard Southeast, looking for the school on the right in 0.8 miles. (Do not use the Church of Jesus Christ of Latter Day Saints parking lot on Duthie Hill Road.) **By bus:** Metro bus route 927 gets within 3 miles of park; continue east on Issaquah–Fall City Road, then take Duthie Hill Road to parking lot. GPS: N47 35.035' / W121 58.618'

THE RIDE

Did you ever wonder what became of those neighborhood kids who would place a brick under one end of an old piece of lumber to make a homemade bicycle jump? Undoubtedly some of them ended up on the work gangs that built the fast single track and soaring jumps at Duthie Hill Park.

Hundreds of volunteers turned the 130-acre King County park into a world-class wonderland for mountain biking that opened in 2010. The facility has received widespread recognition, not only for the trails and free-ride lines, but also for the cooperation between county officials and the Evergreen Mountain Biking Alliance that led to the park's creation.

Duthie Hill Park is aimed for all skill levels, so don't be alarmed if you see mountain bikers in the parking lot wearing bike helmets with chin bars and Kevlar body armor. That's the appropriate dress for those who plan to go airborne on freestyle jumps scattered throughout the forest. Still, there's plenty of riding for mountain bikers who like to keep their knobbies firmly planted in the dirt.

Four cross-country courses weave through the dense forest of Douglas fir and western hemlock in a cloverleaf pattern. These trails, covering about five miles, are ranked for novice, intermediate, and advanced mountain bikers.

Within the confines of each cloverleaf cross-country route are free-ride lines with ladder drop-ins, fast-flowing berms, and rolling

Bike Shops

Bicycle Center of Issaquah: 121 Front St. North, Issaquah; (425) 392-4588; bicyclecenter.biz
REI–Issaquah: 735 NW Gilman Blvd., Issaquah; (425) 313-1660; rei.com/stores/issaquah.html
Singletrack Cycles: 119 W. North Bend Way, North Bend; (425) 888-0101; stcycles.com

and tabletop jumps. A few of these are feasible for novice riders going slowly, but most are recommended for expert riders who enjoy using their speed to launch themselves skyward. Read the warnings posted at each free-ride line.

All the rides begin and end at the Central Clearing, a 2.5-acre area with a shelter, kiosks, and skill-building setups such as logs and skinny boards at various heights above the ground. This is also where Evergreen holds its mountain-biking clinics.

This ride uses the four cross-country trails: Bootcamp (novice), Movin' On, Step It Up (both intermediate), and Braveheart (advanced).

From the parking lot off Southeast Duthie Hill Road, pass between the boulders to begin the Duthie Hill Trail. This heads down a slight hill to a 600-foot-long boardwalk—wide enough for mountain bikers to pass—that crosses a soggy area filled with alders. You'll climb a couple of switchbacks that lead to the Central Clearing. Here you're likely to see mountain bikers in small groups, sitting around on benches swapping lies, checking the bulletin board, or practicing their balance on logs.

The entrance to the first trail—Bootcamp—is directly across the clearing from the access road. As with all the trails, Bootcamp is a one-way single track that rolls in a clockwise direction; the entrance is clearly marked.

Bootcamp weaves for a little more than a mile through a part of the forest where mature trees are bedecked in moss. The turns are fairly wide and easy

A mountain biker catches air on an expert jump at the Flow Park.

to negotiate; many are bermed so you can ride up on the bank without slowing down. There are a few skinnies and ladder bridges along the route; easier options are clearly marked with arrows.

The single track meanders slightly uphill to a log ride made of up several fallen trees that combine to the length of a football field. Some log sections are wider than others, and confident bikers might want to give the wider parts a try. The single track trends downhill on the way back to the clearing.

Evergreen Mountain Bike Alliance

When your mountain-bike tires roll across a narrow dirt track anywhere in the Puget Sound region, it's likely that members of the Evergreen Mountain Bike Alliance had a hand in it.

Evergreen and its 7,000 members work on advocacy, education, and trail building and maintenance for the mountain-biking community. All those missions came together at Duthie Hill Mountain Bike Park. The group worked with King County to dedicate the park for mountain biking and provided volunteer workers to build the trails. Since the park's opening in 2010, mountain bikers have been going there to ride for fun and attend clinics on improving their skills.

The prototype for Duthie Hill is the I-5 Colonnade Mountain Bike Skills Park, a 2-acre urban skills park with about a mile of single track beneath I-5 near the Lakeview Boulevard East exit in Seattle. At this city park that opened in 2007 the skill features and extensive trails were built by Evergreen volunteers.

The alliance got its start in 1989 as a grassroots group called the Backcountry Trails Club. They were trying to win respect for mountain bikers at a time when two-wheelers were being kicked off some trails and losing others to suburban sprawl. As the membership rolls swelled and experience grew, the club learned how to advocate for trails. Now its members are involved in land-use issues affecting trails at the beginning of the process instead of when the bulldozers appear or the NO MOUNTAIN BIKING signs are posted.

Something to bear in mind is that these trails didn't build themselves. Someone had to design the route through the woods and get approval for it. Then a whole bunch of folks had to cut through brush, move rocks, shovel dirt, and build bridges. In most cases, volunteers fill these roles. Good karma dictates that if you ride the trails, then you should put in some hours helping to build or maintain them. Volunteer opportunities are always posted at the Evergreen Mountain Bike Alliance website—evergreenmtb.org/home/index.php.

The appropriately named Movin' On trail starts just to the left of where Boot-camp ends. The trail heads slightly uphill on a fairly direct course, then bombs down the back side to a clearing, but ends with a climb up a few switchbacks to the Central Clearing.

Movin' On has tighter turns and more roots and rocks to remind you that you're riding in the Pacific Northwest. A couple of short ladder bridges aren't paired with easier options, but all the elevated ladders and skinnies offer alternatives around them.

As you arrive at a small clearing, look for the trail to resume in the forest on the right. You'll want to avoid getting mixed into the fast moving traffic in the Flow Park, although there's a good view of the freestyle action as you head uphill.

Movin' On ends at the Braveheart trail, which is considered advanced. Instead, let's head over to the other intermediate trail, Step It Up, which is the first trail past the Duthie Hill Trail as you skirt the left side of the Central Clearing.

At about 1.5 miles, Step It Up is the longest of the cross-country trails. Although marked intermediate, it seems more challenging than the first two trails. There are more tight turns, especially in the first half, as well as some drops where options aren't available. When alternatives are suggested around technical obstructions, the options can be more challenging.

Several free-ride options—Honey Badger, Ryan's Eternal Flow, Double Trouble, Gravy Train, GHY, and Big Tree—are accessible about 1 mile into the loop. Honey Badger is novice level, but the others are for expert bikers.

Returning to the Central Clearing, go to the right around the perimeter to return to Braveheart. This is the only trail marked advanced. It begins with a steep, rocky drop and then some exacting uphill turns around some roots and over stones. A couple of speedy downhills follow before the final climb up to Central Clearing.

If you haven't already done so, you can practice your balance on some of logs and skinnies in the clearing. Or you can take Bootcamp again at a faster pace or challenge yourself on some more difficult features. You also can just turn left from the Braveheart exit, find the Duthie Hill Trail, and return to the parking lot.

MILES & DIRECTIONS

0.0 Pass through boulders at trailhead to Duthie Hill Trail.

0.1 Begin riding on the boardwalk.

0.3 Finish riding on the boardwalk; follow the trail to the right.

0.5 Arrive at Central Clearing; keep heading in same direction to Boot-camp Trail.

0.6 Begin Bootcamp Trail, which is marked with a sign.

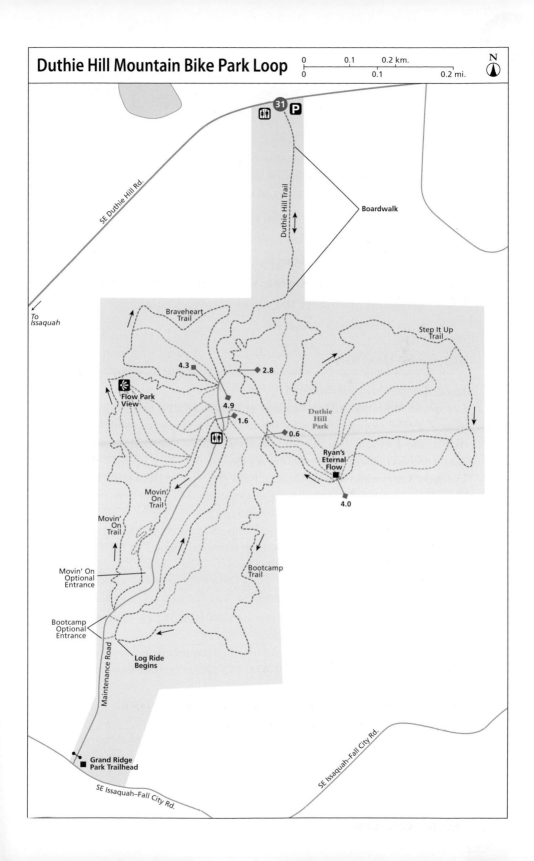

Duthie Hill Mountain Bike Park Loop

0   0.1   0.2 km.

0   0.1   0.2 mi.

N

31 **P**

SE Duthie Hill Rd.

Duthie Hill Trail

Boardwalk

To Issaquah

Braveheart Trail

Step It Up Trail

4.3

2.8

Flow Park View

4.9

1.6

0.6

Duthie Hill Park

Ryan's Eternal Flow

4.0

Movin' On Trail

Movin' On Trail

Movin' On Optional Entrance

Bootcamp Trail

Bootcamp Optional Entrance

Log Ride Begins

Maintenance Road

Grand Ridge Park Trailhead

SE Issaquah–Fall City Rd.

SE Issaquah–Fall City Rd.

1.6 Finish Bootcamp Trail and turn left to begin Movin' On Trail.

1.9 Pass access trail on left to Maintenance Road.

2.5 Enter a small clearing at low end of Flow Park; find continuation of Movin' On Trail directly ahead.

2.7 Finish Movin' On Trail; cross gravel road and left along the edge of Central Clearing toward Step It Up Trail (just past Duthie Hill Trail).

2.8 Turn left to enter Step It Up Trail.

4.0 Pass Ryan's Eternal Flow and other free-ride lines on right.

4.2 Finish Step It Up and follow perimeter of Central Clearing to the right.

4.3 Turn right to begin Braveheart Trail (just after the freestyle-run HLC Line).

4.9 Finish Braveheart Trail, and bear left to return to Duthie Hill Trail.

4.9 Turn left onto Duthie Hill Trail and return to parking lot.

5.4 Arrive at parking lot. End of ride.

RIDE INFORMATION

Local Events and Attractions

Evergreen Mountain Biking Festival at Duthie Hill Park: Vendors show gear and offer mountain bikes for demo rides, races, clinics, food, refreshments, and entertainment in mid-June. Details at Evergreen Mountain Bike Alliance: evergreenmtb.org/home/index.php.

Evergreen mountain-biking classes: Held regularly at Duthie Hill Park in the spring, summer, and fall. Details at Evergreen Mountain Bike Alliance: evergreenmtb.org/education.

Grand Ridge Park: Fifteen miles of mountain-biking trails; connects to south end of Duthie Hill Park from Issaquah–High Point Trail along I-90. See chapter about Grand Ridge Park Trail.

Restaurants

Issaquah Brewhouse: 35 W. Sunset Way, Issaquah; (425) 557-1911; rogue.com/events/pub-events-issaquahpub.php

XXX Root Beer Drive-in: Vintage drive-in with antique cars cruising the parking lot; 98 NE Gilman Blvd., Issaquah; (425) 392-1266; triplexrootbeer.com

Restrooms

Mile 0.0: West end of parking lot (portable toilet)

Mile 1.6: Maintenance Access Road just south of entrance to Movin' On Trail (portable toilet)

32

Grand Ridge Park Trail

Tame to wild in under 30 minutes—that's the time frame for traveling by mountain bike from downtown Issaquah to the quiet depths of Grand Ridge Park. This route promises steep dirt trails that can prove a little tricky up to and down from the ridgelines. Otherwise, the well-maintained single track meanders freely through the dense forest.

Start: Parking lot near I-90 on East Sunset Way in Issaquah

Length: 14.5 miles round-trip

Approximate riding time: 3 to 4 hours

Best bike: Mountain bike

Terrain: Very steep getting up and down the ridge; also a set of switchbacks deep in the park

Traffic and hazards: Watch for other mountain bikers, occasional equestrians, and hikers. The trail can get busy on weekends and summer evenings. Rocky paths and tree roots can be slippery when it's wet.

Things to see: Fanciful sculptures; old coal-mine debris; hand-built bridges; giant Douglas fir and western red cedar; and possible glimpses of deer, bear, owls, and other wildlife

Maps: *DeLorme Atlas & Gazetteer—Washington,* page 46; King County Grand Ridge Park, your.kingcounty.gov/ftp/gis/Web/VMC/recreation/BCT_GrandRidge_brochure.pdf

Getting there: By car: Take I-90 east to Issaquah and take exit 18 toward East Sunset Way. Stay on the right-hand ramp and turn right at the traffic light. Go 1 block downhill and turn left into a dirt parking lot. (If you're concerned about car break-ins, continue 4 blocks west on East Sunset Way and look for street parking around city hall.) Additional parking spaces are located at Issaquah's Central Park on Northeast Park Drive and the Southeast High Point Way at exit 20 on I-90. King County is studying a small parking lot east of the park on 280th Drive Southeast. **By bus:** Metro bus route 554 from downtown Seattle stops next to City Hall at East Sunset Way and 1st Avenue Southeast. GPS: N47 31.787' / W122 01.540'

THE RIDE

The name Grand Ridge Park is no exaggeration. The land mass on the shoulder of the Cascades is grand in terms of both its prominence over the landscape to the west as well as the noble stands of Douglas fir, hemlock, and western red cedar that cover it.

Mountain bikers, hikers, and equestrians for years were drawn to the old logging roads and other raggedy trails that crossed this crease of land owned by private interests. In the late 1990s, however, King County was able to gain title to 1,300 acres up here in a trade-off with developers of the adjacent Issaquah Highlands. With the property in the public domain, the county began working with the local outdoors groups. Volunteers improved the trails leading up the ridge at the south end of the park, then built 7 miles of single track northward through the forest.

That's the destination for this bike route that starts at the Sunset Way Trailhead on East Sunset Way at the corner of 6th Avenue Northeast in Issaquah. Head uphill on Sunset Way to the crosswalk across the I-90 ramp and follow the paved path that goes beneath, then alongside, a raised roadway. You're on the Issaquah–High Point Trail, which soon turns to crushed rock. The trail is the old roadbed of the Northern Pacific Railroad that ran through this east-west corridor between Grand Ridge (on your left) and Tiger Mountain (on your right). Now it's a noisy slot for traffic traveling on I-90.

Bike Shops

Bicycle Center of Issaquah: 121 Front St. North, Issaquah; (425) 392-4588; bicyclecenter.biz
REI–Issaquah: 735 NW Gilman Blvd., Issaquah; (425) 313-1660; rei.com/stores/issaquah.html

Riding uphill from East Fork Issaquah Creek, look on the left for the well-worn Coal Mine Trailhead. Turn left up the quick steep slope and then left again at the first Y. (The right turn is a slightly more direct route named Coal Mine Loop that suffers from loose rock that creates severe traction woes.)

An open spot in the woods just past this left turn is the site of the old Grand Ridge coal mine, which was a going concern here off and on from 1909

The trail follows the ridgeline at the top of the first climb.

to the 1950s. All that remains are a few moss-covered concrete building foundations and a slight depression at the old mine entrance. You're also likely to see small pieces of coal scattered about the trail here or in streambeds.

Next is a section that gains altitude rapidly. Veer right at the next two junctions and try not to lose your momentum, or else you'll be pushing your bike. (Those paths to the left connect to Issaquah's Central Park on Northeast Park Drive.) You've passed the steepest part of the trail when you gain the ridgeline a couple of hundred feet past that second right. You're still gaining altitude, but it's steadier.

Following the canopied contours of this trail for about a half-mile, you reach the junction with the main Grand Ridge Trail coming up the slope from the Issaquah–High Point Trail. Turn left, head uphill, cross a small bridge, and suddenly the road noise from I-90 disappears. Cross Grand Ridge Drive and zoom uphill on the other side. (A short detour left down the road leads to a spectacular view of Bellevue and Seattle.)

The next 5-mile segment heads north through a giant swath of public land that extends eastward and is considered a greenway and wildlife corridor. After loggers ripped through here to harvest lumber to build Seattle in the late nineteenth and early twentieth centuries, this area has been largely untouched. The second-growth forest is home to black bear, coyote, and mule deer, as well as the smaller raccoon and mountain beaver. Residents of the area have reported seeing cougar, bobcat, and elk. Pacific tree frogs and red-legged frogs serenade passersby, and Pacific giant salamanders live in moist areas here.

After running the ridges, you too will descend to the swampy areas. A steep descent takes you to the Canyon Creek Bridge, which volunteers built on site from fallen cedar scavenged nearby. Then the trail meanders through the second-growth forest for more than a mile, passing a trailside boulder deposited by an ancient glacier, to a swampy area that used to swallow the shoes of ardent bicyclists and hikers. Once again, Washington Trails Association volunteers spent a couple of summers building a 600-foot-long puncheon bridge across this swamp. The builders used locally milled lumber for the boardwalk, which even has a hitching post for horses.

A short, winding ride uphill finds the trail end at Southeast Fall City Road. Looking across the road you'll spot the back entrance to Duthie Hill Park, the skills course created by the Evergreen Mountain Bike Alliance. To return, retrace your route all the way back to the trail junction where you first met the Grand Ridge Trail coming uphill at mile 2.5. On your return trip, that junction is at mile 11.5 and it's a left turn. The trail takes a rolling path along the ridge to another junction where you turn left and roll gently downhill.

Suddenly, the trail heads downhill in an exciting descent around eight or nine tight switchbacks marked by steep drops over tree roots or rocks. Hold onto your brakes as you take a pounding for the next half-mile or so to the bottom. After that last rugged stretch, the Issaquah-High Point Trail seems amazingly smooth as you turn right and head down the trail and back to the parking lot.

MILES & DIRECTIONS

0.0 Turn right out of parking lot and head uphill on bike lane or sidewalk.

0.2 Continue across I-90 exit ramp at crosswalk light.

0.4 Go straight ahead toward Preston (instead of Issaquah) at junction on paved trail, which turns into a gravel path named Issaquah–High Point Trail.

1.4 Turn left onto Coal Mine Trail, a well-worn dirt trail that may or may not be marked on the left.

1.5 Turn left at first junction (a right turn is a rockier uphill trail). About 100 yards beyond this junction is the site of an unmarked coal-mine entrance.

1.7 Take the right trail fork (the left heads to a transmission-line trail) and pedal uphill.

1.8 Take the right fork at trail junction and bike along ridge.

2.1 Continue straight at junction. Trail on left is 1.1-mile loop around South Pond.

2.5 Take the left-hand fork at trail junction (right returns to Issaquah–High Point Trail).

Grand Ridge Park Trail

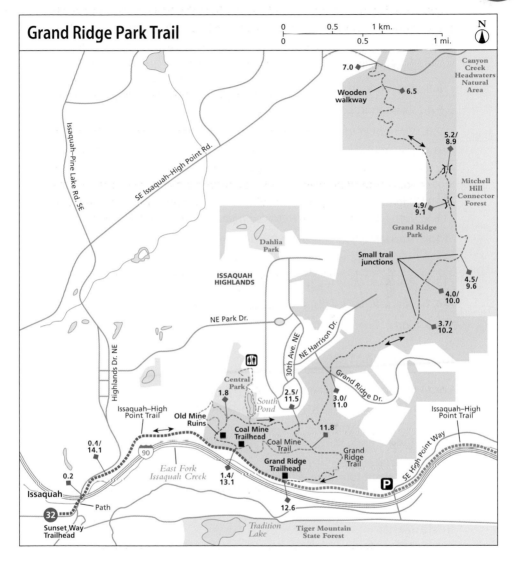

3.0 Cross Grand Ridge Drive (a short detour to left on the road leads to a viewpoint).

3.7 Take left fork at trail junction.

4.0 Take right fork at trail junction.

4.5 Take left fork at trail junction. (Right turn leads to 284th Avenue Southeast trailhead).

4.9 Cross a bridge.

5.2 Cross Canyon Creek Bridge at the bottom of a steep descent.

6.5 Begin crossing a 0.1-mile boardwalk across swamp.

7.0 Turn around at Southeast Issaquah–Fall City Road (entrance to Duthie Hill Park is across the road).

8.9 Cross bridge, followed by steep hill with switchbacks.

9.1 Cross short bridge.

9.6 Go right at trail junction.

10.0 Go left at trail junction.

10.2 Take right fork at junction.

11.0 Cross Grand Ridge Drive.

11.5 Turn left at junction (to retrace original route go right).

11.8 Turn left at junction (right turn is Coal Mine Trail).

12.6 Turn right onto Issaquah–High Point Trail.

13.1 Pass Coal Mine trailhead.

14.1 Bear left toward historic Issaquah.

14.5 End of ride.

RIDE INFORMATION

Local Events and Attractions

Salmon Days Festival: October, streets are closed throughout downtown Issaquah; salmondays.org

Grand Ridge Park, King County: kingcounty.gov/recreation/parks/trails/backcountry/grandridge.aspx

Evergreen Mountain Bike Alliance: Grand Ridge Park Trail wiki; trails.evergreenmtb.org/w/index.php?title=Trail:Grand_Ridge

Restaurants

Issaquah Brewhouse: 35 W. Sunset Way, Issaquah; (425) 557-1911

XXX Root Beer Drive-in: Vintage drive-in with antique cars cruising the parking lot; 98 NE Gilman Blvd., Issaquah; (425) 392-1266; triplexrootbeer.com

Restrooms

Mile 2.1: Turn left at this trail junction, ride about a half-mile on either side of pond, then turn left when you hit the parking lot for Central Park. Restrooms with water are located near the baseball fields.

33

Tiger Mountain State Forest

*If there were a collective mountain bikers' bucket list for the Seattle area, Tiger Mountain State Forest would certainly be at the top. The forested landmark just a half-hour drive east of Seattle is home to a collection of single tracks that, when combined with forest roads, creates a 17-mile mountain-biking loop through mature forests. If there's a drawback, it's the more than 1,600-foot climb on forest service roads to the summit. Anyone who makes it to the top agrees that the gravity-battling labor pays off. **Note:** Mountain-biking trails are closed roughly from Oct 15 to Apr 15, depending on the weather. Take water; no potable water on-site.*

Start: Tiger Mountain parking lot on SR 18

Length: 17.6 miles

Approximate riding time: 3 to 4 hours

Best bike: Mountain bike

Terrain: Long climb to the summit (climbs more than 1,600 feet in 4 miles); mountain-bike trails are mostly downhill with short climbs. Trails are well maintained; the Preston Railroad Grade Trail has more rocks and roots than the others.

Traffic and hazards: Hikers occasionally use these trails; mountain bikers can take them in either direction. Check the kiosk for announcements about trail closures due to logging, flooding, or the seasons. Car break-ins are an occasional problem.

Things to see: Views of western Washington and Mount Rainier from East Tiger Mountain Summit, hang-gliders taking off from Poo Poo Point, thick second-growth as well as recently logged forestland, wildlife

Maps: *DeLorme Atlas & Gazetteer—Washington,* page 46; Green Trails Maps, Map No. 204S: Tiger Mountain

THE RIDE

The grand loop for mountain bikers in the Tiger Mountain State Forest comprises four trails with distinct personalities: the flowy East Tiger Summit Trail, the rooty and rocky Preston Railroad Grade, the smoother Northwest Timber Trail, and the technical Iverson Trail. Also, there's a good chance that volunteer trail-builders for the Evergreen Mountain Bike Alliance will have completed the Silent Swamp Trail between the Preston and Northwest Timber trails by the time this guidebook is published in 2014. Those trails and the various forest roads are the only ones open to mountain bikers in the 13,500-acre state forest. Other trails are set aside for hikers or equestrians.

Tiger Mountain rises prominently in the eastern Seattle suburbs. Its six peaks are part of the so-called Issaquah Alps that march toward the Cascades from the lower Cougar and Squak mountains in the west to the higher Rattlesnake Ridge to the east. The mountain is bordered by I-90, Issaquah-Hobart Road, and SR 18.

The single-track route winds through the thick second-growth forests on the eastern face of the mountain. Like most of western Washington, this area was heavily logged by settlers, and many of the hiking and biking trails we use today have their origins with the roads and railroads loggers built to get their timber to market.

You can ride these single-track trails in any direction and in any order, but here is the route that most prefer. Just make sure the trails are open; they're usually closed from mid-October to mid-April.

The ride starts at a pot-holed parking lot marked Tiger Mountain Summit on SR 18. Find the kiosk and take the gate on the left to West Side Road. Turn into the upper parking lot in about 0.3 miles to find pit toilets. (This short stretch is usually open to

Bike Shops

Bicycle Center of Issaquah: 121 Front St. North, Issaquah; (425) 392-4588; bicyclecenter.biz
REI–Issaquah: 735 NW Gilman Blvd., Issaquah; (425) 313-1660; rei.com/stores/issaquah.html
Singletrack Cycles: 119 W. North Bend Way, North Bend; (425) 888-0101; stcycles.com

Mount Rainier can be seen from the East Tiger Mountain Summit Trailhead.

cars in the summer and you can choose to park here instead of the SR 18 parking lot below. Remember to display your Discover Pass in this state facility.)

Ride through this parking lot and turn right onto the Connector Trail that links to Main Tiger Mountain Road in 0.2 miles. Take a deep breath and start your ascent up this gravel forest road in your stump-puller gear. Although this is a steady climb, the slope changes occasionally and almost levels out on a couple of switchbacks. Look for views off the mountain through occasional breaks in the treeline or look down into ravines that carry rushing water off the mountainside.

At 3.0 miles from the parking lot turn right onto Crossover Road, which continues to ascend. Turn left at mile 3.5 for the final half-mile assault to East Tiger Mountain Summit, at 3,006 feet the highest of six peaks on the mountain. After pausing to enjoy a breathtaking view of Mount Rainier, start off downhill on the marked East Tiger Summit Trail. The single track, completed in 2012, was the first new mountain-biking trail on Tiger Mountain in at least two decades. Volunteers handled the bulk of the hauling, shoveling, and grading.

The silky smooth trail drops about 500 feet through the forest in 1.5 miles on roller-coaster runs and banked turns. Experienced bikers can catch air on these jumps, although novice riders will be fine cutting their tire treads through the dirt as long as their speed doesn't get away from them.

Tiger Mountain State Forest

The older Preston Railroad Grade Trail starts as the East Summit Trail hits a continuation of the Main Tiger Mountain Road. Preston is a much rougher trail through a more mature part of the forest. Bikers dodge rocks and bump over tree roots as they descend more than 900 feet over the next 3.4 miles. The upper portion is fairly level, but the elevations drop as you hit a series of six or seven switchbacks installed by old-time railroaders to get up this steep part of the mountain. In wet weather, water finds its way onto the trail through here.

Preston ends at Crossover Road. Turn left and then make a right onto East Side Road in about 0.2 miles. Take this forest road for 2 miles to the trail-head for Northwest Timber Trail on the right. (With the opening of the Silent Swamp Trail in 2014, you can turn right at Crossover Road, go a short distance, then take Silent Swamp to the left and another left when you get to Joyride Trail. This avoids the East Side Road and meets the Northwest Timber Trail.)

The 2.1-mile Northwest Timber Trail is certainly a kinder and gentler ride after the jarring descent on Preston, but be alert for a couple of dicey root crossings. This part of the mountain is visibly wetter, as moss hangs from the trees and grows up to the edge of the trail. At least a half-dozen bridges cross streams. Riding this trail reminds bikers that this is still a working forest as they cross a steep mountainside cleared of the big trees that stand elsewhere along the trail.

The trail ends at Main Tiger Mountain Road. A left turn returns to the lower parking lot, where bikers can call it quits or launch the final leg toward Iverson Trail. (Iverson Trail is also accessible from the Connector Trail, but that westbound route has more climbing.)

Repeat the earlier leg from the lower parking lot, but instead of turning into the upper lot, continue 1.4 miles to the Iverson Trailhead on the right. After a challenging climb, the 2-mile trail continues over roots and those niggling small stones called "baby heads." The trail passes next to a logged area on the uphill side, but the mature forest surrounding the trail has been spared. After the second bridge the trail makes a steep run downhill to the upper parking lot.

Now you can scratch this ride off your mountain biking bucket list, but you'll probably return.

MILES & DIRECTIONS

Main Loop

0.0　Start at West Side Road, which is the gravel forest road on the left side of a kiosk at the rear of the lower parking lot next to SR 18.

0.3　Right turn into Tiger Mountain Trailhead, also known as upper parking lot. Pass the restrooms on the right and take a short dirt path

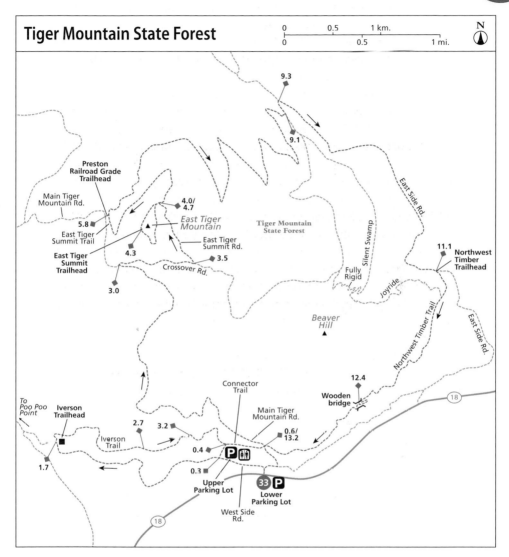

Tiger Mountain State Forest

0   0.5   1 km.
0   0.5   1 mi.

N

9.3

9.1

Preston
Railroad Grade
Trailhead

Main Tiger
Mountain Rd.

4.0/
4.7

5.8

East Tiger
Summit Trail

East Tiger
Mountain

East Tiger
Summit Rd.

Tiger Mountain
State Forest

East Side Rd.

Silent Swamp

11.1

Northwest
Timber
Trailhead

4.3

East Tiger
Summit
Trailhead

3.5

Crossover Rd.

Fully
Rigid

Joyride

3.0

Beaver
Hill

Northwest Timber Trail

East Side Rd.

12.4

Connector
Trail

Wooden
bridge

18

To
Poo Poo
Point

Iverson
Trailhead

2.7

3.2

Main Tiger
Mountain Rd.

0.6/
13.2

Iverson
Trail

0.4

P

1.7

0.3

18

Upper
Parking Lot

33 P

Lower
Parking Lot

West Side
Rd.

18

toward Iverson Railroad Trail, Preston Railroad Trail, and Northwest
Timber Trail.

0.4 Take right fork onto Connector Trail (Iverson Railroad Trail is on
the left).

0.6 Turn left onto Main Tiger Mountain Road.

3.0 Turn right onto Crossover Road 5500, following the signs to East
Tiger Summit.

3.5 Turn left onto the forest service road to East Tiger Summit.

4.0 Cross the East Tiger Summit Trail.

4.3 Stop at East Tiger Mountain Summit to enjoy the views. East Tiger Summit Trail is marked and heads to the left.

4.7 Cross the forest road as you descend.

5.8 Bear to the right onto Preston Railroad Trail (left is Main Tiger Mountain Road).

9.1 Turn left onto Crossover Road 5500 at end of Preston Railroad Trail. (In 2014 and beyond, look for signs to Silent Swamp Trail, which will become a single-track option to Northwest Timber Trail.)

9.3 Turn right onto East Side Road 7000, following the sign toward Northwest Timber Trail.

11.1 Turn right onto an unnamed forest road and make an immediate left onto Northwest Timber Trail.

12.4 Cross a large wooden bridge.

13.2 Trail ends; turn left onto Main Tiger Mountain Summit Road 4000.

13.5 Pass through blue gate into lower parking lot. The ride ends.

Iverson Trail Option

0.0 From the lower parking lot, take West Side Road to the left.

0.3 Pass the Tiger Mountain Trailhead turnoff on the right.

1.7 Turn right through the Iverson Trailhead gate.

2.7 Cross a wooden bridge.

3.2 Cross a bigger bridge with handrails. Begin descent.

3.7 Pass upper parking lot on the right. Trail becomes Connector Trail.

3.9 Turn right on Main Tiger Mountain Road.

4.1 Pass through gate to lower parking lot. End of ride.

RIDE INFORMATION

Local Events and Attractions

Hang-gliding at Tiger Mountain: Poo Poo Point, www.nwparagliding.com .dnnmax.com/PilotInfo/TigerMountain/tabid/236/Default.aspx

Salmon Days Festival: October; streets are closed throughout downtown Issaquah; salmondays.org

Discover Pass: Required at state parks and recreation areas. Available online at discoverpass.wa.gov.

Off-season Biking to Poo Poo Point

If you visit Tiger Mountain when the single-track trails are closed over the winter and early spring (usually Oct 15 to Apr 15), you're free to roam over the forest service roads. You can still pedal to East Tiger Summit, or the other summits, to enjoy the views.

One breathtaking destination is Poo Poo Point, named for the sound made by the whistle signals used by loggers to communicate. The lookout on the west side of Tiger Mountain has views of Issaquah, Bellevue, and Seattle as well as Lake Sammamish and Squak and Cougar Mountains. If the weather is dry, you'll see paragliders running off the edge of the mountain to catch thermals as they drift down to the field below.

Poo Poo Point is a rigorous 15.3-mile round-trip ride that gains 2,800 feet of ascent using the West Side Road from the lower parking lot (the gate to the upper parking lot is usually closed in the winter). After the Fifteen Mile Creek crossing at mile 5.1, cyclists face a 1,000-foot climb in the next 3 miles.

If this sounds like a little too much, the Grand Canyon Trail heads off the road to the right at mile 4.7. This trail is for hikers only, and there are bike racks and hitching posts to lock up your ride at the trailhead. The 1.4-mile round-trip trail passes a closed coal-mining tunnel and other artifacts before it reaches waterfalls in Fifteen Mile Creek.

Restaurants
Issaquah Brewhouse: 35 W. Sunset Way, Issaquah; (425) 557-1911
XXX Root Beer Drive-in: Vintage drive-in with antique cars cruising the parking lot; 98 NE Gilman Blvd., Issaquah; (425) 392-1266; triplexrootbeer.com

Restrooms
Mile 0.3: Tiger Mountain Trailhead (pit toilets; no water)

34

Middle Fork Snoqualmie Trail

This trail follows the pristine, fasting-flowing waters of the Middle Fork Snoqualmie through a mature second-growth forest about 15 miles from North Bend. Although the trail is marked by a few brisk climbs and tricky spots, it's well worth the hour's drive from Seattle to ride your mountain bike at the edge of the wilderness. **Note:** *The trail is only open to mountain biking on odd-numbered days between June 1 and Oct 31, depending on weather conditions. (Equestrians get even-numbered days.) Call the US Forest Service North Bend Office at (425) 888-1421 for details. A Northwest Forest Pass is required.*

Start: Middle Fork Trailhead parking lot operated by US Forest Service, about 15 miles from North Bend

Length: 12.4 miles

Approximate riding time: 2 to 3 hours

Best bike: Mountain bike

Terrain: The loop bike ride follows a dirt road gradually uphill (with one steep climb) for about 6 miles, then makes a gradual return on the trail. The trail has a number of steep climbs that might require some bike pushing. Don't get discouraged.

Traffic and hazards: Very light traffic on FR 56 to the turnoff at Dingford Creek. Only hikers use the trail (equestrians use the trail on even-numbered days). The trail is mostly clay, so it can be slippery when wet, as are the wooden bridge decks and tree roots. This section of the trail is rated for mountain bikers with intermediate skills.

Things to see: Views of Garfield Mountain and Alpine Lakes Wilderness areas, Middle Fork Campground, wildlife, second-growth forest, bald eagles and herons, Goldmyer Hot Springs up the road

Maps: *DeLorme Atlas & Gazetteer—Washington,* page 47; Snoqualmie Ranger District map, Mt. Baker-Snoqualmie National Forest, available at DiscoverNW.org

Getting there: By car: Drive eastbound I-90 toward North Bend and take exit 34 and turn left onto 468th Avenue Southeast. Go 2 blocks and turn right onto Southeast Middle Fork Road (FR 56). This is a very rough road, although it is scheduled for paving (2014–2015). The US Forest Service parking lot marked Middle Fork Trailhead is on the right side of the road. GPS: N47 32.890' / W121 32.217'

THE RIDE

The Middle Fork Snoqualmie Trail pokes deep into the Cascade Mountains, rolling alongside the fast-moving Middle Fork Snoqualmie River for a total of more than 14 miles. Surrounded by thick forests and peaks in the Alpine Lakes Wilderness, it's hard to believe you're only an hour from Seattle.

Safe and scenic access to the trail in the Mt. Baker–Snoqualmie National Forest and improvements to the trail itself represent years of hard work—and cooperation and compromise—by volunteers working with the Forest Service. One group, the Middle Fork Coalition, undertook the job of cleaning up the forest service road corridor that served as a dumping ground for abandoned cars and piles of garbage. The Forest Service installed gates on side roads to limit access and built the Middle Fork Campground near the entrance to the Middle Fork Trailhead.

In the meantime, the Washington Trails Association and Evergreen Mountain Bike Alliance helped to improve and maintain the Middle Fork Trail that runs alongside the upper reaches of the river. To avoid conflicts and reduce trail damage during the rainy months, the parties agreed to limit mountain biking to odd-

Bike Shop

Singletrack Cycles: 119 W. North Bend Way, North Bend; (425) 888-0101; stcycles.com

numbered days from June 1 to Oct 31, depending on weather conditions. (Equestrians are limited to even-numbered days from June 1 to Oct 31.) The 12 miles of pot-holed Southeast Middle Fork Road into the trailhead will be improved from 2014 through 2016. Extended weekday and week-long road closures are anticipated. Check the Western Federal Lands Highway website for details. If you don't encounter deep craters as you turn onto Southeast Middle Fork Road, then you know that work has been completed.

This 12.4-mile bike route covers the least-difficult lower third of the Middle Fork Trail. From the Middle Fork Trailhead parking lot, the route heads

Riverside views reveal mountains upstream that are obscured by smoke from wildland fires.

upriver on FR 56 for 6 miles, crosses the river on a bridge at the Dingford crossing, then follows the trail downriver to another bridge at the trailhead.

This is the easiest way to ride the trail. The Dingford crossing is about 400 feet higher than the Middle Fork Trailhead. Overall, the route gains about 1,300 feet of elevation. Also, you can ride upriver on the trail and return via the road, or simply ride the trail in both directions. Mountain bikes are allowed on the Middle Fork Trail for its entire length, so you can ride past the Dingford crossing for another 8 miles. There are river crossings at Goldmyer Hot Springs and at the head of the trail. Just remember the trail gets wilder and much more technical the farther upstream you go.

The Middle Fork Trailhead has a couple of pit toilets and information displays. The ride starts as you turn right onto FR 56. In less than a mile you'll pass the entrance to the Middle Fork Campground on the left, cross a bridge over Taylor River, and start a steep climb. After the crest, the road descends again and takes a gradual uphill route to the locked gate at the Dingford crossing, named for Dingford Creek just upriver. Turn right down a hillside trail and across a field of moss-covered boulders to the Middle Fork of the Snoqualmie. (A detour through the gate for 4.5 miles leads to the historic Goldmyer Hot Springs, a small resort accessible by mountain bike or foot. Reservations are suggested, as only 20 people on any given day are allowed to soak in the pools fed by the 125-degree Fahrenheit water that flows from a mine shaft.)

A sign marks the way to Middle Fork Trail 1003 and the arching steel bridge crossing the river. You'll turn right onto the Middle Fork Trail after crossing the bridge; the left turn goes to Goldmyer Hot Springs. A short, steep grunt uphill introduces you to the Middle Fork Trail. Then it trends down toward the river as you pass through the forest of second-growth Douglas fir, western hemlock, and cedar that marks this entire region. There are a few small creeks and drainages that cross the trail but don't warrant their own bridges. These can be a little tricky to navigate.

The trail climbs again to a picturesque bridge over the falls at Cripple Creek, and then plunges downhill to a boardwalk over a swampy area at the edge of the river. It seems perennially wet here, with slippery tree roots and moss hanging from branches at the river's edge. As you negotiate the next steep section, you'll encounter a series of challenging sandboxes on the trail. These are essentially steps backfilled with crushed rock to prevent the trail from washing away. Some enthusiasts say this is a good place to practice bike-handling skills.

Soon you return to the river's edge with clear views across the river to granite-topped Garfield Mountain and a series of peaks overlooking the valley upriver. Another steep climb delivers you to some rocky avalanche crossings, where you might consider practicing your bike-pushing skills.

Coming off these, the riding gets easier to manage as the trail picks up the railroad grade of the old North Bend Timber Co. that worked the area in the first half of the twentieth century. Looking uphill, you might spot a Douglas fir or two that the loggers left behind because they were too hard to reach.

The trail pays another visit to the Middle Fork Snoqualmie, then climbs up to the base of a prominent ridge and hiking destination dubbed Stegosaurus Butte. From here it's your final trip downhill to the picturesque archedbeam cable-hung Gateway Bridge that has spanned the river since the early 1990s. Turn right, cross the bridge, and follow the trail into the Middle Fork Trailhead parking lot to finish your route.

MILES & DIRECTIONS

0.0 Turn right onto FR 56 from Middle Fork Trailhead parking lot.

0.3 Pass the entrance to Middle Fork Campground on the left.

Middle Fork Snoqualmie Trail

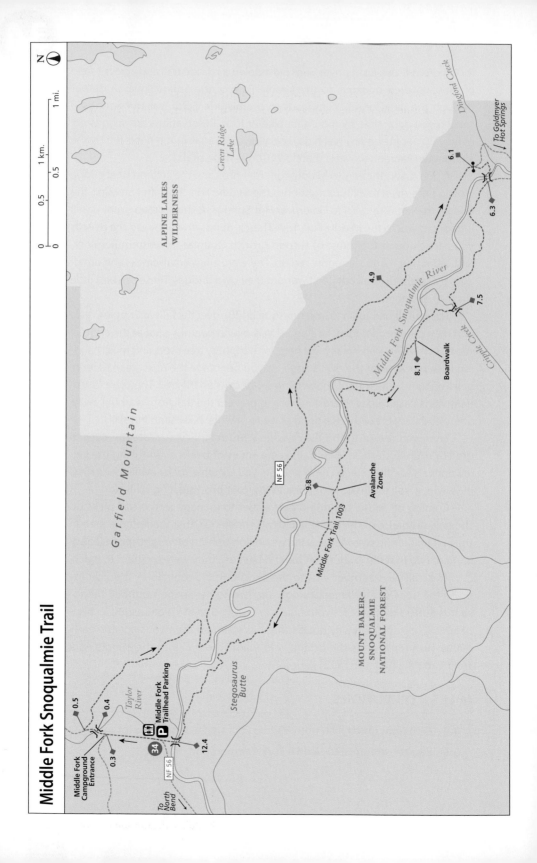

0.4 Cross the bridge over Taylor River.

0.5 Turn right at fork in the road (it's still FR 56). The route climbs for about a half-mile, then drops downhill and makes a tight left at the bottom.

4.9 Pass the Green Ridge Lake hiking trail on the left.

6.1 Road ends at a gate; turn right onto Middle Fork Trail 1003 that heads downhill.

6.3 Cross steel Dingford Bridge and turn right at the trail junction.

7.5 Cross wooden bridge over waterfall on Cripple Creek. A footpath from here heads up to Derrick Lake.

8.1 Cross boardwalk through swampy area.

9.8 Cross over boulder field littering first of two avalanche zones.

11.6 Continue over rocky trail beneath Stegosaurus Butte.

12.4 Turn right and cross bridge over Middle Fork Snoqualmie River.

RIDE INFORMATION

Local Events and Attractions
Goldmyer Hot Springs: Wading pools and campground, 4.5 miles from closed gate on Forest Service Road 56; (206) 789-5631; goldmyer.org/index.php?m=1
Middle Fork Campground: US Forest Service campground about a half-mile past Middle Fork Trailhead on FR 56. Reservations at (877) 444-6777; www.recreation.gov/camping/Middle_Fork_Campground_Wa/r/campground-Details.do?contractCode=NRSO&parkId=75386
Mt. Baker–Snoqualmie National Forest: Snoqualmie District Ranger District, North Bend Office, 902 SE North Bend Way, Building 1, North Bend; (425) 888-1421; www.fs.usda.gov/detail/mbs/about-forest/offices/?cid=fsbdev7_001660
Western Federal Lands Highway: Federal Highway Administration website for Middle Fork Road construction updates in 2014–2016, www.wfl.fhwa.dot.gov/projects/wa/snoqualmie/

Restrooms
Start: Middle Fork Trailhead (pit toilets)

35

John Wayne Pioneer Trail

Did you ever want to take a long bike ride that was all downhill? Well, this can be that ride. The John Wayne Pioneer Trail is a rail trail that rolls over the Cascades on its way across two-thirds of the state. The most popular ride, however, is the 21-mile one-way downhill stretch that starts with a spin through a dark tunnel and features awesome views from railroad trestles. It requires a car shuttle between Cedar Falls and Hyak. **Note:** *The Snoqualmie Tunnel is usually closed between November and May because of snow. Access to the trail is limited, and the shuttling doesn't work if the tunnel is closed. You'll need a state park Discover Pass (discoverpass.wa.gov) to use the parking lot.*

Start: Hyak Trailhead in Iron Horse State Park, with a shuttle stop at Cedar Falls Trailhead

Length: 21.4 miles one-way

Approximate riding time: 2 to 3 hours

Best bike: Hybrids and mountain bikes with tires greater than 28 mm width

Terrain: The trail is crushed rock. From Hyak, it's a continuous downhill grade.

Traffic and hazards: The trail is closed to motor vehicles. The 2.2-mile Snoqualmie Tunnel is pitch black and lots of lighting is necessary to spot a possible fallen rock or unlit pedestrian. Jacket and mittens are recommended, even in the summer.

Things to see: The Snoqualmie Tunnel, various trailside displays that recount life on the railroad, vistas from railroad trestles, vintage railway gear along the side of the trail, Cedar River Watershed Education Center

Maps: *DeLorme Atlas & Gazetteer—Washington,* page 61; Snoqualmie Ranger District, Mt. Baker–Snoqualmie National Forest, US Forest Service Map

Getting there: Cedar Falls Trailhead: Head east on I-90 to exit 32, turn right on 436 Avenue SE, which becomes Cedar Falls Road, then follow it uphill approximately 3.5 miles to the entrance for Iron Horse State Park parking lot on the left. A state Discover Pass must be displayed to use the parking lot (discoverpass.wa.gov). If you're shuttling to Hyak, leave a car at Cedar Falls and proceed to the Hyak Trailhead. **Hyak Trailhead:** Return to I-90 on Cedar Falls Road and continue east on I-90 to exit 54. Turn right at the exit onto SR 906, then the first left onto NFR 2219. Following the signs to Iron Horse State Park, take the second right in 0.4 miles, then right again into parking lot entrance. Cedar Falls Trailhead GPS: N47 25.954' / W121 45.985'; Hyak Trailhead GPS: N47 23.519' / W121 23.525'

THE RIDE

We can be glad that the old steam locomotives had difficulty battling gravity to get through the mountains. It resulted in abandoned railroad beds that are now bicycle paths with easy grades.

Nowhere is that more true than the John Wayne Pioneer Trail. Acquired by the state in 1980, the western section gains 1,568 feet of elevation over 21 miles into the picturesque Cascades. Bicyclists taking the trail uphill enjoy a barely perceptible grade that's never more than 2 percent from the trailhead at Cedar Falls to Snoqualmie Pass at Hyak.

In spite of the easy grade, many visitors prefer to shuttle to the top for a leisurely downhill ride. This works especially well for families. People can shuttle themselves between Cedar Falls and Hyak with two or more cars. (A shuttle bus that provided this service has been discontinued.)

This ride starts at the Hyak Trailhead after you've shuttled to the top. Mountain peaks, some capped with snow in the spring and early summer, rise on three sides. Be sure to fill up your water bottles at the restrooms here because there's no safe drinking water until the Cedar River Watershed Education Center, located past the Cedar Falls Trailhead.

Bike Shop

Singletrack Cycles: 119 W. North Bend Way, North Bend; (425) 888-0101; stcycles.com

Directly across from the restroom is an informational sign for the Iron Horse State Park. Turn right here, and soon you'll come to the East Portal of the 2.2-mile-long, straight-as-a-rifle-shot Snoqualmie Tunnel. Running 1,500 feet beneath the summit, the tunnel is cold and pitch black inside. If there's no fog blowing through the tunnel, you can see a pinpoint of light at the other entrance (you can't see this heading east because the trail makes a sharp turn after the East Portal). Carry a bright light in here to spot fallen rocks, other bicyclists, or hikers.

The flat surface of crushed rock emerges on the other side in a much grander portal structure emblazoned with the Snoqualmie Tunnel name over the dates 1912–1914. Workers drilled from both ends of the tunnel, which opened for passenger service in 1915.

The Milwaukee Road

The Chicago, Milwaukee, St. Paul, and Pacific Railroad, known by the nickname Milwaukee Road, originally traveled this route beginning in 1909. Steam, then electric, then diesel locomotives hauled freight and passengers until 1980, when the state received title to the land.

The abandoned railway crosses two-thirds of the state from the Cedar Falls Trailhead near North Bend to Tekoa on the Idaho border, a distance of about 320 miles. It was named the John Wayne Pioneer Trail after the John Wayne Pioneer Wagon and Riders group that spearheaded efforts to turn the abandoned railway into a trail. The western trail section from Cedar Falls to the Columbia River crossing near Beverly is confined in the narrow Iron Horse State Park. Bicyclists, hikers, and equestrians can travel this improved trail for 110 miles from the wet western slopes of the Cascades, through the 2.2-mile Snoqualmie Tunnel, down through the scenic Yakima River canyon, and into the arid eastern plateaus above the Columbia River. The remaining 200 miles of railway bed are unimproved to the Idaho border.

In 2009, the state closed five railroad tunnels because of hazardous conditions; the Snoqualmie Tunnel was reopened in 2011 and the other four were reopened in 2013.

The abandonment of the Milwaukee Road contributed to other rail-to-trail bikeways in King County. The Snoqualmie Valley Regional Trail that links with the John Wayne Pioneer Trail at Cedar Falls Trailhead heads north for 31 miles to Duvall. That branch of the railroad once went to Everett.

The main branch rolled through the Cedar River Watershed and made tracks for Seattle and Tacoma. While no trail exists in the watershed, which supplies Seattle's drinking water, the right-of-way between Landsburg and Renton became the Cedar River Trail.

Oxeye daises thrive at the side of the trail.

Except for a couple of dips, you'll be riding downhill for the next 18 miles. It isn't steep enough to coast, but you can build up quite a bit of steam by easy pedaling. Mountain peaks are always in view to your right; Granite Mountain is the first to catch the eye. I-90 runs alongside the South Fork of the Snoqualmie River far below.

Less than two miles after exiting the tunnel you'll come to a basin hemmed in by Humpback Mountain, Silver Peak, and Abiel Peak. Below a scarred avalanche zone here, you'll come across a rebuilt snow shed used to protect the railroad from snow slides. The wet climate on this side of the Cascades and cooler mountain temperatures contribute to a riot of wildflowers in the clearings up here until late in the summer. You'll find Turks cap, cinquefoil, and lupine, but oxeye daisies seem to thrive best alongside the trail.

The high steel trestles over the deep ravines provide the most spectacular views. The first is the Hansen Creek Trestle, which soars above the trees growing alongside the creek more than 100 feet below. You'll see scars on the mountainsides where repeated avalanches have scraped the slopes bare.

Occasionally, you'll come across signs for the old train stations—Rockdale (at the West Portal of Snoqualmie Tunnel), Bandera, Garcia, Ragnar, and Cedar Falls—along the trail. Some of these were water stops before the steam locomotives were replaced by electric engines. Cedar Falls was a full-fledged station, although not at the location of today's sign.

John Wayne Pioneer Trail

Cyclists ride across the trestle over the Mine Creek canyon in Iron Horse State Park.

Some bicyclists make this ride an overnight affair. The first campground at Carter Creek (mile 8.3) is the most popular with tent sites perched next to the tumbling creek. Three miles down trail (mile 11.2), the Alice Creek Campground sits right on the path. That apparent lack of privacy isn't a problem, however, as most of the hikers and bicyclists have passed by early evening and these tent sites can catch the morning sun.

You'll cross more trestles at Mine Creek and Hull Creek before arriving at the Deception Crags rock-climbing area at the Change Creek Trestle. This is a busy destination for beginning and intermediate climbers. Some climbing routes are closed in the spring so as not to disturb peregrine falcon nests. Watch out for unattended children meandering around on the trail while mom or dad swing from ropes above.

Also, keep your eyes open for trailside artifacts left over from the railroading days. Many telegraph poles, some with wire still hanging from them, can be seen in the second-growth forest that hugs the trail. Look for concrete foundations for train signals and miscellaneous railroad ties, rails, and iron spikes lying about. Scaffolding over the trestles carried wires when the railroad was electrified. Mileage signs posted along the trail note the distance to Chicago, the railroad's final destination. A collection of rusting semaphores and other equipment can be found by exploring a storage yard at the Ragnar train stop.

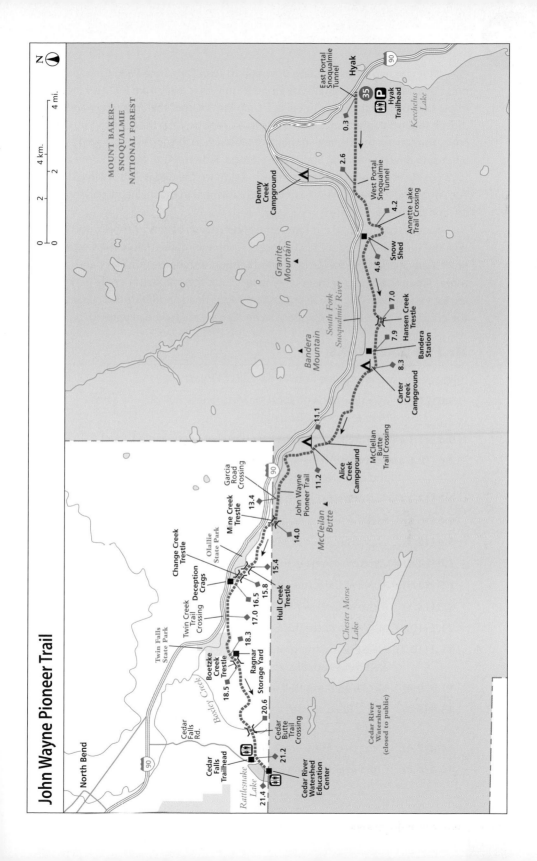

John Wayne Pioneer Trail

North Bend

MOUNT BAKER–
SNOQUALMIE
NATIONAL FOREST

East Portal
Snoqualmie Tunnel

Hyak

Hyak
Trailhead

West Portal
Snoqualmie Tunnel

Keechelus
Lake

0.3

2.6

Denny Creek
Campground

Annette Lake
Trail Crossing

4.2

Snow
Shed

4.6

7.0

Hansen Creek
Trestle

7.9

Bandera
Station

Granite
Mountain

South Fork
Snoqualmie River

Bandera
Mountain

Carter
Creek
Campground

8.3

11.1

McClellan
Butte Crossing

Alice
Creek
Campground

11.2

Garcia Road
Crossing

Mine Creek
Trestle

13.4

John Wayne
Pioneer Trail

14.0

McCleilan
Butte

Ollallie
State Park

Change Creek
Trestle

Deception
Crags

Twin Creek
Trail Crossing

Twin Falls
State Park

15.4

15.8

16.5

17.0

Hull Creek
Trestle

Boetzke
Creek
Trestle

Ragnar
Storage Yard

18.3

18.5

Boxley Creek

20.6

Cedar Butte
Trail Crossing

Cedar
Falls Rd.

Cedar Falls
Trailhead

21.2

21.4

Cedar River
Watershed
Education
Center

Rattlesnake
Lake

Chester Morse
Lake

Cedar River
Watershed
(closed to public)

N

0   2   4 km.

0   2   4 mi.

After crossing a trail heading downhill to Twin Falls State Park, the road noise dissipates as the John Wayne Pioneer Trail veers away from I-90 and the forest canopy gets thicker with tall firs. Lush ferns carpet the understory and moss hangs from tree branches. The Boetzke Creek trestle is the last one you'll cross. You can see the distinctive shape of Mount Si to the northwest as well as a housing development on Snoqualmie Ridge. Ride through this thick forest for a couple more miles before you reach a sign for the Cedar Falls Trailhead. Turn right and follow this short, windy path downhill to the trailhead, parking lot, and pit toilets.

If you first want a cold drink and some flush toilets before you finish, don't take the turn for the Cedar Falls Trailhead. Continue on the trail to the Cedar River Watershed Education Center. The building also houses displays and a three-dimensional map of the route you just took. You can return to the parking lot via the John Wayne Trail or the Cedar Falls Road Southeast that passes the education center on its way back to the Cedar Falls Trailhead parking lot.

MILES & DIRECTIONS

(Mileages in parentheses are from Cedar Falls to Hyak)

0.0 (21.4) Bike ride starts on John Wayne Pioneer Trail directly across from restrooms. Turn right.

0.3 (21.1 exit tunnel) Enter the East Portal of Snoqualmie Tunnel.

2.6 (18.8 arrive tunnel) Emerge from tunnel's West Portal. Picnic tables and pit toilet are nearby.

4.2 (17.2) The Annette Lake Trail for hikers crosses the trail.

4.6 (16.8) Pass the snow shed and informational sign for Avalanche Alley.

6.4 (15.3) Cross over Rainey Creek.

7.0 (14.4) Cross over Hansen Creek Trestle.

7.9 (13.6) Arrive at the former Bandera station site.

8.3 (13.1) Arrive at Carter Creek Campground.

11.1 (10.3) McClellan Butte Trail heads downhill toward parking lot.

11.2 (10.1) Alice Creek Campground. Another spur of McClellan Butte Trail comes uphill and crosses the trail nearby.

11.5 (9.8) McClellan Butte Trail heads uphill.

13.4 (8.0) Garcia Road crosses the trail. Signs for former Garcia station follow.

14.0 (7.4) Cross over Mine Creek Trestle.

15.4 (6.0) Cross over Hull Creek Trestle.

15.8 (5.6) Cross Change Creek Trestle and enter the Deception Crags Climbing Area. A hiking trail heads downhill to South Fork Snoqualmie River from here.

16.5 (4.9) Pass a restricted-access gravel road that goes downhill.

17.0 (4.4) Pass a hiking trail to Twin Falls State Park that heads downhill.

18.3 (3.2) Pass by the Ragnar storage yard.

18.5 (2.9) Cross over Boetzke Creek Trestle.

20.6 (0.9) Pass by Cedar Butte Trail, which heads uphill.

21.2 (0.2 turn left onto JWPT) Turn right off the John Wayne Pioneer Trail on the path to Cedar Falls Trailhead. Follow winding path to pit toilet restrooms and parking lot. (Left turn if heading from Cedar Falls to Hyak.)

21.4 (0.0) End of ride at Cedar Falls parking lot.

RIDE INFORMATION

Local Events and Attractions
Iron Horse State Park: parks.wa.gov/
Cedar River Watershed Education Center: 19901 Cedar Falls Rd. Southeast, North Bend; (206) 733-9421; seattle.gov/util/EnvironmentConservation/Our Watersheds/CedarRiverWatershed/CedarRiverEducationCenter/index.htm
Mountains to Sound Greenway: Check the website for events on John Wayne Pioneer Trail; mtsgreenway.org

Restrooms
Mile 0.0: Hyak Trailhead (water)
Mile 2.6: West Portal (pit toilet; no water)
Mile 8.3: Carter Creek Campground (pit toilet; no water)
Mile 11.2: Alice Creek Campground (pit toilet; no water)
Mile 15.8: Deception Crags (portable toilet; no water)
Mile 21.4: Cedar Falls Trailhead (pit toilet; no water)

Westside

Port Gamble's twin water tanks stand at entrance to commercial area of the historic company town.

A simple ferry ride across the Puget Sound to bicycle routes on the islands or Olympic Peninsula can seem like a voyage far from home. Vashon and Bainbridge Islands and the peninsula towns of Port Gamble, Poulsbo, and Port Orchard have a nautical flavor that's very different than Seattle and its suburbs.

Roads with little traffic link coastal towns that at one time thrived when commerce moved around the Puget Sound on small boats. Some roads, like those on Bainbridge and Vashon Islands, can be hilly. Conversely, the scenic road that follows the shoreline from Southworth to Port Orchard is fairly flat.

Beachcombing can be a major sidelight on some rides, and there are old lighthouses and fortifications to explore in parks along the way. Bicyclists will find the downtowns that once thrived on coastal boat traffic and the lumber business now cater to tourists with antiques shops and cafes.

For mountain bikers, the 1-square-mile Banner Forest Heritage Park near a ferry stop offers miles of single track among mature conifers.

Vashon–Maury Island Loop

Bicyclists who ride the ferry over to Vashon-Maury Island are treated to a bike route that rolls through dense forests, past old farms and pastures with views of the Olympic Peninsula, and alongside picturesque harbors. There's a historic lighthouse to visit and countless quirky shops and art galleries on this island that has resisted the dense development of the rest of the Seattle area.

Start: Ferry dock at north end of Vashon Island

Length: 35.1 miles

Approximate riding time: 3 to 4 hours

Best bike: Road or hybrid

Terrain: Some hilly sections; all on paved roads.

Traffic and hazards: Traffic is light on these rural roads except for Vashon Highway, which has shoulders.

Things to see: The child's red bicycle in a tree, Quartermaster Harbor, Point Robinson Lighthouse, Uptown and Burton communities, Puget Sound beaches, horse pastures, winery

Maps: *DeLorme Atlas & Gazetteer—Washington,* pages 45 and 59; Vashon-Maury Island Chamber of Commerce Map, shows bike routes and business locations; available at John Scott Realty, 13401 Vashon Hwy. Southwest, at corner of Cedarhurst Road

Getting there: By car: Fauntleroy Ferry: From north or south I-5, take exit 163 to West Seattle Bridge. After crossing the bridge, follow the arterial as it becomes Fauntleroy Way Southwest (follow signs to the ferry). Turn right into the Lincoln Park parking lot. After leaving your car, coast downhill on the shoulder or sidewalk next to Fauntleroy Way and turn right into the Fauntleroy Ferry Terminal. GPS: N47 31.881' / W122 23.654'. King County Water Taxi: Leaves from downtown Seattle Pier 50 at intersection of Alaska Way with Yesler Way. Street parking and parking garages are available in area. GPS: N47 36.102' / W122 20.219'. **By bus:** Metro buses 116, 188, 119, and 673 serve the Fauntleroy Ferry.

THE RIDE

Some say that going to Vashon-Maury Island is like taking a trip back in time. Others say it's like visiting an artist's colony. Still others say it's a New Age commune. Of course, the 10,000-person population of the island is too diverse to be labeled, but visitors agree the flavor of life here is much different than the Seattle metro area, just twenty-some minutes away by ferry.

What bicyclists notice first is the thigh-busting 1-mile climb right after departing the ferry onto Vashon Highway Southwest. Just about every ferry landing on the Puget Sound is followed by some kind of ascent, but this one is unforgettable.

After the road levels out, the route turns right onto Cedarhurst Road Southwest and plunges downhill in a breathtaking descent through a dense cedar forest. Don't go full speed here, as there are surprising turns and rough road ahead.

Road crews built this section of Cedarhurst Road up to the ridgetop in the early 1920s to connect the west side of the island with the auto ferry that began running in 1919. Heading south for the next 8 miles, you'll follow older roads that haven't changed much since they were first constructed in the early 1890s. They connected several small agricultural communities on the west side of Vashon Island to docks that shipped produce to market.

Bike Shop

Vashon Island Bicycles: 9925 SW 178th St., Vashon; (206) 463-6225; vashonislandbicycles.com

After the road becomes Westside Highway Southwest, look for the Colvos Store on the right. Built in 1923 to serve west-islanders with food, gasoline, and auto repair, it's preserved as a residence with the vintage fuel pump still out in front. Many of the barns and outbuildings along this stretch date to the 1900s to 1920s, as do two churches you'll pass (one is now a synagogue and the other is a home).

The route continues south as the Westside Highway ends at Southwest 220th Street, and after a couple of turns, becomes Wax Orchard Road Southwest. The road name refers to the island's agricultural history, as orchards and strawberries once contributed to the island's economy. There are still small farms here, as evidenced by the occasional unattended fruit stands. You'll notice many horse pastures and stables here now.

The route takes a sharp left turn onto the shoulder of Vashon Highway Southwest. As you head downhill, you'll pass a potential viewpoint named Inspiration Point Overlook. On my visits, the overlook has been overgrown and crying out for some inspired brush clearing. It's a better idea to keep coasting downhill to Magnolia Beach on Quartermaster Harbor.

When the Native Americans were moved off the island by treaty, this was the first area settled in 1877. It soon became a center of commerce with logging, fishing, and brick-making operations. Today the harbor is lined with beach homes—some swank and others ramshackle. The National Audubon Society designates this as an "Important Bird Area" for the western grebe that spend the winter here, as well as thirty-six other bird species. An inviting beach offers a good viewing spot of the harbor and Maury Island across the way.

Just around the bend, still on Vashon Highway, and up a small hill is the crossroads community of Burton. A well-stocked general store, Harbor Mercantile, is located at one corner, and the two-story Burton Masonic Hall, built in 1894 and now an art gallery, sits at another. Next door to the gallery is the Burton Coffee Stand with outdoor seating.

The Point Robinson Lighthouse first lit the way for ships plying the Puget Sound in 1915.

36

The Red Bicycle

One of Vashon Island's most popular attractions, at least for bicyclists, is an old red bicycle that's embedded in a tree. It's not just stuck in the tree; it's encased in the wood of the tree trunk.

According to the local newspaper, an island boy left the bicycle in the woods back in 1964. Apparently the bike was too small for him and he didn't care for its hard rubber tires. So one day, playing with some friends near his house, he just ditched it in the woods.

The bike was discovered lodged in the tree many years later, setting off a lot of conversation and speculation on the island. That ended when a retired sheriff's deputy visited the site with his mother, who still lived on the island, and stated that it was the bike he'd left behind.

The little red bike was featured in the 1997 children's book *Red Ranger Came Calling,* written by Berkeley Breathed, also known for his political Bloom County comic strip. He lived on the island for about ten years beginning in 1988.

Although the red bike plays a role in a popular children's book and is the namesake of the Red Bicycle Bistro and Sushi establishment in town, there are no signs to its location. To find it on this bicycle route, make the right turn from Southwest 204th Street to 99th Avenue Southwest / Vashon Highway Southwest. Immediately after passing the second building on the right (both were vacant on my last visit), look for a path that goes 10 to 20 feet off into the woods from a gravel parking lot. It leads right to the tree with the bike embedded about 12 feet off the ground.

Passing through Burton and alongside the harbor, turn right onto Southwest Quartermaster Drive toward Maury Island. Maury was separate from Vashon until a narrow connection was built in 1916. Ride over this just before you turn right onto Dockton Road Southwest. The route veers left onto Southwest Point Robinson Road at a Y intersection and heads toward the Point Robinson Lighthouse. There is a steep climb on this road that rivals the initial hill at the ferry dock. For a slightly easier route, turn left onto Southwest Luana Beach Road and follow it for 2.5 miles to the signs for the lighthouse once you rejoin Point Robinson Road.

A lighthouse and foghorn have been located on the driftwood-laden beach since 1887, and the current 38-foot-tall tower was built in 1915. Vashon Parks Department leases the facility from the Coast Guard; the two lighthouse-keeper dwellings are available for vacation rentals. Lighthouse historians give tours on weekends.

Return to Vashon Island via Southwest Luana Beach Road, which you pick up as you leave Point Robinson Park. You'll rejoin Southwest Point Robinson Road/Dockton Road and cross the man-made isthmus on Quartermaster Drive. Turn right onto Monument Road Southwest and climb the last hill. After turning left onto Southwest 204th Street, you'll come to a right turn onto the 99th Avenue Southwest shoulder.

Just past two buildings on the right corner is the short path into the woods to the old red bicycle in the tree (see sidebar).

Traffic picks up as you proceed through Center, the old commercial center of the island, to Uptown, the local name for the main business district. Along the way, you'll notice that many of the island's older buildings have been repurposed into antiques stores and art galleries, helping create the island's reputation as an artists' colony. There are restaurants, groceries, and coffee shops in the commercial district, and inviting places to relax at Ober Park.

From here, the trip back to the ferry is mostly level or downhill. Along the way, you might want to consider stops at the Labyrinth—one of eight paths on the island designed for introspection—at the Episcopal Church of the Holy Spirit, as well as the Palouse Winery, which you passed coming off the ferry.

You'll see signs directing you back to the ferry from Vashon Highway. Turn left onto 103rd Avenue Southwest, zoom down the hill to the intersection with Vashon Highway, then turn left and ride to the gate in front of the waiting cars. If there's time, you can grab a snack at the outdoor counter at the La Playa Restaurant as you wait for the ferry to carry you back to the hubbub of Seattle.

MILES & DIRECTIONS

0.0 Depart the ferry and start riding uphill on Vashon Island Highway. The road bends right at the top of the hill, passes 103rd Avenue Southwest, and then curves to the left.

1.9 Turn right at the fork onto Southwest Cedarhurst Road.

3.9 Road curves to the left and becomes Westside Highway Southwest.

7.3 Pass the Vashon Island Center Forest on the left.

7.9 Turn right onto Southwest 196 Street (Southwest Cemetery Road from the left). The road curves left and becomes Westside Highway Southwest again.

9.6 Turn right onto Southwest 220th Street.

9.8 Turn left onto Wax Orchard Road Southwest.

12.6 Pass Camp Sealth on the right.

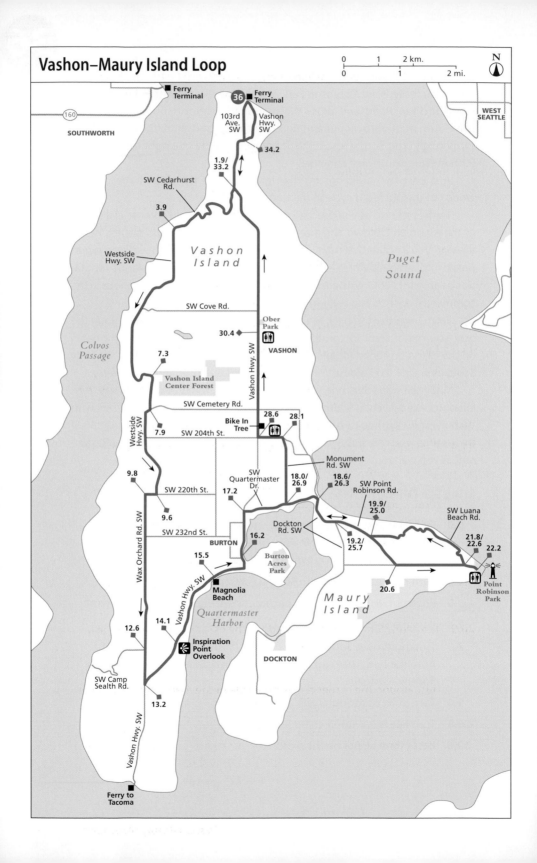

Vashon–Maury Island Loop

0 1 2 km.

0 1 2 mi.

N

Ferry Terminal

160

SOUTHWORTH

WEST SEATTLE

36 **Ferry Terminal**

103rd Ave. SW

Vashon Hwy. SW

34.2

1.9/ 33.2

SW Cedarhurst Rd.

3.9

Vashon Island

Puget Sound

Westside Hwy. SW

SW Cove Rd.

Ober Park

30.4

VASHON

Colvos Passage

7.3

Vashon Island Center Forest

Vashon Hwy. SW

SW Cemetery Rd.

Westside Hwy. SW

28.6

28.1

Bike In Tree

7.9

SW 204th St.

Monument Rd. SW

9.8

SW Quartermaster Dr.

18.0/ 26.9

18.6/ 26.3

SW Point Robinson Rd.

SW 220th St.

17.2

9.6

SW 232nd St.

Dockton Rd. SW

19.9/ 25.0

SW Luana Beach Rd.

BURTON

16.2

Wax Orchard Rd. SW

19.2/ 25.7

21.8/ 22.6

22.2

Burton Acres Park

Maury Island

15.5

20.6

Point Robinson Park

Magnolia Beach

14.1

Quartermaster Harbor

Inspiration Point Overlook

DOCKTON

12.6

SW Camp Sealth Rd.

Vashon Hwy. SW

13.2

Ferry to Tacoma

13.2 Sharp left turn onto Vashon Highway Southwest. (A 1-mile detour straight ahead goes to the landing for the Port Defiance–Tahlequah Ferry at the sound end of the island.)

14.1 Pass the Inspiration Point Overlook on the right.

15.5 Ride through Magnolia Beach community, passing Quartermaster Harbor on the right.

16.2 Enter the small community of Burton and pass Southwest Burton Drive on the right. There is a grocery store on one corner, coffee stand on another. (A 2.6- mile side-trip on Southwest Burton Drive loops around Burton Acres and kayak rentals at Jenson Point. Water views are blocked by houses, except at the dock.)

17.2 Turn right onto Southwest Quartermaster Drive.

18.0 Pass the turn on your left to Monument Road Southwest.

18.6 Turn right onto Dockton Road Southwest.

19.2 Take the left at the road split onto Southwest Point Robinson Road (right turn heads toward Dockton).

19.9 Ride past Southwest Luana Beach Road on your left (take a left here if you're looking for a less hilly route to Point Robinson).

20.6 Follow Southwest Point Robinson Road as it veers to the left.

21.8 Turn right at T intersection, following Southwest Point Robinson Road.

22.2 Follow circuitous route downhill to lower parking lot. From here, you can walk out to the lighthouse at Point Robinson Park. Retrace your route uphill when you're done.

22.6 Go straight through intersection onto Southwest Luana Beach Road, passing Southwest Point Robinson Road on the left.

25.0 Turn right onto Southwest Point Robinson Road.

25.7 Southwest Point Robinson Road joins Dockton Road Southwest.

26.3 Turn left onto Southwest Quartermaster Drive.

26.9 Turn right onto Monument Road Southwest and climb another hill.

28.1 Turn left onto Southwest 204th Street.

28.6 Turn right onto 99th Avenue Southwest / Vashon Highway Southwest (just around the corner on the right side of the road is the location of Vashon's famous bicycle in the tree).

30.4 Look for food, beverages, restrooms in Uptown, the business district of Vashon Island. This is the corner of 99th Avenue Southwest / Vashon Highway Southwest and Southwest Bank Road.

31.8 Pass the Episcopal Church of the Holy Spirit, which has a complex labyrinth open to the public.

33.2 Pass the Cedarhurst Drive Southwest turnoff on the left; remain on Vashon Highway Southwest.

34.2 Look for sign for ferry traffic and turn left onto 103rd Avenue South west. The road goes downhill and curves right. Follow it to the ferry dock, look for traffic, and turn left onto the dock and ride to the head of the line of cars to board the ferry.

35.1 End of ride.

RIDE INFORMATION

Local Events and Attractions

Docton Forest and Natural Area: 400-acre natural area with 9 miles of trail for mountain bikers, hikers and equestrians operated by King County on Maury Island; map at your.kingcounty.gov/ftp/gis/Web/VMC/recreation/BCT _Dockton_brochure.pdf

Vashon Island Garden Tour: A weekend in late June; vashonalliedarts.org

Vashon Island Strawberry Festival: Parades, music, carnival rides on a week-end in mid-July; vashonchamber.com/strawfest

Point Robinson Lighthouse: Open Sundays in the summer, 3705 SW Point Robinson Rd., Vashon; lighthousefriends.com/light.asp?ID=113

Palouse Winery: 12431 Vashon Hwy. Southwest, Vashon; palousewinery.com

Chamber of Commerce: Information on attractions and lodging; (206) 463-6217; vashonchamber.com

Restaurants

Burton Coffee Stand: 23919 Vashon Hwy. Southwest, Burton

LaPlaya Mexican Restaurant: Snack counter at the ferry dock, 10824 Vashon Hwy. Southwest, Vashon Island, (206) 567-0020

Red Bicycle Bistro & Sushi: 17618 Vashon Hwy. Southwest, Vashon, (206) 463-5959

Vashon Island Coffee Roasterie: 19529 Vashon Hwy. Southwest, Vashon, (206) 463-9800

Restrooms

Mile 22.2: Point Robinson Park (portable toilets)

Mile 28.4: Vashon Pool

Mile 30.5: Ober Park in Vashon (Uptown business district)

Bainbridge Island Loop

Bainbridge Island is easily reached by a ferry ride from a terminal in downtown Seattle. It's the destination for thousands of hardy bicyclists in the Chilly Hilly Bicycle Classic at the end of February every year. If the idea of pedaling along on narrow roads on a damp winter day doesn't excite you, then you can follow this modified route around the island and pick your season and your companions.

Start: The ferry landing in Winslow, Bainbridge Island

Length: 34.4 miles

Approximate riding time: 3 to 4 hours

Best bike: Road or hybrid

Terrain: There are a dozen climbs on this ride, many of which are short and steep.

Traffic and hazards: There's heavy traffic in Winslow when cars and trucks come off the ferry, but the roads in town have wide shoulders, bike lanes, or sharrows. There are two crossings of SR 305, but both are at traffic lights.

Things to see: Downtown Winslow, Fay Bainbridge Park, Port Madison, Frog Rock, Fort Ward Park, shoreline views too numerous to mention

Maps: *DeLorme Atlas & Gazetteer—Washington,* page 45; Bainbridge Island Map, street maps available on board ferry

Getting there: By car: Go to the Seattle Ferry Terminal at 801 Alaskan Way Pier 52, Seattle, to catch the ferry to Winslow on Bainbridge Island. From northbound I-5, take exit 164A and follow the signs; from southbound I-5, take 165B and follow the signs. Parking on-site is limited, so you'll have to look for on-street parking or use a parking garage. **By transit:** Metro bus routes 16, 66, and 99 all stop in the vicinity of the ferry terminal on Alaska Way. **By bike:** Park at Smith Cove on the Alaska Way–Alki bike route; the ride passes the ferry terminal about mile 4.6. GPS: N47 36.113' / W122 20.224'

37

THE RIDE

Only a 35-minute ferry ride from Seattle, Bainbridge Island is considered a bedroom community for the metro area. Still, the islanders are dedicated to controlling residential and commercial development and preserving green space.

Many Bainbridge Island residents have discovered bicycling as a cost-effective method of transportation to and from the city. In fact, the island has earned a bronze-level Bicycle-Friendly Community award from the League of American Bicyclists. You'll notice many of those improvements as you ride off the ferry in Winslow. The Bike Barn of Bainbridge Island, just up the hill from the ferry terminal, provides indoor bike parking and lockers for bicyclists. The local streets either have wide shoulders, bike lanes, or sharrow markings.

Riding off the ferry onto SR 305, head up the hill to the first traffic light and turn left onto Winslow Way East. Here's a shopping district with a food store, coffee shops, cafes, and plenty of places to lock up your bike. Turn right at the end of the street and head uphill on Madison Avenue North. As the houses start to thin out, you'll turn left onto Northeast New Brooklyn Road, then right onto Sportsman Club Road Northeast before crossing SR 305 at a traffic light. The road briefly becomes Madison Avenue again before you bear to the right at the Y and pick up Manitou Beach Drive Northeast.

Soon you're zooming along a scenic waterfront stretch of road that faces across Murden Cove to the Seattle skyline. There's a break in Manitou Beach Drive as you begin uphill; bicyclists and pedestrians are allowed on the narrow paved path that continues straight. The road curves to the left and passes the historic Messenger House Care Center—now a nursing home but in 1909 a hotel for Chautauqua Park where people listened to speeches from William Jennings Bryan and music from John Philip Sousa.

This is one of the notable hills on the ride, as the route turns left onto Valley Road then right onto Sunrise Drive Northeast. Then it's a rolling downhill to Fay Bainbridge Park on the right. This is a popular destination for anyone

---

Bike Shops

Bainbridge Island Cycle Shop: 124 Bjune Dr. Southeast, Bainbridge Island; (206) 842-6413; b-i-cycle.com
Bike Barn Rentals: 260 Olympic Dr. Southeast, Bainbridge Island; (206) 842-3434; bikebarnrentals.com
Classic Cycle: 740 Winslow Way East, Bainbridge Island; (206) 842-9191; classiccycleus.com/home

---

These sun-bleached derelict boats on Port Orchard Bay are slowly decaying.

making an overnight camping trip from Seattle. The small campground has tent sites, water, and restrooms and shares a road that heads down to a 1,400-foot-long beach strewn with driftwood.

Just past Fay Bainbridge Park, the route turns left onto Northeast Lafayette Avenue and then right onto Washington Avenue Northeast. A sweeping left turn onto Euclid Avenue Northeast overlooks Port Madison Inner Harbor, at one time a center of commerce for this side of the Puget Sound. Settled in the mid-1800s, the townsfolk made their fortunes in the lumber and ship-building business industries here. When it became the center of government for Kitsap County in 1856, the town boasted a courthouse, jail, hotel, post office, and schoolhouse. As the lumber, fishing, and shipping industries faded away, so did the town.

Climbing away from the water, you'll soon come to Frog Rock, probably the most photographed site on the island. Legend has it that a local dairy farmer dynamited the rock in two sometime in the first half of the twentieth century, and later a road crew working at the intersection stacked the smaller half on top of the large one. In the late 1960s or early '70s, local high-school students painted the frog face you see today, although the local community has taken responsibility for its upkeep.

Passing Frog Rock on Phelps Road Northeast, turn right onto Northeast Day Road and immediately cross SR 305 at the traffic light (turn right here to cross the Agate Pass Bridge and join the North Kitsap bike route). Crossing the island, you'll turn left on Manzanita Road Northeast, skirt Manzanita Bay, turn left onto Northeast Bergman Road, and then right onto the aptly named Peterson Hill Road. Turn right again onto the shoulder of Miller Road Northeast, then right again on Northeast Arrow Point Drive, which descends before taking a steep climb up to Battle Point Park. The park is named for a battle between a local tribe, led by Chief Kitsap, and invaders from the north before white settlement.

Japanese Relocation

A bleak chapter in Bainbridge Island's history is remembered at the Bainbridge Island Japanese American Exclusion Memorial, located on Taylor Avenue Northeast just off Eagle Harbor Drive Northeast. That's the point in 1942 where the 221 Japanese-American men, women, and children had been rounded up for relocation to internment camps, in spite of the fact that two-thirds of them were born in the United States. They unwillingly left their homes for the dusty Manzamar internment camp at the edge of the Mojave Desert, and later moved to the Minidoka camp in Idaho.

Executive Order 9066 at the beginning of World War II required that all Japanese Americans be moved inland. Eventually, some 110,000 Japanese Americans across the US ended up in relocation camps. Those from Bainbridge Island were the first in the nation to be uprooted, possibly because of concerns about the proximity of sophisticated radio equipment in use at Fort Ward. The ancestors of many had lived on the island since the late 1800s, first working in the logging industry and later responsible for the thriving strawberry-growing and canning industry. Only about half of the 276 Japanese Americans (55 chose to leave before the Army's roundup) returned to Bainbridge Island.

In 1988, Congress passed legislation to pay reparations to the internees and their survivors, and President Ronald Reagan apologized for the injustice.

A 276-foot-long Story Wall names every Japanese American on the island in 1942 and retraces the steps of those who had to leave their homes behind.

Crossing through the park, follow Battle Point Drive Northeast all the way back to Miller Road Northeast. The road becomes Fletcher Bay Road Northeast, which rolls through the Island Center community. If you're getting tired, keep your eyes open for Northeast High School Road, which takes you eastward across the island to Madison Avenue North in Winslow.

Turn right onto Lynwood Center Road Northeast and right again on Northeast Baker Hill Road. This starts a challenging 300-foot climb in less than a mile, but ends in a 6-mile stretch with no ascents along Port Orchard Bay and the narrow Rich Passage ferry route between Seattle and Bremerton. This can be daunting if there are headwinds, however.

Point White Drive Northeast heads to Lynwood Center, a historic island community that has undergone renewal in recent years and is a good place to stop for baked goods and coffee. Turn right onto Pleasant Beach Drive Northeast and follow it into Fort Ward Park, which turns into a bicycle path along the waterfront.

The Army built Fort Ward Park in the 1900s and armed it with gun batteries to protect the passage to the Puget Sound Naval Shipyard in Bremerton. The Navy took over in 1938 and installed radio antennas that were useful in World War II and the Korean War. Decommissioned in 1958, some relics and buildings from the military days remain. Today, scuba divers and birders flock to the park.

Taking a sharp left after exiting the park, follow Fort Ward Hill Road Northeast past some old brick barracks to Blakely Harbor Put-In Park, a sheltered cove that marks the former site of another bustling island seaport that rivaled Port Madison.

Turning right on Blakely Avenue Northeast, the road splits. Take the straight-ahead rolling Halls Hill Road that soon curves left into Rockaway Beach Road Northeast. You'll pass many homes on the seaward side of the bluff with stunning views of Seattle. Wait until the road narrows to one lane at a washout for an unobstructed view of Seattle.

The route turns left along Eagle Harbor Drive Northeast, with good views of Winslow and the ferry terminal across the busy Eagle Bay Harbor. Look for the entrance to the Bainbridge Island Japanese American Exclusion Memorial before Taylor Avenue. Follow the road around the end of Eagle Bay to Wyatt Way and turn right toward town. You'll face one last hill before turning right onto Madison Avenue and then left to the coffee shops and bakeries on Wyatt Way.

As you return to the ferry on SR 305, keep to the far right of the traffic and follow a bike path down to the ferry boarding area.

0.0 Disembark from ferry and continue straight on Olympic Drive Southeast (SR 305).

0.2 Turn left on Winslow Way East.

0.5 Turn right on Madison Avenue North.

1.7 Turn left on Northeast New Brooklyn Road.

2.1 Turn right on Sportsman Club Road Northeast.

2.9 Road becomes Madison Avenue North as you cross SR 305.

3.0 Turn right onto Manitou Beach Drive Northeast. It curves left after passing Murden Cove.

3.7 Continue ahead on path marked PEDESTRIANS AND BICYCLISTS KEEP RIGHT.

4.4 Turn left onto Northeast Valley Road.

4.7 Turn right onto Sunrise Drive Northeast.

7.3 Pass Fay Bainbridge Park (Side trip: Turn right into entrance and follow road that passes campground, water, and restrooms. There's a loop that goes down to shore. After exploring, retrace your path and turn right on Sunrise.) Turn left onto Northeast Lafayette Avenue in about 500 feet.

8.0 Take sharp right onto Washington Avenue Northeast.

8.2 Follow sharp curve to left; road becomes Euclid Avenue Northeast.

8.9 Turn right onto Phelps Road Northeast.

9.0 Pass Frog Rock.

9.4 Turn right into Hidden Cove Ballfields if you need restrooms.

10.4 Turn right onto Northeast Day Road, then cross SR 305 at traffic signal. (SR 305 crosses Agate Bridge and connects with the Port Gamble–Poulsbo Loop.)

11.5 Turn left onto Manzanita Road Northeast.

11.8 After passing tiny cove the road curves to the left and becomes Northeast Bergman Road.

12.1 Turn right on Peterson Hill Road Northeast.

12.5 Turn right onto Miller Road Northeast.

13.0 Turn right onto Northeast Arrow Point Drive, which curves to the right at Battle Point Park.

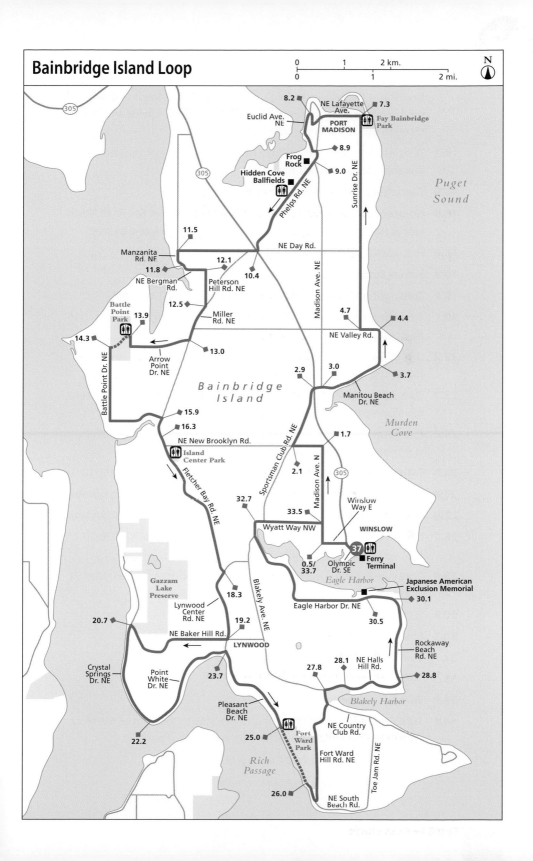

Bainbridge Island Loop

0   1   2 km.

0   1   2 mi.

N

8.2
NE Lafayette Ave.
7.3
Euclid Ave. NE
PORT MADISON
Fay Bainbridge Park
305
8.9
Frog Rock
9.0
Hidden Cove Ballfields
Phelps Rd. NE
305
Sunrise Dr. NE

Puget Sound

11.5
Manzanita Rd. NE
12.1
NE Day Rd.
11.8
10.4
NE Bergman Rd.
Peterson Hill Rd. NE
Madison Ave. NE
12.5
4.7
4.4
Battle Point Park
Miller Rd. NE
13.9
NE Valley Rd.
14.3
13.0
Battle Point Dr. NE
Arrow Point Dr. NE
2.9
3.0
3.7
Manitou Beach Dr. NE

Bainbridge Island

Murden Cove

15.9
16.3
1.7
NE New Brooklyn Rd.
Island Center Park
Sportsman Club Rd. NE
2.1
Madison Ave. N
305
Fletcher Bay Rd. NE
32.7
Winslow Way E
33.5
WINSLOW
Wyatt Way NW
37
Ferry Terminal
0.5/33.7
Olympic Dr. SE
Eagle Harbor
Japanese American Exclusion Memorial
30.1
Gazzam Lake Preserve
18.3
Eagle Harbor Dr. NE
30.5
Lynwood Center Rd. NE
20.7
19.2
Blakely Ave. NE
NE Baker Hill Rd.
LYNWOOD
Rockaway Beach Rd. NE
Crystal Springs Dr. NE
Point White Dr. NE
23.7
28.1
NE Halls Hill Rd.
27.8
28.8
Blakely Harbor
Pleasant Beach Dr. NE
22.2
25.0
Fort Ward Park
NE Country Club Rd.
Fort Ward Hill Rd. NE
Toe Jam Rd. NE
Rich Passage
26.0
NE South Beach Rd.

13.9 Turn left into Battle Point Park. On the left of the green multipurpose building at the entrance, take the paved path that leads to a restroom building. Continue on that path to the soccer fields and ride through the adjacent parking lot to the park exit.

14.3 Turn left onto Battle Point Drive Northeast as you exit the park. Follow the road as it curves to the left.

15.9 Turn right on Miller Road Northeast.

16.3 Go straight as Miller Road Northeast becomes Fletcher Bay Road Northeast at Northeast New Brooklyn Road intersection, a four-way stop.

16.6 Pass Island Center Park.

18.3 Turn right onto Lynwood Center Road Northeast.

19.2 Turn right on Northeast Baker Hill Road, a steep 0.7-mile hill.

20.7 Turn left onto Crystal Springs Drive Northeast at stop sign; cross traffic does not stop.

22.2 Crystal Springs Drive Northeast becomes Point White Drive Northeast.

23.7 Turn right onto Pleasant Beach Drive Northeast at Lynwood Center development.

25.0 Enter Fort Ward Park. Road soon becomes a paved path. Pit toilets, water, and picnic areas are located in the park.

26.0 Turn left on Fort Ward Hill Road Northeast.

27.5 Turn left onto Northeast Country Club Road; cross traffic does not stop.

27.8 Turn right onto Blakely Avenue Northeast; cross traffic does not stop.

28.1 Go straight through intersection, taking Northeast Halls Hill Road that veers to the left uphill.

28.8 Continue as road curves left and becomes Rockaway Beach Road Northeast.

30.1 Turn left onto Eagle Harbor Drive Northeast.

30.5 Entrance to Japanese American Exclusion Memorial.

32.7 Turn right on Wyatt Way Northwest.

33.5 Turn right on Madison Avenue North.

33.7 Turn left on Winslow Way East.

34.1 Turn right on Olympic Drive Southeast. Stay to the right of the ferry fee entrance and follow bike lane on right side of parking.

34.4 Arrive at ferry dock to wait for ferry. End of ride.

RIDE INFORMATION

Local Events and Attractions

Chilly Hilly Bike Ride: An early-season (late Feb) 33-mile bike ride around Bainbridge Island presented by the Cascade Bicycle Club; cascade.org/ride-major-rides/chilly-hilly

Bainbridge Island Summer Challenge: An August or September bicycle ride with options of 16 to 52 miles presented by the Kiwanis Club; membermanager.net/summerchallengeride

Fay Bainbridge Park: Camping and beachcombing at 15446 Sunrise Dr., Bainbridge Island; (206) 842-3931; biparks.org/parksandfacilities/pkfay bainbridge.html

Fort Ward Park: Picnicking, beachcombing at 2241 Pleasant Beach, Bainbridge Island; biparks.org/parksandfacilities/pkftward.html

Bainbridge Island Japanese American Exclusion Memorial: 4192 Eagle Harbor Dr., Bainbridge Island; bijac.org/index.php?p=MEMORIALVisitor Information

Restrooms

Mile 0.0: Ferry terminal
Mile 7.3: Fay Bainbridge Park
Mile 9.4: Hidden Cove Ballfields
Mile 13.9: Battle Point Park
Mile 16.6: Island Center Park (in community building)
Mile 25.0: Fort Ward Park
Mile 34.4: Ferry terminal

Port Gamble–Poulsbo Loop

This bicycle route encircles northern Kitsap County, a land of forests, farms, and miles of shoreline. The ride starts after a scenic half-hour ferry ride to Kingston. It passes through two historic towns—one preserving its hardscrabble past as a mill town, the other relishing its Norwegian heritage. This ride follows a route offered by the Cascade Bicycle Club during its Kitsap Color Classic in the fall.

Start: Ferry terminal in Kingston (leave your car in Edmonds)

Length: 36.9 miles

Approximate riding time: 2.5 to 4 hours

Best bike: Road

Terrain: The entire route is on paved streets and highways. The terrain includes several ascents where the route leaves the shoreline.

Traffic and hazards: Traffic can be heavy on the state highways, but they have wide shoulders for riding a bike. The other roads are low traffic, except in the area of Suquamish, which can be congested.

Things to see: Water and mountain views, beachcombing, sightseeing, antique shopping in Port Gamble and Poulsbo, Indian Reservation casino, gravesite of Chief Seattle (namesake of Seattle)

Maps: *Delorme Atlas & Gazetteer—Washington,* page 45; Kitsap County Bike Map, kitsapgov.com/PW/maps/Bike_Route_2004.pdf

Getting there: By car: Take I-5 north from Seattle to exit 177 and follow it toward Edmonds and the Kingston Ferry. Follow SR 104 into town and look for on-street parking, being careful not to get in the waiting lines for ferry traffic (you don't want to drive onto the ferry). Parking at a city park adjacent to the ferry port is limited to four hours. Find the passenger terminal and purchase your ticket. **By bus:** Community Transit Route 416 travels between downtown Seattle and Edmonds. **By bike:** See the Green Lake to Edmonds Loop (ride 8). GPS: N47 48.785' / W122 23.059'

THE RIDE

The past is readily at hand more than 150 years after the first white settlers arrived on this finger of land that juts into the Puget Sound from the Olympic Peninsula.

Descendants of the Suquamish and other Native American tribes still make their homes on reservations on the northern Kitsap Peninsula. A mill town—Port Gamble—owned by early industrialists is preserved as a National Historic Landmark. The former fishing village of Poulsbo continues to celebrate the tidal wave of Norwegian immigrants who settled the area in the nineteenth century.

The bike ride starts in Kingston, a town created as a hideaway and resort for city folk in the late 1800s. With its natural harbor, however, it soon became a busy port for freight and the logging industry and passengers plying the Puget Sound.

As is natural for ferry stops on the glacier-carved Puget Sound, the terrain immediately begins to rise as soon as you pedal ashore onto SR 104. It's a steady, but not steep, uphill slog for nearly four miles. About halfway, turn right onto Hanesville Road Northeast, and then left at the crest of the hill on Northeast 288th Street. The route plunges into forests that have regrown since the first logging operations started in the mid-1800s to supply gold-rush boomtowns like San Francisco with lumber. You'll catch glimpses of open water to the right through the woods here, and the forest gets thicker after you make a right turn back onto SR 104.

Soon you arrive at historic Port Gamble. It's the site of the longest continuously operating sawmill in the US—1853 to 1995—and a prime example of a company town. The Puget Mill Co. owned the sawmill (located on the shoreline below the bluff), the homes where workers lived, the stores where they shopped, and the dance halls and movie houses where they relaxed. The preserved houses and buildings have a distinctive New England flavor. It's no surprise to learn that the original owners came from Maine and coaxed many of their former neighbors to follow them as skilled craftsmen at the facility.

Bike Shops

Harvy's Bike Shop: 19920 SR 99, Suite C, Lynnwood; (425) 774-8951; harvysbikeshop.com
Silverdale Cyclery: 9242 Silverdale Way Northwest, Silverdale; (360) 692-5508; silverdalecyclery.com

The bike route follows SR 104 to the left. (A detour straight ahead on North Rainier Avenue takes you past more historic buildings to the cafe and museum in the Port Gamble General Store [circa 1916] at the end of the street.

The main drag in Poulsbo sports a Norwegian flair.

Turn left and head uphill on Walker Street to the Buena Vista Cemetery, which commands views of the Hood Canal and mountains beyond. It's easy to see why the local tribe called the town site Teekalet for "brightness of the noon-day sun." Return to the bike route by going half a block to Kitsap Avenue, turn left, and then turn right back onto SR 104.)

Returning to SR 104, follow the bike route downhill. Continue straight ahead on the wide shoulder of SR 3 as SR 104 heads to the right over the Hood Canal Bridge. The Hood Canal is on your right side, hidden behind the trees for the next 3 miles. Checking behind you for traffic, move into the left-turn lane at Big Valley Road and turn left at the traffic light. This winding 6-mile stretch passes pastures and farm lots where early settlers supplied the peninsula with food and later helped make Northern Kitsap the biggest chicken-producing location in the nation for a time.

Leaving the quiet rural road behind, turn right onto the shoulder of Bond Road and then left onto Front Street Northeast at a busy three-way intersection. Soon you catch glimpses of Liberty Bay on the right. There's a pullout at the American Legion Park that provides views of the scenic bay once called Dog Fish Bay for the plentiful chum salmon that were caught here and used for their oil.

Continue on Front Street Northeast into Poulsbo, known as Little Norway. The town celebrates its Norwegian heritage in its festivals—Viking Fest,

Bicycling by Ferry

It's hard not to feel a sense of excitement when one of the Washington State Ferries pulls into the dock to whisk you away for a bicycling adventure across the Puget Sound.

The five bike routes west of Seattle are most easily reached by ferry. The Bainbridge Island ferry leaves from Pier 52 in downtown Seattle, the ferry to Vashon and Southworth leaves from the Fauntleroy Ferry Terminal in West Seattle, and the Kingston ferry to the Port Gamble–Poulsbo Loop departs from the ferry terminal in Edmonds.

King County Metro also runs two water taxis from Pier 50 in downtown Seattle that go to Alki Beach in West Seattle and Vashon Island. Unlike the large motor-vehicle ferries operated by the state, bicyclists have to carry their bikes onto the water taxi and there's only space for sixteen bikes on the West Seattle water taxi and eighteen bikes on the one that serves Vashon.

Bicyclists on state ferries traveling east to west must pay for themselves as passengers as well as a small fee for the bicycle. The return trip is free. The rules for the Metro Water Taxi are a little different. Bicyclists pay going in each direction, but they don't pay an extra fee for their bicycle. Also, the water-taxi hours to Vashon are limited to the commute hours in the morning and evening.

Bicyclists are always the first to board the ferries. They're directed to wait in front of lined-up cars and trucks and then to walk their bikes onto the ferry where they ride to the bow. Cyclists must either secure their bikes with rope hanging from ferry fixtures or hook the handlebars over the railing. Because they are at the bow of the ferry, bicyclists are also the first to depart at the destination. Cleats, including bike-shoe cleats, are not allowed to be worn in the ferry cabins. It's okay to walk around in your socks, though.

The routine is a little different at each departure. Bicyclists arriving at Pier 52 in downtown Seattle must purchase their tickets at the same tollbooth as the motorists upon entering the facility. In Edmonds, the bicyclists pay for their passage in the passenger terminal, which is at the entrance to the ferry dock. At the Fauntleroy Terminal in West Seattle, bicyclists buy tickets in the ferry building at the end of a walkway that goes to the head of the dock.

None of the ferry terminals have parking. If you drive to the terminal, you'll have to use on-street parking or find a parking garage or lot.

Bon voyage!

Midsommer Fest, and Julefest—and the business district that sports Norwegian names on buildings and streets. Passing the Poulsbohemian Coffeehouse, you turn right onto King Olaf Vei to Liberty Park, where you can relax in the Kvelstad Pavilion. The town owes its Norwegian heritage to Ole Stubb, who settled on Dog Fish Bay in 1875. Stubb extolled the area's virtues to friends and relatives, and they began arriving in droves in the 1880s and '90s. They made their livelihoods in farming, logging, and fishing. At one time the bay was home to cod- and oyster-processing facilities.

The route continues through Poulsbo and along the narrow Liberty Bay inlet until you turn right onto the shoulder of SR 305. Soon you're entering the reservation of the Suquamish tribe, who at one time controlled most of North Kitsap Peninsula. Settlers adopted the name Kitsap for the Suquamish war chief who defeated marauding tribes from the north several times. The father of Chief Seattle, who aided white settlement of the city by the same name, was a member of the Suquamish tribe.

Today the tribe is known for owning the sprawling Suquamish Clearwater Casino, which you pass just before turning left onto Suquamish Way from SR 305. Riding uphill, turn left onto Division Avenue Northeast. (To see the gravesite of Chief Seattle, who died in 1866, turn right at Northeast South Street and left in 2 blocks to the Suquamish Cemetery.)

The route continues through thick forest on the way back to Kingston. After 6 miles, it returns to the shoulder of SR 104. Turn right onto Barber Cutoff Road Northeast to avoid the cars in a holding pattern for the ferry and follow the bike route back to the business district near the ferry. There are plenty of coffee shops or cafes here as you wait to roll your bicycle back onto the ferry.

MILES & DIRECTIONS

0.0 The bike ride begins as you roll off the ferry in Kingston onto SR 104.

2.6 Turn right onto Hanesville Road Northeast.

3.6 Turn left onto Northeast 288th Street. Road becomes Gamble Bay Road Northeast.

5.8 Turn right onto SR 104.

8.9 Enter Port Gamble.

9.2 Turn left onto Pope Street, also SR 104.

9.4 Pass Kitsap Avenue on the right (goes to Buena Vista Cemetery).

10.5 Continue straight onto SR 3 at stop light. (SR 104 turns right and crosses the Hood Canal Bridge.)

Port Gamble–Poulsbo Loop

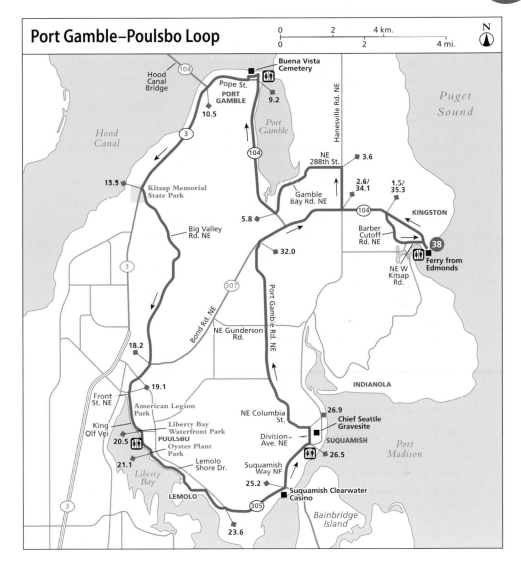

13.5 Slide into left-turn lane and turn left at traffic signal onto Big Valley Road Northeast.

18.2 Turn right at Bond Road Northeast (SR 307).

18.6 Cross SR 305 at traffic signal.

19.1 Get into left-turn lane to turn left at traffic signal onto Front Street Northeast.

19.7 Pass entrance to American Legion Park.

20.1 Turn right at King Olaf Vei to Liberty Bay Park (gazebo and restrooms).

20.2 To leave park, retrace your route on King Olaf Vei and turn right onto Front Street Northeast. Follow the arterial to the left as it becomes Northeast Hostmark Street.

20.5 Turn right onto Fjord Drive Northeast, which becomes Lemoro Shore Drive Northeast.

21.1 Oyster Plant Park is on the right.

23.6 Turn right onto SR 305 at stop sign.

25.2 Merge into left-turn lane at traffic signal and turn left at Suquamish Way Northeast. This is a busy intersection as the Suquamish Clearwater Casino Resort is on the right and SR 305 heads straight across the Agate Pass Bridge to Bainbridge Island and the ferry to Seattle.

26.5 Left turn on Division Avenue Northeast. (A detour to the gravesite of Chief Seattle is a right turn at Northeast South Street, 2 blocks downhill, and turn left at sign for Suquamish Cemetery.)

26.9 Turn left on Northeast Columbia Street.

27.7 Stay on Northeast Columbia Street as it branches to the left at Middle Street Northeast. Northeast Columbia Street becomes Port Gamble Road Northeast.

29.9 Caution; cross traffic does not stop at intersection of Gunderson Road Northeast.

32.0 Turn right onto Bond Road Northeast (also marked as SR 307, which becomes SR 104).

35.3 Bear right onto Barber Cutoff Road Northeast.

36.4 At four-way stop, continue straight (bearing slightly to the left) as the road turns into Northeast West Kingston Road.

36.7 Turn right onto eastbound SR 104; pass through Kingston business district.

36.9 End of ride at ferry terminal on the right. Restrooms are located in the terminal and the Mike Wallace Park behind it.

RIDE INFORMATION

Local Events and Attractions
Viking Fest: Poulsbo, May; vikingfest.org
St. Hans Mid-Sommerfest: Poulsbo, June; poulsbosonsofnorway.com

Chief Seattle Days: Suquamish, third weekend in August; suquamish.org/ChiefSeattleDays.aspx

Port Gamble Old Mill Days: Carnival, lumberjack competition, July; oldmill days.com

Kitsap Color Classic: Cascade Bicycle Club, September/October; cascade .org/kitsap-color-classic

Julefest: Poulsbo, December; poulsbochamber.com

North Kitsap Trails Association: Biking, hiking, and kayaking trails; north kitsaptrails.org

West Sound Cycling Club: westsoundcycling.com

Port Gamble: portgamble.com

Greater Poulsbo Chamber of Commerce: poulsbochamber.com

Restaurants

Port Gamble General Store and Cafe: 32340 NE Rainier Ave. #3, Port Gamble; (360) 297-7636

Sluy's Poulsbo Bakery: 18924 Front St. Northeast, Poulsbo; (360) 779-2798

Poulsbohemian Coffeehouse: 19003 Front St., Poulsbo; (360) 779-9199

Restrooms

Mile 0.0: Kingston Ferry Terminal

Mile 9.2: Port Gamble General Store and Cafe

Mile 19.7: American Legion Park

Mile 20.1: Liberty Bay Park, Poulsbo

Mile 26.5: Suquamish Village Shell station

Mile 36.9: Kingston Ferry Terminal or Mark Wallace Park

The Ride to Port Orchard

Cyclists who enjoy riding flat, waterfront roads can commune with the tidal zone on this Kitsap Peninsula bike ride from the Southworth ferry landing to historic Port Orchard. Bicycle riders cast their gazes across Puget Sound tributaries for most of the way as they pass through small seaside villages that dot the route.

Start: Southworth Ferry Terminal in Kitsap County via Fauntleroy-Vashon-Southworth ferry

Length: 29.4 miles round-trip

Approximate time: 2 to 4 hours

Best bike: Road or hybrid

Terrain: A few very small hills, but flat on long stretches of waterfront

Traffic and hazards: Two-lane roads with narrow shoulders and light traffic; watch for speed bumps in Manchester State Park; roadside can be a little hacked up in places.

Things to see: Historic waterfront communities of Southworth, Manchester, Annapolis, and Port Orchard; farmers' market; surviving fortifications at Manchester State Park; broad tidal zone on Puget Sound and Sinclair Inlet; wide variety of seabirds

Maps: Kitsap County Bicycle Route System, kitsapgov.com/pw/maps/Bike_Route_2004.pdf; *Delorme Atlas & Gazetteer—Washington,* page 45

Getting there: By car: Fauntleroy Ferry in West Seattle: From north or south I-5, take exit 163 to West Seattle Bridge. After crossing the bridge, follow the arterial as it becomes Fauntleroy Way Southwest (follow signs to the ferry). Turn right into the Lincoln Park parking lot. Bike downhill on the shoulder or sidewalk next to Fauntleroy Way and turn right into the Fauntleroy Ferry Terminal. **By bus:** Metro buses 116, 188, 119, and 673 serve the Fauntleroy Ferry. GPS: N47 31.881' / W122 23.654'

THE RIDE

The squawks and cries of gulls replace the sounds of traffic on this waterfront bike ride, especially if you arrive in Port Orchard for the annual Seagull Calling Festival each May. Tourism now boosts the maritime economy of this historic seaport, and visiting bicyclists can linger in antiques shops and cafes or wander among booths at the weekly farmers' market.

The out-and-back ride starts at the Southworth, a 30- or 40-minute ferryboat ride from West Seattle, depending on whether or not there's a stop at Vashon Island. Visitors can stop in at the Southworth Grocery and Deli on the right for a light meal and coffee.

Unlike other ferry stops across the Puget Sound, there's no grueling uphill climb from the shoreline here, just a rolling rise that quickly drops to a stretch of road alongside an aged seawall. Southeast Southworth Drive veers left at the community of Harper, which housed the state ferry dock until it relocated to Southworth in 1967.

Riding alongside Yukon Harbor, you next come to Colby, another hamlet that at one time sported a public ferry dock. After crossing the small Curly Creek Bridge, look for Yukon Harbor Road Southeast that veers to the right off the main road. This follows the shoreline and offers views across the Puget Sound to the Seattle skyline. It hooks up with Colchester Drive Southeast, which ends in Manchester.

The Family Inn Restaurant is a Sunday brunch (as well as other meals) destination for bicyclists. It's also reminiscent of the town's regional prominence in the travel industry, as a car ferry landed here from the early 1920s until 1949. The site of the ferry dock is now Pomeroy Park at the foot of Main Street, where visitors walk the beach and enjoy views across to Seattle. The route becomes Beach Drive East and passes through Manchester Fuel Depot, a naval fueling station. A few pipes and storage tanks are visible as you ride through this area that has served several military missions since 1898.

Bike Shop

Olympic Bike and Skate: 744 Bay St., Port Orchard; (360) 895-2127

Manchester State Park used to be part of this sprawling facility, located across Rich Passage from Fort Ward on Bainbridge Island. Now it's a wooded, 111-acre park that's popular with campers, hikers, and beachcombers. A former torpedo warehouse sees service for social events and is listed on the National Register of Historic Places, as are a nearby command post and gun battery.

After leaving the park, the route returns to the waterfront along Port Orchard Bay. Although there isn't much of a shoulder, the route is lightly

A bicycle rack takes a familiar form at Pomeroy Park in Manchester as Seattle's skyline rises on the horizon.

traveled. Heading southwest, bicyclists enjoy views across the water to Bremerton and the Puget Sound Naval Shipyard with Green Mountain and the Olympic Mountains looming in the background. Wildflowers and small bushes grow in the thin, grassy strip between the road and the tidal flats where shorebirds pick at shells and small crabs.

Homes with expansive water views sit opposite the road from the water, although occasional cottages are located on the waterfront side of the road. Most look sound and sturdy, while a few others appear rather weatherbeaten and perch precariously on pilings over the beach.

One of the small waterfront communities is Annapolis. An original settler, John Mitchell, adopted the name of the US Naval Academy's hometown on this point in 1890 hoping to convince the Navy to build the Puget Sound Naval Shipyard here. Instead, the Navy chose a location in what is now Bremerton, located directly across Sinclair Inlet from Port Orchard. Workers who live in communities on both sides of the inlet have built and repaired thousands of Navy ships there in the past century. A large number of inactive ships, including four aircraft carriers that are clearly visible from Port Orchard, are currently mothballed at the shipyard.

The route into Port Orchard crosses Black Jack Creek and passes motels, car lots, and gas stations before arriving in the old downtown. Port Orchard

Mosquito Fleet

Many of the small towns that dot the waterfront of the Kitsap Peninsula looked to the Puget Sound for commerce and transportation throughout the second half of the nineteenth and early twentieth centuries. Wagon roads between many communities were few and in abysmal shape. It was easier to travel from town to town by rowboat, dinghy, or steamboat in those early days.

The use of steam-powered paddleboats grew to the point where a thousand such watercraft carried supplies and passengers between these small towns and back and forth to major ports of Tacoma and Seattle.

Loosely called the Mosquito Fleet for the way they flitted around the Puget Sound in large numbers, the boats helped sustain the economies of many isolated communities along the shoreline. They largely disappeared in the 1920s with the construction of reliable roads and use of trucks and autos.

was founded as Sidney in 1886 after the area had served the logging industry since the late 1850s. Construction and operation of the naval shipyard buoyed the economy over the years. It became the county seat for a while and changed its name to Port Orchard, after the bay, in 1903.

While much of Port Orchard's commerce shifted to the shopping centers uphill on the south side of town, the downtown has been rejuvenated with antiques shops, boutiques, cafes, and community events such as the Seagull Calling Festival and weekly farmers' markets at Port Orchard Marina Park. The Olympic Bicycle and Skate shop at the corner of Bay Street and Sidney Avenue is worth a visit for a tire patch or a tour of antique bicycles stored in the shop.

A visit to Bremerton with your bike is as simple as boarding the foot ferry that embarks from the base of Sidney Avenue. A similar ferry also operates from Annapolis. Fees and schedules are posted.

To return to Southworth, merely turn left onto Beach Drive East at the east side of town and retrace your route back to the ferry.

MILES & DIRECTIONS

0.0 Disembark the ferry and go straight on Southeast Southworth Drive.

0.9 Turn right to remain on Southeast Southworth Drive.

1.6 Turn left to remain on Southeast Southworth Drive.

3.1 Bear right onto Yukon Harbor Road Southeast.

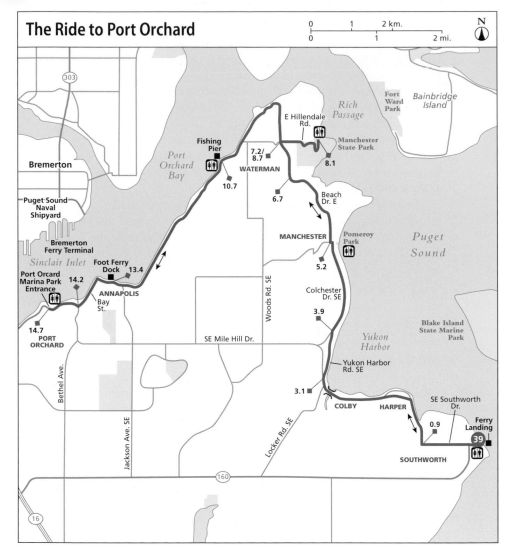

The Ride to Port Orchard

0   1   2 km.
0   1   2 mi.

N

3.9 Merge onto Colchester Drive Southeast.

5.2 Turn left onto East Main Street in Manchester, and then turn right onto Beach Drive East.

6.7 Turn right to stay on Beach Drive East.

7.2 Turn right onto East Hilldale Road to enter Manchester State Park.

8.1 Arrive at Manchester State Park beach. Retrace your route.

8.7 Turn right onto Beach Drive East.

10.7 Pass public fishing pier on Waterman's Cove.

13.4 Pass foot ferry terminal in Annapolis; road name changes to Bay Street.

14.2 Bear right to remain on Bay Street, which becomes SR 166.

14.6 Pass entrance to Port Orchard Marina Park on the right.

14.7 Turn right onto Sidney Avenue. Explore downtown and retrace route to Southworth Ferry Terminal.

29.4 End of ride.

RIDE INFORMATION

Local Events and Attractions

Port Orchard Farmers' Market: 9 a.m. to 3 p.m. Sat, Apr through Oct at Port Orchard Waterfront Marina Park

Seagull Calling Festival: Memorial Day weekend, Port Orchard Waterfront Marina Park; www.portorchard.com/joomla/index.php/seagull-calling-festival-eventsfestivals-246

Manchester State Park: 7767 E. Hilldale Rd., Port Orchard; camping reservations, https://secure.camis.com/WA/ManchesterStatePark

Banner Forest and Long Lake Park: kitsapgov.com/parks

Restaurants

Family Inn at Manchester: 2386 Colchester Dr. East, Manchester; (360) 871-8199

Carters Chocolates: 160 Bethel Ave., Port Orchard; (360) 876-4424

Slaughter County Brewery: 1307 Bay St., Port Orchard; (360) 329-2340

Restrooms

Mile 0.0: Ferry terminal at Southworth

Mile 5.2: Turn right onto East Main Street in Manchester to access Pomeroy Park, which has restrooms in the parking lot

Mile 8.1: Manchester State Park, on beach

Mile 10.7: Public fishing pier (portable toilet)

Mile 14.6: Turn right into entrance for Port Orchard Marina Park and bear right through parking lot to restroom building

Banner Forest Heritage Park

Mountain bikers who enjoy easygoing single track or challenging trails with lots of tight turns will both be happy in this square mile of second-growth forest near the Southworth Ferry Terminal in southern Kitsap County. Keep your eyes open for wildlife in this remote area.

Start: Banner Forest Heritage Park parking lot on Banner Road, southern Kitsap Peninsula

Length: 9.5-mile ride; more than 20 miles of trails in the park

Approximate riding time: 2.5 to 3.5 hours

Best bike: Mountain bike

Terrain: No long hills, but plenty of short climbs. Mostly hard-packed trail surface, but tends to drain into frequent puddles in rainy weather. Trails around the perimeter are drier than those in the middle. Some trails are smooth and straight, while others are twisty with roots.

Traffic and hazards: Joggers, equestrians, and dog walkers on the trails

Things to see: Dense forest and 139 acres of wetlands in the park, Southworth Ferry Terminal, nearby towns of Manchester, Port Orchard

Maps: *DeLorme Atlas & Gazetteer—Washington,* page 45; Kitsap County Parks website, kitsapgov.com/parks/Parks/Pages/heritageparks/banner _forest.htm

Getting there: By car: From I-5, take exit 163 toward West Seattle Bridge. Follow signs to ferry via Fauntleroy Way Southwest. Turn right at ferry terminal and board ferry for Southworth. Disembark at landing and turn left on SR 160 (Southeast Sedgewick Road). Turn left at mile 2.5 onto Banner Road. Forest is another mile on the right. **By bicycle:** To avoid the car charge on the ferry, roll your bicycle onto the ferry (bring food and water with you as there are no services). At Southworth, take the first left onto the shoulder of SR 160 (Southeast Sedgewick Road). Turn left at mile 2.5 onto Banner Road and proceed another mile to Banner Forest on the right. GPS: N47 29.349' / W122 32.755'

THE RIDE

Banner Forest Heritage Park on the southern Kitsap Peninsula is one of those places where it's hard to believe that so many miles of single track for mountain biking can be crammed into such a small space.

In this case, more than 20 miles of trails wind through the 1-square-mile Kitsap County Park. Even so, you'll never see another trail except the one you're riding or the one you cross. The second-growth forest is so thick that, although you might hear other bikers yipping and hollering nearby, you never see them unless your paths cross.

The park is in a wild setting in a sparsely populated part of Kitsap Peninsula. On the way there in the morning, you'll likely see deer browsing in open fields. Be aware that the park has had a history of spring and early summer black-bear sightings in recent years.

Visitors can drive or reach the park by bicycle from the Southworth ferry landing, which is served from West Seattle's Fauntleroy ferry terminal. It's a 3.6-mile ride that gains about 100 feet per mile (it's a breeze on the return trip when you're tired).

The trails are just a spaghetti maze through the park, and you can ride for hours without rolling over the same ground. The single track occasionally emerges onto a service road that runs through the park and is useful for orienting. If you find a park map, you'll see that all the trails have names. Some of those trail names are posted on signs about 10 feet high in the trees.

Banner Forest has been a publicly owned forest since statehood, and the state sold logging rights on different tracts to lumber companies to raise funds for school construction. In the early 1990s, the state was ready to close a land swap with a developer to gain more land for Tiger Mountain State Forest in return for giving away Banner Forest as a housing development. Local residents reacted vehe-

Bike Shop

Olympic Bike and Skate: 744 Bay St., Port Orchard; (360) 895-2127

mently, the plan eventually died, and Kitsap County bought the land. Today, the trails in Banner Forest serve hikers, dog walkers, joggers, and equestrians, as well as a variety of mountain-biking styles.

Some trails—such as Fusion Loop, Wild Hare Loop, Sashay, and Donald Duck—are mostly flat or rolling with a fairly smooth surface. Others—consider Bonzer Loop or Oakland/San Francisco Loop—are a challenging series of tight turns where bikers coax their wheels up and down hills as they negotiate countless tree roots. In between are long trails like Capitulate and Mishmash that weave among tall trees and rise and fall over terrain, giving bikers a chance to find their rhythm.

One obstacle you'll find on many trails in the winter and spring is standing water. Although the trail surface is hard-packed and doesn't generally get muddy, there are countless small puddles where water collects in rainy weather. Trail etiquette encourages bikers to ride through the middle of these, instead of seeking detours that widen the trail and trample surrounding vegetation. That's okay, as most of the puddles are fairly shallow. Use caution, however, as there are a few puddles where you can lose sight of your front wheel nearly to the hub. The trails through the center of the park, the location of wetlands, tend to have more problems during wet weather. Banner Slough, for instance, has water standing in deep pools where the only reasonable passage is on paths that have been hacked through the woods a few feet uphill.

Here's a nearly 10-mile ride that encompasses just about everything the trails in Banner Forest can throw your way.

Whether you drive or ride from Southworth, the marked entrance on Banner Road is the easiest trailhead to find. A dirt path leads uphill to a packed-gravel access road. This makes a semi-loop through the park to Southeast Olalla Valley Road.

Take the third right junction off the road to enter PR2. This runs a short distance to Mishmash, a fun loopy single track that rolls for 2 miles through an older part of the forest. There are some challenges here, but none are too technical. This ends at an intersection with Foxy Deer. Wild Hare Loop, which also can be reached from the access road, is an easy stretch with a couple of hills. The brushy foliage encroaching onto Oh Crap makes that a little troublesome, especially with low-hanging limbs and a fallen tree. Next, the tight, twisty Bonzer Loop with its legions of tree roots is a challenge that seems much longer than its 0.5-mile length. (See the map and directions on how to avoid this trail.)

Riding the trails in this order, Sashay is aptly named as it feels like a casual stroll after Bonzer. Back to the access road briefly, the Fusion Loop heads off into the woods and, in spite of a couple of climbs, is smooth sailing. There's an old wrecked car that's slowly rusting into the forest floor down one of the side trails, and some others head over to an abandoned gravel pit at the edge of the park.

Just for laughs, take Donald Duck to return to the main access road, then cross the road onto Banner Slough. If it's winter or spring, there's a large pond up ahead, so take a right trail junction onto Capitulate. This is another long, winding route headed south on a twisty trail that starts out a little reminiscent of Bonzer Loop but ends up as an easier version of Mishmash. Some of the fallen Douglas firs on this trail have been hewn into log rides.

Lizard King is a more direct trail that returns to the wide, tame Banner Slough Trail. Large puddles, or small ponds, may convince you to take Banner Alley to the right. This heads north to Greek Row, a backbone trail whose side trails are named for fraternity houses. The Gamma trail returns to the access road and it's an easy coast back to the parking lot.

MILES & DIRECTIONS

0.0 Leave the parking lot and use the trail to the right of the kiosk. Turn left on the access road.

0.3 Turn right onto second trail on the right, PR2. Bear left at next trail junction.

0.7 Take right fork onto Mishmash.

1.9 Mishmash arrives at access road; take hard right to stay on a newer section of Mishmash.

2.6 Turn right on Foxy Deer within sight of access road. Then three trails come together—Bonzer Loop, Foxy Deer, and Wild Hare Loop. Take Wild Hare Loop to the right.

2.8 Go straight through cross trail.

3.0 Turn left onto Oh Crap.

3.2 Turn left onto Foxy Deer and then right at the next two forks.

3.3 Pass by a trail on the right, and then turn right onto next trail, which is Bonzer Loop. (To skip the roughest section of the 0.6-mile Bonzer Loop, go straight instead of turning right.)

3.9 Turn right at trail junction after loop and stay on main trail.

4.1 Turn left on Roller Coaster, then first right onto Sashay.

4.2 Take a quick succession of three lefts for Bent Pedal and return to Sashay.

4.5 Turn left at junction with Roller Coaster, and take next left junction.

4.7 Turn right onto access road.

4.8 Turn right onto Fusion Loop (the second right from access road). Stay on main trail and keep momentum for short hill after trail junction.

Banner Forest Heritage Park

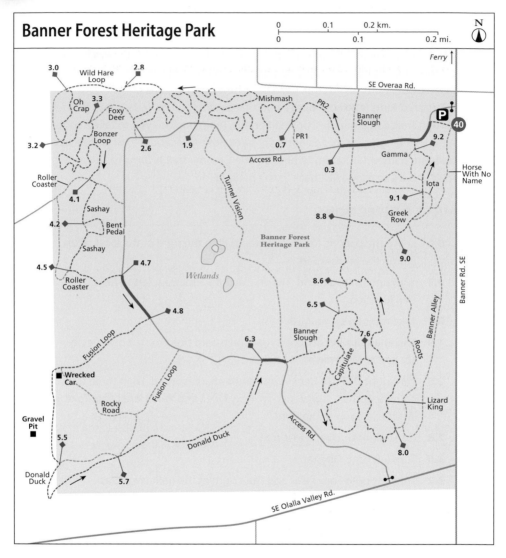

5.1 Pass Rocky Road Trail on left, which is marked by a rusting car. Several trails split off to the right to an old gravel pit.

5.5 Take right fork to pick up Donald Duck (Fusion Loop goes left), then follow it to the left after it goes uphill (Pulverizer is the right fork).

5.7 Keep to Donald as a series of trails splits off to the right.

6.1 Take left fork to stay on Donald Duck.

6.3 Turn right onto access road, then second left onto the wide trail named Banner Slough.

6.5 Take first right off main trail onto Capitulate.

7.6 Take left fork to remain on Capitulate. Several fallen logs in this area have been shaved flat to practice balance.

8.0 Left turn onto Lizard King.

8.6 Turn right on a wide trail, Banner Slough.

8.8 Turn at first right onto narrower Banner Alley.

9.0 Turn left at intersection onto Greek Row (straight is Worm Hole). Stay on main trail and bear left at fork with K2 Land trail.

9.1 Cross Iota trail.

9.2 Bear left onto Gamma, and then turn right at a junction after a short rise.

9.3 Turn right onto access road, then left onto path that returns to the parking lot.

9.5 Return to parking lot. End of ride.

RIDE INFORMATION

Local Events and Attractions
Port Orchard Farmers' Market: 9 a.m. to 3 p.m. Sat, Apr through Oct at Port Orchard Waterfront Marina Park
Seagull Calling Festival: Memorial Day weekend, Port Orchard Waterfront Marina Park

Restaurants
Family Inn at Manchester: 2386 Colchester Dr. East, Manchester; (360) 871-8199
Carters Chocolates: 160 Bethel Ave., Port Orchard; (360) 876-4424
Slaughter County Brewery: 1307 Bay St., Port Orchard; (360) 329-2340

Restrooms
No facilities at the park. Closest facilities at Southworth Ferry Terminal; also commercial district at intersection of SR 16 and SR 160.

Rides at a Glance

ROAD AND RAIL-TRAIL RIDES

Under 20 Miles

2. Discovery Park Loop: 4.7 miles
4. Space Needle–Fishermen's Wharf Loop: 10.1 miles
1. Lake Union–Ship Canal Loop: 10.4 miles
29. Preston-Snoqualmie Trail: 11.3 miles
22. Mercer Island Loop: 13.4 miles
3. Magnolia Loop: 13.6 miles

20 to 30 Miles

13. Green River–Interurban Trails Loop: 20.1 miles
7. Seattle Waterfront to Alki Beach Round-Trip: 21.4 miles
35. John Wayne Pioneer Trail: 21.4 miles
25. Lake Sammamish Loop: 23.5 miles
23. Cougar Mountain–May Valley Loop: 23.7 miles
6. South Lake Washington Loop: 23.7 miles
8. Green Lake to Edmonds Loop: 24.5 miles
30. Rattlesnake Lake and Snoqualmie Falls Loop: 25.2 miles
9. Snohomish–Monroe Loop (Three-River Loop): 26 miles
24. Sammamish River Trail: 26.2 miles
39. The Ride to Port Orchard: 29.4 miles
16. Foothills Trail Ride: 29.5 miles
28. Fall City–Carnation Loop: 30.3 miles

31 to 40 Miles

15. Cedar River Trail: 31.6 miles
37. Bainbridge Island Loop: 34.4 miles
14. Black Diamond–Green River Gorge Loop: 34.5 miles
36. Vashon–Maury Island Loop: 35.1 miles
38. Port Gamble–Poulsbo Loop: 36.9 miles
11. Snohomish–Granite Falls Loop: 37.7 miles
5. North Lake Washington Loop: 39.1 miles

More than 40 Miles

10. Centennial Trail: 59.6 miles

MOUNTAIN-BIKE RIDES

5 to 10 Miles

31. Duthie Hill Mountain Bike Park Loop: 5.4 miles
17. Towers of Power: 6.6 miles
26. Saint Edward State Park and Big Finn Hill Park: 9.0 miles
20. Taylor Mountain Forest Loop: 9.3 miles
40. Banner Forest Heritage Park: 9.5 miles

More than 10 Miles

21. Carbon River Road: 10.2 miles
18. Dash Point State Park Trails: 10.4 miles
12. Paradise Valley Conservation Area: 11 miles
34. Middle Fork Snoqualmie Trail: 12.4 miles
32. Grand Ridge Park Trail: 14.5 miles
19. Henry's Ridge Open Space/Black Diamond Natural Area/Summit Ridge Mountain Bike Area: 14.2 miles
33. Tiger Mountain State Forest: 17.6 miles
27. Thrilla in Woodinvilla Loop: 18.6 miles

Resources

CLUBS AND ADVOCACY GROUPS

Joining a bicycle club is a good way to meet other people who ride. Most clubs have daily or weekly bike rides, in addition to major event rides every year. A membership also is a good way to support the local efforts to make streets safer for cyclists.

B.I.K.E.S. Club: Snohomish County bicycle club; bikesclub.org

Boeing Employees Bicycle Club: Past and present Boeing employees eligible; bebc-seattle.org

Capital Bicycling Club: Advocacy and recreational bicycling based in Olympia; capitalbicycleclub.org

Cascade Bicycle Club: Advocacy, daily rides, major cycling events in Puget Sound region; cascade.org/Home

Cyclists of Greater Seattle: Recreational cycling in Seattle area; cyclistsof greaterseattle.org

Evergreen Mountain Bike Alliance: Advocacy, classes, trail-building, and maintenance in Washington; evergreenmtb.org/home/index.php

Evergreen Tandem Club: Greater Seattle area; evergreentandemclub.org

Seattle Bicycle Touring Club: Recreational cycling in Seattle area; seattle biketours.org

Seattle International Randonneurs: Long-distance bicycling; seattle randonneur.org

Squeaky Wheels Bicycle Club: Based on Bainbridge Island; squeakywheels.org

Tacoma Wheelmen: Pierce County-based; twbc.org

Washington Bikes (formerly Bicycle Alliance of Washington): Statewide bicycle issue advocacy; wabikes.org

West Sound Cycling Club: Advocacy and bicycling west of Puget Sound; westsoundcycling.com

BIG BIKE RIDES AND EVENTS

Here is a sampling of bike rides and other bike events in the Seattle area. Find more at bikingbis.com/washington-bicycle-ride-calendar-index.

Stinky Spoke: Charity mountain bike ride, Woodinville, January; stinkyspoke .org

Chilly Hilly: Loop ride around Bainbridge Island opens bicycling season, February; cascade.org/chillyhilly

Seattle Bike Expo: Bikes, gear, demos, vendors, and displays, March; www .cascade.org/expo

Daffodil Classic: Three options, Orting, April; twbc.org

Bicycle Sundays: Lake Washington Boulevard closed to traffic in Seattle, selected Sundays May through Sept; seattle.gov/parks/bicyclesunday

7 Hills of Kirkland: Late May; 7hillskirkland.com/index.htm

Evergreen Mountain Bike Festival: Duthie Hill Mountain Bike Park, June; evergreenmtb.org/home/index.php

Flying Wheels: Metric century and century, Redmond, June; cascade.org/ flying-wheels-summer-century

Tour de Pierce: Three options, Puyallup, late June or early July; piercecounty wa.org/index.aspx?nid=1277

Seattle to Portland Classic: 200 miles in 1 or 2 days, July; cascade.org/ ride-major-rides/group-health-stp

Tour de Kitsap: Multiple route options on westside of Puget Sound, July; westsoundcycling.com

RAPSody: Loop around Puget Sound begins in Tacoma, August; rapsody bikeride.com

Cycle the WAVE: Women-oriented ride, September; thewavefoundation.org/ cycle-the-wave/

About the Author

Gene Bisbee is an avid bicyclist who has ridden thousands of miles around Washington since settling in Bellevue fourteen years ago. His Biking Bis blog (bikingbis.com) is followed by cyclists interested in recreational bicycling and charity rides in the Pacific Coast states. A newspaper reporter and editor for twenty-five years, he has written bike-touring articles for *Adventure Cyclist* and *Recreation News* magazines. Having made his first overnight bike tour in Ohio as a teenager, he years later fulfilled a lifelong dream of traveling with a friend on bicycles across the United States. He currently lives in Bellevue, Washington, where he writes his blog.

IMBA

INTERNATIONAL MOUNTAIN BICYCLING ASSOCIATION

Come Ride With Us!

You've just purchased, or are about to purchase, the mountain bike of your dreams. Where will you take your new steed? Who will you ride with? Joining IMBA's network of chapters, clubs and patrols taps you into a friendly network of experienced mountain bikers. They host rides for all skill levels, build trails and get together before and after rides to share stories and plan the next adventure. Find a local group by visiting imba.com/near-you.

FIVE RECENT ACCOMPLISHMENTS

1) *Built incredible trails.* IMBA's trailbuilding pros teamed with volunteers around the nation to build sustainable, fun singletrack like the 32-mile system at Pennsylvania's Raystown Lake.

2) *Won grants to build or improve trails.* Your contributions to IMBA's Trail Building Fund were multiplied with six-figure grants of federal money for trail systems.

3) *Challenged anti-bike policies.* IMBA works closely with all of the federal land managing agencies and advises them on how to create bike opportunities and avoid policies that curtail trail access.

4) *Made your voice heard.* When anti-bike interests moved to try to close sections of the 2,500-mile Continental Divide trail to bikes, IMBA rallied its members and collected more than 7,000 comments supporting keeping the trail open to bikes.

5) *Put kids on bikes.* The seventh edition of National Take a Kid Mountain Biking Day put more than 20,000 children on bikes.

FIVE CURRENT GOALS

1) *Host regional bike summits.* We're boosting local trail development by hosting summits in distinct regions of the country, bringing trail advocates and regional land managers together.

2) *Build the next generation of trail systems* with innovative projects, including IMBA's sustainably built "flow trails" for gravity-assisted fun!

3) *Create "Gateway" trails* to bring new riders into the sport.

4) *Fight blanket bans against bikes* that unwisely suggest we don't belong in backcountry places.

5) *Strengthen its network* of IMBA-affiliated clubs with a powerful chapter program.

FOUR THINGS YOU CAN DO FOR YOUR SPORT

1) *Join IMBA.* Get involved with IMBA and take action close to home through your local IMBA-affiliated club. An organization is only as strong as its grassroots membership. IMBA needs your help in protecting and building great trails right here.

2) *Volunteer.* Join a trail crew day for the immensely satisfying experience of building a trail you'll ride for years to come. Ask us how.

3) *Speak up.* Tell land-use and elected officials how important it is to preserve mountain bike access. Visit IMBA's web site for action issues and talking points.

4) *Respect other trail users.* Bike bans result from conflict, real or perceived. By being good trail citizens, we can help end the argument that we don't belong on trails.

YOU BELONG WITH IMBA **JOIN**

Join IMBA at www.imba.com or call 1-888-442-IMBA